PRIVATE FOUNDATION
LAW MADE EASY

T0313752

PRIVATE FOUNDATION LAW MADE EASY

Bruce R. Hopkins

WILEY

John Wiley & Sons, Inc.

For general information on our other products and services, or technical support, please contact our Customer Care Department within the United States at 800-762-2974, outside the United States at 317-572-3993 or fax 317-572-4002.

Wiley also publishes its books in a variety of electronic formats. Some content that appears in print may not be available in electronic books.

For more information about Wiley products, visit our Web site at http:// www.wiley.com.

Library of Congress Cataloging-in-Publication Data:

ISBN: 978-1-118-65337-1

10 9 8 7 6 5 4 3 2 1

Contents

Preface

This book came into existence principally because it wanted to join its companions, the books *Nonprofit Law Made Easy* and *Charitable Giving Law Made Easy*. (It was also fueled by a desire to distill private foundation law, so as to help trustees, directors, and management of foundations obtain some grasp of this complex body of law.) In format, style, and length, it parallels its siblings. The hope is that these three books, in tandem, will be of assistance in guiding nonlawyers through the maze of law concerning private foundations, other types of nonprofit tax-exempt organizations, and charitable giving.

This book also, however, blatantly mimics still another Wiley book (the one that started it all): *Not-for-Profit Accounting Made Easy*. Lawyers and accountants in the nonprofit realm populate overlapping universes, so these three companion volumes about the law are a natural fit with the book on nonprofit accounting rules.

As was noted in the preface to *Nonprofit Law Made Easy*, I have never had the opportunity to discuss this accounting book with its author, Warren Ruppel. I cannot imagine, nonetheless, that he extracted as much enjoyment from this writing process as I did. After years of writing technical (and long) books about various aspects of nonprofit law, writing the private foundation, nonprofit organizations, and charitable giving books with this approach was pure pleasure. The biggest challenge, not surprisingly, was the decisions as to what to include and what to leave out. This book thus reflects my take on what constitutes the fundamentals of the law concerning private foundations.

In any event, I had an easier time of it than Mr. Ruppel did. He had to *create* his book; I had merely to *imitate* it. The substance obviously is different but the format is unabashedly copied. Consequently, the three law books are about the same length as his, there are likewise a dozen chapters in each, every chapter of these books opens with an inventory of what is coming and ends with a chapter summary, and there are no footnotes. (The lack of footnotes came the closest to derogating from the pleasure of writing these books.) The three books share a similar dust jacket. So Mr. Ruppel and Wiley designed the original vessel; I poured my descriptions of the law into it.

Back to this matter of what to include and what to exclude. I included in this book the absolute basics, namely, a description of the differences between a private foundation and a public charity, and the special foundation rules concerning mandatory payouts, prohibited expenditures, self-dealing, excess business holdings, and jeopardizing investments. But, wanting to do more, I added prudent investment standards to the chapter on jeopardizing investments and blended the unrelated business rules into the chapter on excess business holdings. A chapter on charitable giving law is provided, tilted toward the unique aspects of giving to private foundations.

Being unable to stop there, I toyed with some new law and emerging concepts. As to the former, I looked at supporting organizations (heavily and wrongfully damaged by 2006 legislation) and donor-advised funds, and offered comparisons to private foundations. As to the latter, I ventured into the realm of emerging principles as to governance and traditional rules as to liability, and treated them from the singular perspective of foundations.

Nonprofit law continues to be as dynamic as law can get; consequently, trying to capture what appears to be the basics of elements of this law at any point in time can be tricky business. Congress, the Treasury Department, the IRS, the courts, and others in federal and state government are certain to contribute their share of new law. For the sake of the private foundation community, I hope coming law changes are not too tough on foundations, which are a meaningful component of the nonprofit sector and our society in general, and an important part of American philanthropy.

As a nonaccountant in the nonprofit field, I am glad to have *Not-for-Profit Accounting Made Easy* as a guide to the basics of the accounting rules and principles applicable to nonprofit organizations. I have once again tried to emulate Mr. Ruppel's work, to provide an equally valuable volume for the nonlawyer who needs a grounding in private foundation law.

I extend my thanks to Dexter Gasque, senior production editor, and to Susan McDermott, senior editor, for their support and assistance in creating this book.

Bruce R. Hopkins
October, 2008

About the Author

Bruce R. Hopkins is a senior partner in the law firm of Polsinelli Shalton Flanigan Suelthaus PC, practicing in the firm's Kansas City, Missouri, and Washington, D.C., offices. He specializes in the representation of private foundations and other tax-exempt organizations. His practice ranges over the entirety of law matters involving exempt organizations, with emphasis on the formation of nonprofit organizations, acquisition of recognition of tax-exempt status for them, the private inurement and private benefit doctrines, the intermediate sanctions rules, legislative and political campaign activities issues, public charity and private foundation rules, unrelated business planning, use of exempt and for-profit subsidiaries, joint venture planning, tax shelter involvement, review of annual information returns, Internet communications developments, the law of charitable giving (including planned giving), and fundraising law issues.

Mr. Hopkins served as Chair of the Committee on Exempt Organizations, Tax Section, American Bar Association; Chair, Section of Taxation, National Association of College and University Attorneys; and President, Planned Giving Study Group of Greater Washington, D.C.

Mr. Hopkins is the series editor of Wiley's Nonprofit Law, Finance, and Management Series. In addition to *Private Foundation Law Made Easy*, he is the author of *The Law of Tax-Exempt Organizations, Ninth Edition*; the *Planning Guide for the Law of Tax-Exempt Organizations: Strategies and Commentaries*; *IRS Audits of Tax-Exempt Organizations: Policies, Practices, and Procedures*; *The Tax Law of Charitable Giving, Third Edition*; *The Law of Fundraising, Third Edition*; *The Tax Law of Associations*; *The Tax Law of Unrelated Business for Nonprofit Organizations*; *The Nonprofits' Guide to Internet Communications Law*; *The Law of Intermediate Sanctions: A Guide for Nonprofits*; *Starting and Managing a Nonprofit Organization: A Legal Guide, Fifth Edition*; *Nonprofit Law Made Easy*;

Charitable Giving Law Made Easy; *650 Essential Nonprofit Law Questions Answered*; *The First Legal Answer Book for Fund-Raisers*; *The Second Legal Answer Book for Fund-Raisers*; *The Legal Answer Book for Nonprofit Organizations*; *The Second Legal Answer Book for Nonprofit Organizations*; and *The Nonprofit Law Dictionary*; and is the co-author, with Jody Blazek, of *Private Foundations: Tax Law and Compliance, Third Edition*; also with Ms. Blazek, *The Legal Answer Book for Private Foundations*; with Thomas K. Hyatt, of *The Law of Tax-Exempt Healthcare Organizations, Third Edition*; with David O. Middlebrook, of *Nonprofit Law for Religious Organizations: Essential Questions & Answers*; and with Douglas K. Anning, Virginia C. Gross, and Thomas K. Schenkelberg, *The New Form 990: Law, Policy, and Preparation*. He also writes *Bruce R. Hopkins' Nonprofit Counsel*, a monthly newsletter, published by John Wiley & Sons.

Mr. Hopkins received the 2007 Outstanding Nonprofit Lawyer Award (Vanguard Lifetime Achievement Award) from the American Bar Association, Section of Business Law, Committee on Nonprofit Corporations. He is listed in *The Best Lawyers in America*, Nonprofit Organizations/Charities Law, 2007–2008.

Mr. Hopkins has served as a member of the adjunct faculty at the George Washington University National Law Center and the University of Missouri-Kansas City, teaching courses on the law of tax-exempt organizations. He currently teaches that course as a member of the adjunct faculty at the University of Kansas School of Law.

Mr. Hopkins earned his JD and LLM degrees at the George Washington University National Law Center and his BA at the University of Michigan. He is a member of the bars of the District of Columbia and the state of Missouri.

PRIVATE FOUNDATION
LAW MADE EASY

1

PRIVATE FOUNDATIONS AND PUBLIC CHARITIES

The purpose of this chapter is to explain the distinctions between *private foundations* and *public charities*. There are, however, different types of private foundations and likewise different types of public charities. Specifically, this chapter will:

- Provide a generic and a technical definition of the term *private foundation*.

- Explain the terms *private operating foundations, exempt operating foundations, conduit private foundations*, and *nonexempt charitable trusts*.

- Explain the concept of a *public charity*.

- Define the public charities that are the *institutions*.

- Define the public charities that are the *donative publicly supported charities*.

- Define the public charities that are the service provider publicly supported charities.

- Provide a comparative analysis of publicly supported charities.

- Define the public charities that are *supporting organizations*.

- Define the public charities that *test for public safety*.

- Summarize the rules as to the excise tax on net investment income.

- Explain the significance of the private foundation-public charity dichotomy.

- Review some of the most recent IRS statistics on these subjects.

PRIVATE FOUNDATION DEFINED

A *private foundation* is a form of tax-exempt charitable organization. In this context, the term *charitable* includes program undertakings that are classified as *educational*, *scientific*, and *religious*. Generically, however, a private foundation typically has four other characteristics:

1. A private foundation is usually funded from a single source, often an individual, a family, or a corporation.

2. This funding is usually a one-time occasion, by means of a sizeable charitable contribution. While a private foundation may receive an ongoing flow of gifts, that is a rarity.

3. The year-by-year revenue derived by a private foundation is almost always in the form of investment income earned on their assets (also known as *principal* or *corpus*).

4. The typical private foundation makes grants for charitable purposes to other persons (individuals and/or organizations), rather than conduct its own programs.

The *private* aspect of the concept of a private foundation, then, principally reflects the nature of its financial support, particularly its initial funding. The *private* nature of a foundation, however, is often reflected in its governing board structure (see Chapter 12).

Because private foundations are generally exempt from federal income tax, the term *private foundation* appears in the Internal Revenue Code. This technical tax law definition, however, does not match the generic definition. Congress could have crafted a definition of private foundation in accord with the four unique attributes of foundations but it elected another approach. The reason for this distinction is rooted in the history of private foundation law, which came into being in 1969.

When most of the law as to private foundations was created in that year, Congress was in a horrific anti-foundation mood. The antipathy toward foundations at that time was substantial, largely because members of Congress were being regaled with tales of foundation abuse (mostly apocryphal) and many were in a populist mind-set, with foundations seen as playthings (and pocketbooks) of the wealthy. Consequently, when fashioning a definition of the term *private foundation*, Congress was careful to write it in such a way as to minimize the likelihood that crafty tax lawyers would find ways around the foundation laws.

Thus, the technical definition of *private foundation* has two key characteristics:

1. Despite the fact that the Internal Revenue Code purports to define the term, it does not. Instead, the Code defines what a private foundation isn't. (A private foundation is a tax-exempt charitable organization that is not a public charity.)

2. A unique feature in the law causes every tax-exempt charity in the United States to be *presumed* to be a private foundation. Among other outcomes, this forces nearly all charities that are not private foundations to convince the Internal Revenue Service of that fact and be officially classified as public entities. Put another way, a charitable organization that cannot, or subsequently fails to, qualify as a public charity is, by operation of law, a private foundation.

PRIVATE OPERATING FOUNDATIONS

As noted, one of the characteristics of a conventional private foundation is that it is a grant-maker. That is, the typical foundation serves as a funder of the charitable programs of other organizations. There are some private foundations, however, that, instead of grant-making, use their funds principally to administer their own charitable programs. This type of private foundation is known as a *private operating foundation*, with the word *operating* intended to convey this feature of internal program operations (rather than external funding). (These foundations are exempt from the standard income distribution requirement [see Chapter 4].) Some museums, libraries, housing and health care facilities, and scientific research entities, for example, are structured as private operating foundations. To qualify as an operating foundation, a private foundation must meet an income test and one of three other tests: an assets test, an endowment test, or a support test.

A private foundation satisfies the *income test* if it expends at least 85% of the lesser of its (1) *minimum investment return* (which, as explained in Chapter 4, is an amount equal to 5% of the foundation's investment assets) or (2) adjusted net income for the direct, active conduct of charitable activities. *Adjusted net income* is the amount of income from charitable functions, investment activities, set-asides, unrelated business, and short-term capital gains that exceeded the cost incurred in earning the income.

To meet the *assets test*, a private foundation must directly use at least 65% of its assets for the active conduct of charitable activities. Satisfaction of the *endowment test* requires that the foundation regularly make distributions for the active conduct of charitable activities in an amount not less than two-thirds of its minimum investment return. To meet the *support test*, a private foundation must regularly receive substantially all of its support (other than from gross investment income) from the public or from five or more qualifying exempt organizations; receive no more than 25% of its support (other than from gross investment income) from any one qualifying exempt organization; and receive no more than 50% of its support in the form of gross investment income.

EXEMPT OPERATING FOUNDATIONS

Certain private operating foundations are exempt from the excise tax on net investment income paid by most private foundations (discussed later in this chapter). This type of operating foundation must maintain public support for a minimum of 10 years; maintain a governing body at all times that is broadly representative of the public, where no more than 25% of that board consists of disqualified individuals; and not have at any time during the year an officer who is a disqualified individual. These foundations are also exempt from the expenditure responsibility requirements (see Chapter 5).

CONDUIT FOUNDATIONS

A *conduit private foundation* is not a separate category of private foundation; it is a standard private foundation that, under certain circumstances, is regarded as a public charity for charitable contribution deduction purposes. A foundation functions as a conduit when it makes qualifying distributions (see Chapter 4) that are treated as distributions from its corpus in an amount equal to 100% of all contributions received in the year involved, whether as money or property. These distributions, to qualify, must be made not later than the 15th day of the third month after the close of the foundation's tax year in which the contributions were received. The foundation must not have any remaining undistributed income for the year.

These distributions are treated as made first out of contributions of property and then out of contributions of money received by the private foundation in the year involved. The distributions cannot be made to an organization controlled, directly or indirectly, by the distributing foundation or by one or more disqualified persons (see Chapter 2) with respect to the foundation or to a private foundation that is not a private operating foundation.

NONEXEMPT CHARITABLE TRUSTS

Nonexempt charitable trusts are trusts that are not tax exempt but are treated as private foundations for federal tax law purposes. These trusts are funded and operated in nearly identical fashion as exempt private foundations. This type of trust has exclusively charitable interests; donors to them are allowed to claim a tax deduction for charitable contributions. Unlike private foundations, nonexempt charitable trusts are required to pay an annual tax on income that is not distributed for charitable purposes.

CONCEPT OF PUBLIC CHARITY

The dichotomy thus established in the Internal Revenue Code forces every U.S. charity to be classified as a public charity or a private foundation. This is by no means an equal division, in that, while there are millions of public charities, there are about 80,000 private foundations. (This disparity as to numbers, however, is not reflected in any balancing of the volume of federal tax law concerning charitable organizations; there are many pages of rules in the Internal Revenue Code that are applicable only to private foundations.)

As noted, a private foundation is a tax-exempt charitable organization that is not a public charity. The Code "definition" of *private foundation* focuses on the meaning of the term *public charity*. There are many categories of public charities. From a big-picture standpoint, however, there are four types of public charities: the *institutions, publicly supported charities, supporting organizations,* and (of minor import) *public safety testing organizations.*

As will be seen, public charities tend to be organizations with inherently *public* activity, entities that are financially supported by the public, or entities that have a close operating relationship with one or more other public charities. The term *public* can, however, be misleading; it is not used in the sense of a governmental entity (department, agency, etc.). The confusion is emblematic in the notion that a private school is a public charity. (Governmental entities are public charities.)

Most private foundations confine their grant-making to public charities. Therefore, it is essential (to avoid tax penalties [see Chapter 4]) that foundations having that approach understand the various ways in which a tax-exempt charitable organization can also be a public charity.

INSTITUTIONS

A category of public charity is loosely defined as *institutions*. These are entities that have inherently public activity. Embraced by the ambit of the institutions are churches, certain other religious organizations, schools, colleges, universities, hospitals, medical research organizations, and governmental units.

Churches

A *church* (including a synagogue and a mosque) is a public charity. The federal tax law is imprecise in defining this term, largely due to constitutional law (First Amendment) constraints. Although the term is not defined in the

Internal Revenue Code, the IRS formulated criteria that it uses to ascertain whether a religious organization constitutes a *church*. Originally, these criteria (unveiled in 1977) were in a list of 14 elements, not all of which needed to be satisfied. These elements include:

- A distinct legal existence
- A recognized creed and form of worship
- An ecclesiastical government
- A formal code of doctrine and discipline
- A distinct religious history
- A literature of its own
- Established places of worship
- Regular congregations
- Regular religious services
- Schools for the religious instruction of youth and preparation of its ministers

Over the ensuing years, however, the IRS has added criteria and become more rigid (and inconsistent) in its interpretation of the term *church*. It is currently the position of this agency that, to be a church, an organization must—in addition to being *religious*—have a defined congregation of worshippers, an established place of worship, and regular religious services. Some of the criteria in the original 14-element list have been downgraded in importance, as being common to tax-exempt organizations in general.

Associations and Conventions of Churches

Some religious entities are public charities because all of their members are churches. An *association of churches* is a church-membership entity where the membership is confined to churches in a state. A *convention of churches* is a church-membership entity where the membership embraces a multistate region of the United States or perhaps the entire nation.

Educational Institutions

An *educational institution* is a public charity. The concept of what is *educational* is much broader than *educational institution*, so it is insufficient for these purposes that an organization is merely educational in nature. To be an educational institution, an organization must normally maintain a regular faculty and curriculum, and normally have a regularly enrolled body of pupils or students in attendance at the place where its educational activities are regularly carried on. This type of institution is generically a *school*;

consequently, it must have as its primary function the presentation of formal instruction.

Educational institutions that qualify for public charity status include primary, secondary, preparatory, and high schools and colleges and universities. (Public schools are public charities by virtue of being units of government.) An organization cannot achieve public charity status as an operating educational institution where it is engaged in educational (institution-type) and educational (non-institution-type) activities, unless the latter activities are merely incidental to the former. For example, an organization cannot qualify as this type of public charity if its primary function is the operation of a museum, rather than the presentation of formal instruction.

A *university* generally is an institution of higher learning with teaching and research facilities, comprising an undergraduate school that awards bachelor's degrees and a graduate school and professional schools that award master's or doctor's degrees. A *college* is generally referred to as a school of higher learning that grants bachelor's degrees in liberal arts or sciences; the term is also frequently used to describe undergraduate divisions or schools of a university that offer courses and grant degrees in a particular field. The term *school* is defined as a division of a university offering courses of instruction in a particular profession; the term is also applicable to institutions of learning at the primary and secondary levels of education.

An organization may be regarded as presenting formal instruction even though it lacks a formal course program or formal classroom instruction. For example, an organization that conducted a survival course was classified as a public charity, even though its course periods were only 26 days and it used outdoor facilities more than classrooms; it had a regular curriculum, faculty, and student body. By contrast, an organization, the primary activity of which was providing specialized instruction by correspondence and a five- to ten-day seminar program of personal instruction for students who completed the correspondence course, did not qualify as an operating educational institution.

Even if an organization qualifies as a school or other type of formal educational institution, it will not be able to achieve public charity (or tax-exempt) status if it maintains racially discriminatory admissions policies or if it benefits private interests to more than an insubstantial extent. As an illustration of the latter, an otherwise qualifying school that trained individuals for careers as political campaign professionals was denied exempt status because of the private benefit accruing to a national political party and its candidates, inasmuch as nearly all of the school's graduates became employed by or consultants to the party's candidates.

Hospitals

A tax-exempt organization, the principal purpose or functions of which are the provision of medical or hospital care, medical education, or medical research, if the organization is a hospital, is a public charity. The term *hospital* includes exempt federal government hospitals; state, county, and municipal hospitals that are instrumentalities of governmental units; rehabilitation institutions; outpatient clinics; extended-care facilities or community mental health or drug treatment centers; and cooperative hospital service organizations. This term does not include convalescent homes, homes for children or the elderly, or institutions whose principal purpose or function is to train disabled individuals to pursue a vocation, nor does it include free clinics for animals. The term *medical care* includes the treatment of any physical or mental disability or condition, whether on an inpatient or outpatient basis, as long as the cost of the treatment is deductible by the individual treated.

Medical Research Organizations

A *medical research organization* directly engaged in the continuous active conduct of medical research in conjunction with a public charity hospital can qualify as a public charity. The term *medical research* means the conduct of investigations, experiments, and studies to discover, develop, or verify knowledge relating to the causes, diagnosis, treatment, prevention, or control of physical or mental diseases and impairments of human beings. To qualify, an organization must have the appropriate equipment and professional personnel necessary to carry out its principal function. *Medical research* encompasses the associated disciplines spanning the biological, social, and behavioral sciences.

An organization, to be a public charity under these rules, must have the conduct of medical research as its principal purpose or function and be primarily engaged in the continuous active conduct of medical research in conjunction with a qualified hospital. The organization need not be formally affiliated with an exempt hospital to be considered primarily engaged in the active conduct of medical research in conjunction with the hospital. There must, however, be a joint effort on the part of the research organization and the hospital to maintain close cooperation in the active conduct of the medical research. An organization is not considered to be primarily engaged directly in the continuous active conduct of medical research unless it, during a computation period, devotes more than one-half of its assets to the continuous active conduct of medical research or it expends funds equaling at least 3.5% of the fair market value of its endowment for the continuous active conduct of medical research.

If an organization's primary purpose is to disburse funds to other organizations for the conduct of research by them or to extend research grants or scholarships to others, it is not considered directly engaged in the active conduct of medical research.

Public College Support Foundations

Public charity status is accorded to certain organizations providing support for public (governmental) colleges and universities. This type of organization must normally receive a substantial part of its support (exclusive of income received in the performance of its tax-exempt activities) from the United States and/or direct or indirect contributions from the public. It must be organized and operated exclusively to receive, hold, invest, and administer property and to make expenditures to or for the benefit of a college or university that is a public charity and that is an agency or instrumentality of a state or political subdivision of a state, or that is owned or operated by a state or political subdivision or by an agency or instrumentality of one or more states or political subdivisions.

These expenditures include those made for any one or more of the regular functions of these colleges and universities, such as the acquisition and maintenance of real property comprising part of the campus; the construction of college or university buildings; the acquisition and maintenance of equipment and furnishings used for or in conjunction with regular functions of these colleges and universities; or expenditures for scholarships, libraries, and student loans.

Governmental Units

The United States, possessions of the United States, the District of Columbia, states, and their political subdivisions are classified as *governmental units*, which are public charities. This type of a unit qualifies as a public charity without regard to its sources of support, partly because it is responsive to all citizens. The concept of a governmental unit also embraces government instrumentalities, agencies, and entities referenced by similar terms.

Other Institutions

One of the many anomalies of the federal tax law is that some of the charitable institutions in U.S. society that are not generically private foundations are not accorded a public charity classification, unlike churches, schools, hospitals, and the like. Organizations in this position include museums, libraries, and organizations that operate orchestras and operas. To be public charities, these entities must be publicly supported or (much less likely) be structured as supporting organizations (as discussed later in this chapter). Some of these types of organizations are private operating foundations or exempt operating foundations (as discussed previously in this chapter).

DONATIVE PUBLICLY SUPPORTED ORGANIZATIONS

A way for a tax-exempt charitable organization to be a public charity is to receive its financial support from a suitable number of sources. A publicly supported charity is the antithesis of a private foundation, in that a foundation customarily derives its funding from one source, whereas a publicly supported charitable organization is (by definition) primarily or wholly supported by the public. One type of publicly supported charity—the *dona-tive* type—is an organization the revenues of which are in the form of a range of contributions and grants.

General Rules

An organization is a donative publicly supported entity if it is a tax-exempt charitable organization that normally receives a substantial part (defined later in this section) of its support (other than income from the performance of one or more exempt functions) from a governmental unit or from direct or indirect contributions from the public. It is this focus on support in the form of gifts and grants that causes this type of organization to be considered a *donative* one.

Organizations that qualify as donative publicly supported entities generally are organizations such as museums of history, art, or science; libraries; community centers to promote the arts; organizations providing facilities for the support of an opera, symphony orchestra, ballet, or repertory drama group; organizations providing some other direct service to the public; and organizations such as the American National Red Cross or that conduct federated fundraising campaigns.

The principal way for an organization to be a publicly supported charity under these rules is for it to normally derive at least one-third of its financial support from qualifying contributions and grants. (This one-third threshold is the definition of the phrase *substantial part* in this context.) Thus, an organization classified as this type of publicly supported charity must maintain a *support fraction*, the denominator of which is total gift and grant support received during the computation period (defined later in this chapter) and the numerator of which is the amount of support qualifying in connection with the one-third standard from eligible public and/or governmental sources for the period. The cash basis method of accounting is used in making these calculations.

2% Rule

A 2% ceiling is generally imposed on contributions and grants in determining public support. Only this threshold amount of a particular gift or grant is counted as public support, under this rule, irrespective of whether the contributor or grantor is an individual, corporation, trust, private foundation, or other type of entity (taking into account amounts given by related parties). In computing public support in this manner, the IRS has traditionally used a four-year measuring period, consisting of the organization's most recent four years. Beginning with the 2008 tax year, however, the measuring period is the organization's most recent five years.

An illustration will undoubtedly be helpful. Consider a charitable organization that received total gift and grant support in the amount of $1 million during the measuring period. In that instance, all contributions and grants up to $20,000 each are counted as public support (the total of them being the numerator of the support fraction). The amount of all gifts and grants during the period comprise the denominator of that fraction. If a person gave, for example, $80,000 during the measuring period, only $20,000 is public support from that source for that period. This organization thus must receive, during the period, at least $333,334 in contributions or grants of $20,000 or less each. It could receive $666,666 from one source and $10,000 each from 34 sources, or $20,000 each from 17 sources, for example.

A meaningful exception to this rule is available. Support received by a donative publicly supported charity from governmental units and/or other donative publicly supported charities is considered to be a form of *indirect* contributions from the public (in that these grantors are regarded as conduits of direct public support). This type of support is public support in its entirety. That is, this form of funding is not limited by the 2% rule. The same is true with respect to support from charitable organizations that satisfy the donative publicly supported organization definition, even though they are classified as some other form of public charity (such as a church).

For these purposes, the legal nature of the donors and/or grantors is not relevant. That is, in addition to individuals, charities, and governments, public support can be derived from for-profit entities (such as corporations and partnerships) and nonprofit entities (including various forms of charitable and noncharitable tax-exempt organizations). In another example of the English language failing in this regard, private foundations can be sources of public support. Generally, the fact that contributions or grants are restricted or earmarked does not detract from their qualification as public support.

Nonetheless, the 2% limitation applies with respect to support received from a donative publicly supported charitable organization or governmental unit if the support represents an amount that was expressly or impliedly earmarked by a donor or grantor to the publicly supported organization or unit of government as being for or for the benefit of the organization asserting status as a publicly supported charitable organization.

Support Test

A matter that can be of considerable significance in determining whether a charitable organization can qualify as a donative publicly supported entity is the meaning of the term *support*. For this purpose, *support* means amounts received in the form of, as noted, contributions (including corporate sponsorships) and grants, along with net income from unrelated business activities (see Chapter 8), gross investment income, tax revenues levied for the benefit of the organization and paid to or expended on behalf of the organization, and the value of services or facilities (exclusive of services or facilities generally furnished to the public without charge) furnished by a governmental unit to the organization without charge. All of these items comprise the denominator of the support fraction. (The larger the denominator, the greater the amount of public support that is allowed by the 2% threshold.) *Support* does not include gain from the disposition of property that is gain from the sale or exchange of a capital asset; the value of exemption from any federal, state, or local tax or any similar benefit; or funding in the form of a loan.

In constructing the support fraction, an organization must exclude from the numerator and the denominator any amounts received from the exercise or performance of its exempt purpose or function and contributions of services for which a charitable contribution deduction is not allowable. An organization will not be treated as meeting this support test, however, if it receives *almost all* of its support in the form of gross receipts from related activities and an insignificant amount of its support from governmental units and/or the public. Moreover, the organization can exclude from the numerator and the denominator of the support fraction an amount equal to one or more unusual grants (discussed later in this chapter).

Concept of *Normally*

In computing the support fraction, the organization's support that is *normally* received must be reviewed. This means that the organization must meet the one-third support test for a period encompassing the five tax years immediately preceding the year involved, on an aggregate basis. (Prior to 2008, this measuring period was four years.) When this is accomplished, the organization is considered as meeting the one-third support test for its current tax year and for the tax year immediately succeeding its current tax year. For example, if an organization's current tax year is calendar year 2009, the computation period for measuring public support pursuant to these rules is calendar years 2004–2008; if the support fraction requirement is satisfied on the basis of the support received over this five-year period, the organization satisfies this support test for 2009 and 2010. (A five-year period for meeting this support test is available for organizations during the initial five years of their existence.)

Unusual Contributions or Grants

Under the *unusual grant* rule, a contribution or grant may be excluded from the public support fraction. A gift or grant is *unusual* if it is an unexpected and substantial amount attracted by the public nature of the organization and received from a disinterested party. (Thus, this term is somewhat of a misnomer. The exception is not confined to grants and the operative word should be *unexpected*, not *unusual*.)

A number of factors are taken into account in this regard; no single factor is determinative. The positive factors follow, with their opposites (negative factors) in parentheses:

- The contribution or grant is from a person with no connection to the charitable organization. (The contribution or grant is received from a person who created the organization, is a substantial contributor (see Chapter 2) to it, is a board member, an officer, or is related to one of these persons.)

- The gift or grant is in the form of cash, marketable securities, or property that furthers the organization's exempt purposes. An example of the latter is a gift of a painting to a museum. (The property is illiquid, difficult to dispose of, and/or not suitable in relation to the organization's functions.)

- No material restrictions or conditions are placed on the transfer.

- The organization attracts a significant amount of support to pay its operating expenses on a regular basis, and the gift or grant adds to an endowment or pays for capital items. (The gift or grant is used for operating expenses for several years; nothing is added to an endowment.)

- The gift is a bequest. (The gift is an *inter vivos* [lifetime] transfer.)

- An active fundraising program attracts significant public support. (Gift and grant solicitation programs are limited or unsuccessful.)

- A representative and broad-based governing body controls the organization. (Related parties are in control.)

- Prior to the receipts of the unusual grant, the organization qualified as a publicly supported entity. (The unusual grant exclusion was relied on in the past to satisfy the test.)

Facts-and-Circumstances Test

One of the defects of the donative organization support rules is that organizations that are not private foundations in a generic sense, because they have many of the attributes of a public organization, may nonetheless be classified as private foundations because they cannot meet the somewhat mechanical one-third support test. Charitable organizations with this dilemma can include entities such as museums and libraries that heavily rely on their endowments for financial support and thus have little or no need for contributions and grants. Although the statutory law is silent on the point, the tax regulations somewhat ameliorate this rigidity of the general rule by means of a *facts-and-circumstances test*.

The history of an organization's programmatic and fundraising efforts, and other factors, can be considered as an alternative to the rather strict mechanical formula for qualifying as a public charity under the general donative publicly support charitable organization rules. These factors must be present for this test to be met:

- Public support (computed pursuant to the general rule) must be at least 10% of the total support, and the higher the better.

- The organization must have an active "continuous and bona fide" fundraising program designed to attract new and additional public and governmental support. Consideration will be given to the fact that, in its early years of existence, the charitable organization may limit the scope of its gift and grant solicitations to those persons deemed most likely to provide seed money in an amount sufficient to enable it to commence its charitable activities and expand its solicitation program.

- Other favorable factors must be present, such as:
  - The composition of the organization's governing board is representative of broad public interests.
  - Support is derived from governmental and other sources representative of the public.
  - Facilities and programs are made available to the public.
  - The organization's programs appeal to a broad range of the public.

As to the governing board factor, the organization's public charity status will be enhanced where it has a governing body that represents the interests of the public, rather than the personal or private interests of a limited number of donors. This can be accomplished by the election of board members by a broad-based membership or by having the board composed of public officials, individuals having particular expertise in the field or discipline involved, community leaders, and the like.

As noted, one of the important elements of this facts-and-circumstances test is the availability of facilities or services to the public. Example of entities meeting this standard are a museum that holds its building open to the public, a symphony orchestra that gives public performances, a conservation organization that provides services to the public through the distribution of educational materials, and a home for the elderly that provides domiciliary or nursing services for members of the public.

Issues

Nine issues can arise in computing the public support component (the numerator) of the support fraction for donative publicly supported organizations. They are:

1. Proper calculation of the denominator of the support fraction

2. Whether a payment constitutes a contribution or a grant

3. Whether a membership fee can be treated as a contribution rather than a payment for services

4. Whether a payment pursuant to a contract is a grant rather than revenue from a related activity (exempt function revenue)

5. Whether a grant is from another donative publicly supported charity (or a charity *described in* the rules)

6. Whether a grant from a publicly supported charity or governmental unit is a pass-through transfer from another grantor

7. Whether a grant constitutes an unusual grant

8. Whether an organization is primarily dependent on gross receipts from related activities

9. Whether the organization needs to rely on the facts-and-circumstances test

The fourth item warrants additional mention. When the term *contract* is used in this context, it usually connotes a payment for services rendered or goods provided, which means that the funds involved are exempt function revenue and thus must be excluded from the support fraction. Confusion can arise because a grant is often the subject of a contract, although in that setting the term used usually is *agreement*. While sometimes it is difficult to differentiate between the two, a *grant* is a payment made to a charitable organization to enable it to operate one or more programs, while a payment pursuant to a contract is for the acquisition of a good or service.

The principal point with these issues is that the resolution of them can materially affect the construct of the support fraction and thus the public support percentage. Sometimes, an organization will want to exclude a large amount from the fraction (such as a payment made in accordance with a contract) so as to increase the support percentage. It is not uncommon for a support fraction to be improperly computed, so that the resulting public support percentage is below the one-third threshold. It can be a great joy for a tax lawyer to review a draft of an anemic public support fraction calculation, and discover, for example, that a grant that was limited by the 2% threshold can in fact be counted in full as public support (issue 5) or that a large grant can in fact be excluded from the fraction as an unusual grant (issue 7), thereby enabling the charitable organization to report a public support ratio that is considerably in excess of the one-third minimum.

Community Foundations

In the world of charities, the term *foundation* is often used in conjunction with an organization that is not a *private foundation*. An illustration of this word interplay is the *community foundation*, which usually is a donative publicly supported charity. These foundations almost always attract, receive, and depend on financial support from members of the public on a regular, recurring basis. Community foundations are designed to attract large contributions of a capital or endowment nature, with the gifts often received and maintained in separate trusts or funds. These entities are generally identified with a particular community and are controlled by a representative group of persons in that area.

For classification as a public charity, however, a community foundation wants to be regarded as a single entity, rather than an aggregation of funds. To be treated as a component part of a community foundation, a trust or fund must be created by gift or similar transfer and may not be subjected by the transferor to any material restriction. A community foundation must, to be considered a single entity, be appropriately named, be so structured as to subject its funds to a common governing instrument, have a common governing body, and prepare periodic financial reports that treat all funds held by the foundation as its assets. The board of a community foundation must have the power to modify any restriction on the distribution of funds where it is inconsistent with the charitable needs of the community, must commit itself to the exercise of its powers in the best interests of the foundation, and must commit itself to seeing that the funds are invested in accordance with standards of fiduciary conduct.

A private foundation may make a grant to a designated fund within a community foundation (often a donor-advised fund [see Chapter 11]). The private foundation can receive a payout credit (see Chapter 4) for this type of grant, even though it acquires the ability to make recommendations as to distributions to other charitable organizations from the fund, as long as there are no prohibited material restrictions. Grants of this nature are regarded as made to the community foundation as an entity and not to a discrete fund.

SERVICE PROVIDER PUBLICLY SUPPORTED ORGANIZATIONS

The second way that a tax-exempt charitable organization can be a publicly supported entity is to be a *service provider* organization. As is the case with the donative organization rules, qualification for public charity status focuses on sources of revenue, although there are considerable differences between the two ways to compute public support. Public support in this context includes gifts and grants, but also includes forms of exempt function revenue. Thus, this type of publicly supported charity usually has a major portion of its support in the form of fees and like charges derived from the conduct of its programs, such as exempt dues-based entities, theaters, arts organizations, educational publishers, day care centers, and animal shelters.

A two-part support test must be met for an organization to qualify as this type of publicly supported charity:

- Investment income cannot exceed one-third of total support. *Total support* basically is all of the organization's gross revenue normally received (discussed later in this chapter), other than capital gains and the value of exemptions from local, state, and federal taxes.

- More than one-third of total support must be a combination of:

  ○ Contributions, grants, and membership dues from sources other than disqualified persons (see Chapter 2)

  ○ Admission fees to exempt function facilities or activities, such as payments for theater tickets, access to a museum or historical site, seminars, lectures, and athletic events

  ○ Fees for performance of services, such as day care fees, counseling fees, testing fees, laboratory fees, library fines, animal neutering charges, and athletic activity fees

  ○ Sales of merchandise related to the organization's exempt purpose, including books and other educational literature, pharmaceuticals and medical devices, handicrafts, reproductions and copies of original works of art, byproducts of a blood bank, and goods produced by disabled workers

Exempt function revenue from one source may not be treated as public support to the extent it is in excess of $5,000 or 1% of the total support of the organization, whichever is higher.

Permitted Sources

Generally, to be public support under these rules, the support must be derived from *permitted sources*. Consequently, a charitable organization seeking to qualify as a publicly supported entity under these rules must construct a support fraction, with the amount of support from permitted sources constituting the numerator of the fraction and the total amount of support being the fraction's denominator.

Permitted sources are certain public and publicly supported charitable organizations, governmental units, and persons other than disqualified persons (see Chapter 2) with respect to the organization. Thus, in general, support (other than from disqualified persons) from another service provider publicly supported organization, a supporting organization (see below), any other tax-exempt organization (other than the institutions and donative publicly supported organizations, a for-profit organization, or an individual constitutes public support for this type of organization, albeit limited in some instances (see next section). The cash basis method of accounting is used in making these determinations.

Support

The term *support* means (in addition to the categories of public support, which may include corporate sponsorships) (1) net income from any unrelated business (see Chapter 8), (2) gross investment income, (3) tax revenues levied for the benefit of the organization and either paid to or expended on behalf of the organization, and (4) the value of services or facilities (other than services or facilities generally furnished to the public without charge) furnished by a governmental unit. These items of support are combined to constitute the denominator of the support fraction.

The concept of support does not include (1) any gain from the disposition of a capital asset; (2) the value of local, state, and/or federal tax exemptions or similar benefits, and (3) the proceeds of a loan.

Limitations on Support

The support taken into account in determining the numerator of the support test under these rules must come from permitted sources. Thus, transfers from disqualified persons (see Chapter 2) cannot qualify as public support under the service provider publicly supported organizations rules. The fact that a contribution or grant is restricted or earmarked does not detract from its qualification as public support.

In determining the amount of support in the form of gross receipts that is allowable in calculating the numerator of this support fraction, gross receipts from related activities (other than membership fees) from any person or from any bureau or similar agency of a governmental unit are includible in any tax year only to the extent that these receipts do not exceed the greater of $5,000 or 1% of the organization's total support for that year.

The phrase *bureau or similar agency* of a government means a specialized operating (rather than a policy-making or administrative) unit of the executive, judicial, or legislative branch of a government, usually a subdivision of a department of a government. Therefore, an organization receiving gross receipts (a grant) from both a policy-making or administrative unit of a government (e.g., the Agency for International Development [AID]) and an operational unit of a government's department (e.g., the Bureau for Latin America, an operating unit within AID) is treated as receiving gross receipts from two sources, with the amount from each agency separately subject to the $5,000/1% limitation.

A somewhat similar *permitted sources* limitation excludes support from a disqualified person, including a substantial contributor (see Chapter 2). In general, a *substantial contributor* is a person who contributes, grants, or bequeaths an aggregate amount of more than $5,000 to a charitable organization, where that amount is more than 2% of the total contributions, grants, and bequests received by the organization before the close of its tax year in which the contribution or the like from the person is received. As noted, however, grants from governmental units and certain public charities are not subject to this limitation.

The federal tax law defines and distinguishes the various forms of support referenced in the service provided publicly supported organizations rules: *contributions* or *gross receipts*, *grant* or *gross receipts*, *membership fees*, *gross receipts* or *gross investment income*, and *grant* or *indirect contribution*. For example, the term *gross receipts* means amounts received from the conduct of an activity related to an exempt function where a specific service, facility, or product is provided to serve the direct and immediate needs of the payor; a *grant* is an amount paid to confer a direct benefit for the public. A payment of money or transfer of property without adequate consideration generally is a *contribution* or a *grant*. The furnishing of facilities for a rental fee or the making of loans in furtherance of an exempt purpose will likely give rise to *gross receipts* rather than *gross investment income*. The fact that a membership organization provides services, facilities, and the like to its members as part of its overall activities will not result in the fees received from members being treated as *gross receipts* rather than *membership fees*.

Investment Income Test

An organization, to be classified as a service provider publicly supported charity, must normally receive no more than one-third of its support from (1) gross investment income, including interest, dividends, royalties, rent, and payments with respect to securities loans, and (2) any excess of the amount of unrelated business taxable income over the amount of tax on that income. To qualify under this test, an organization must construct a *gross investment income fraction*, with the amount of gross investment income and any unrelated income (net of the tax paid on it) constituting the numerator of the fraction and the total amount of support being the denominator. On occasion, there may be an issue as to whether a revenue item is a *gross receipt* from the performance of an exempt function or is *gross investment income*.

Concept of Normally

These public support and investment income tests are computed on the basis of the nature of the organization's *normal* sources of support. An organization is considered as *normally* receiving at least one-third of its support from permitted sources and no more than one-third of its support from gross investment income for its current tax year and immediately succeeding tax year if, for the *measuring period*, the aggregate amount of support received over the period from permitted sources is more than one-third of its total support and the aggregate amount of support over the period from gross investment income is not more than one-third of its total support.

In computing support under these rules, the IRS has traditionally used a four-year measuring period, involving the organization's most recent years. Beginning with the 2008 tax year, however, the measuring period is the organization's most recent five years. For example, if an organization's current tax year is calendar year 2009, the computation period for measuring support pursuant to these rules is calendar years 2004–2008; if the support fraction is satisfied on the basis of the support received over this five-year period, the organization satisfies this support test for 2009 and 2010. (A five-year period for meeting these support tests has long been available for organizations during the initial five years of their existence.)

Issues

The issues that arise in connection with calculation of public support under the service provider publicly supported organization rules are somewhat the same as those that can emerge in the donative publicly supported organization context ("discussed previously"). Of the nine issues in that setting, numbers 1 through 4 and 7 apply equally here. (A facts-and-circumstances test is not available for service provider entities.) There are five other potential issues (and thus a total of ten issues) for service provider publicly supported organizations:

1. Accurate identification of the organization's disqualified persons (see Chapter 2)

2. Correct computation of exempt function revenue

3. Correct application of the 1% rule

4. Whether a grant is from another service provider publicly supported organization (or a charity described in the rules)

5. Correct ascertainment of gross investment income

COMPARATIVE ANALYSIS OF PUBLICLY SUPPORTED CHARITIES

The two principal types of publicly supported charities can simultaneously meet both public support tests if they have a broad base of financial support in the form of contributions and grants. Indeed, many charities can easily satisfy either test at any time.

A significant deviation arises, however, concerning the matter of *exempt function revenue*. In the case of donative publicly supported charities, exempt function revenue is omitted from the fraction and too much of it can prevent or cause loss of public charity status. By contrast, some or all of exempt function revenue can be public support for service provider publicly supported charities. This distinction is one of the principal determinants for a charitable organization in deciding which category of publicly supported charity is appropriate. A dues-based charitable organization, for example, would almost always select the service provider publicly supported charity classification.

There are other considerations. The donative publicly supported charity calculates its public support using a rather mechanical formula, while the service provider publicly supported charity must go through the machinations of determining whether any of its financial support has been derived from disqualified persons. The donative publicly supported charity status has a preferred aura, if only because the service provider publicly supported charity (usually being fee-based) can appear too commercial in nature. Most service provider publicly supported charities are not permitted to maintain a pooled income fund (see Chapter 9), although today this is not much of a distinction because these funds are out of favor.

SUPPORTING ORGANIZATIONS

A category of tax-exempt charitable organization that is a public charity is the *supporting organization*. Charitable supporting organizations usually are entities that do not qualify as *institutions* or *publicly supported charities* but are sufficiently related to one or more charitable organizations that are institutions or are publicly supported organizations so that the requisite degree of public control and involvement is considered present. Certain types of noncharitable tax-exempt organizations also may be supported organizations.

A supporting organization must be organized and at all times operated exclusively for the benefit of, to perform the functions of, or to carry out the purposes of one or more eligible supported organizations. Also, a supporting organization must be operated, supervised, or controlled by one or more qualified supported organizations, supervised or controlled in connection with one or more such organizations, or operated in connection with one or more such organizations. A parsing of this rule has led to a quadruple classification of supporting organizations:

- Parents and subsidiaries (also known as Type I supporting organizations)
- Commonly controlled organizations (Type II)
- Functionally integrated organizations (Type III)
- Nonfunctionally integrated organizations (also Type III)

A third fundamental requirement is that a supporting organization must not be controlled, directly or indirectly, by one or more disqualified persons (other than foundation managers or eligible supported organizations).

A supporting organization may be created by one or more donors or by an organization that becomes the supported organization. To qualify as a supporting organization, a charitable entity must meet an organizational test and an operational test.

Organizational Test

A supporting organization must be organized exclusively to support or benefit one or more specified public institutions, publicly supported charitable organizations, or certain noncharitable organizations. Its articles of organization must limit its purposes to one or more of the purposes that are permissible for a supporting organization, may not expressly empower the organization to engage in activities that are not in furtherance of these purposes, must state the specified entity or entities on behalf of which it is to be operated, and may not expressly empower the organization to operate to support or benefit any other organization.

To qualify as a supporting organization, an organization's stated purposes may be as broad as, or more specific than, the purposes that are permissible for a supporting organization. Thus, an organization that is formed "for the benefit of" one or more eligible supported organizations will meet this organizational test, assuming the other requirements are satisfied. An organization that is *operated, supervised, or controlled by* (a Type I entity) or *supervised or controlled in connection with* (Type II) one or more qualified supported organizations to carry out their purposes will satisfy these requirements if the purposes stated in the articles of organization are similar to, but no broader than, the purposes stated in the articles of the supported organization or organizations.

An organization will not meet this organizational test if its articles of organization expressly permit it to operate to support or benefit any organization other than its specified supported organization or organizations. The fact that the actual operations of the organization have been exclusively for the benefit of one or more specified eligible supported organizations is not sufficient to permit it to satisfy this organizational test.

Operational Test

A supporting organization must be operated exclusively to support or benefit one or more specified qualified supported organizations. Unlike the definition of the term *exclusively*, as applied in the context of charitable organizations generally, which has been held by the courts to mean *primarily* (see Chapter 3), the term *exclusively* in the supporting organization context means *solely*.

A supporting organization must engage solely in activities that support or benefit one or more eligible supported organizations. One way to do this, although it is not mandated but will be in certain instances (see Chapter 11), is for the supporting organization to make grants to the supported organization; this is often done, for example, where the supporting organization houses an endowment for the benefit of a supported organization. Another form of support or benefit occurs where a supporting organization carries on a discrete program or activity on behalf of a supported organization. In one instance, a tax-exempt hospital wanted a facility near the hospital in which patients about to undergo serious surgery, and their families and friends, could stay in immediate advance of the surgical procedure; the hospital created a supporting organization, which purchased a nearby motel and converted it into the facility the hospital needed. In another case, a supporting organization, supportive of the academic endeavors of the medical school at an exempt university, was used to operate a faculty practice plan in furtherance of the teaching, research, and service programs of the school. A supporting organization may engage in fundraising activities, such as solicitation of contributions and grants, special events, and unrelated business, to raise funds for one or more supported organizations or other permissible beneficiaries.

The allowable activities of a supporting organization may include making payments to or for the use of, or providing services or facilities for, members of the charitable class benefited by the charitable supported organization. A supporting organization may make a payment indirectly through an unrelated organization to a member of a charitable class benefited by a supported charitable organization but only where the payment constitutes a grant to an individual rather than a grant to the organization.

A supporting organization has many characteristics of a private foundation, such as the absence of any requirement that it be publicly supported. Thus, like a private foundation, a supporting organization can be funded entirely by investment income. It can satisfy this organizational test by engaging solely in investment activity, assuming charitable ends are being served.

Specification Requirement

As noted, a supporting organization must be organized and operated to support or benefit one or more *specified* supported organizations. This specification must be in the supporting organization's articles of organization, although the manner of the specification depends on which of the types of relationships with one or more eligible supported organizations is involved.

Generally, it is expected that the articles of organization of the supporting organization will designate (i.e., *specify*) each of the supported organizations by name. If the relationship is one of *operated, supervised, or controlled by* (Type I) or *supervised or controlled in connection with* (Type II), however, designation by name is not required as long as the articles of organization of the supporting organization require that it be operated to support or benefit one or more beneficiary organizations that are designated by class or purpose and that include one or more supported organizations, as to which there is one of these two relationships, or organizations that are closely related in purpose or function to supported organizations as to which there is one of the two relationships (in either instance, where there is no designation of the organization(s) by name). If the relationship is one of *operated in connection with* (Type III), the supporting organization must designate the supported organization or organizations by name.

A supporting organization is deemed to meet the specification requirement, even though its articles of organization do not designate each supported organization by name—irrespective of the nature of the relationship—if there has been a historical and continuing relationship between the supporting organization and the supported organizations and, by reason of that relationship, there has developed a substantial identity of interests between the organizations.

Nonetheless, in practice, it is common to specify the supported organization or organization in the supporting organization's articles of organization, irrespective of the type of supporting organization.

Required Relationships

As noted, to meet these requirements, an organization must be operated, supervised, or controlled by or in connection with one or more eligible supported organizations. Thus, if an organization does not stand in at least one of the required relationships with respect to one or more eligible supported organizations, it cannot qualify as a supporting organization. Regardless of the applicable relationship (Type I, II, or either of the IIIs), it must be ensured that the supporting organization will be *responsive* to the needs or demands of one or more eligible supported organizations and that the supporting organization will constitute an *integral part* of or maintain a *significant involvement* in the operations of one or more qualified supported organizations. (Additional information about these relationships and other supporting organization rules is in Chapter 11.)

Operated, Supervised, or Controlled By

The distinguishing feature of the relationship between a supporting organization and one or more eligible supported organizations encompassed by the phrase *operated, supervised, or controlled by* is the presence of a substantial degree of direction by one or more supported organizations in regard to the policies, programs, and activities of the supporting organization. This is a relationship comparable to that of a parent and subsidiary (Type I).

Supervised or Controlled in Connection With

The distinguishing feature of the relationship between a supporting organization and one or more eligible supported organizations encompassed by the phrase *supervised or controlled in connection with* is the presence of common supervision or control by the persons supervising or controlling the supporting organizations and the supported organization(s) to ensure that the supporting organization will be responsive to the needs and requirements of the supported organization(s). Therefore, in order to meet this requirement, the control or management of the supporting organization must be vested in the same individuals who control or manage the supported organization(s) (Type II).

Operation in Connection With

Qualification as a supporting organization by reason of the *operated in connection with* relationship entails the least intimate of the relationships between a supporting organization and one or more supported organizations. This relationship usually is more of a programmatic one than a governance one. This type of relationship (Type III), prevalent for example in the health care field, is often structured so as to avoid legal liability, from the standpoint of a supported organization, for something done by the supporting organization.

The distinguishing feature of the relationship between a supporting organization and one or more supported organizations encompassed by this phrase is that the supporting organization must be responsive to and significantly involved in the operations of the supported organization or organizations. Generally, to satisfy the criteria of this relationship, a supporting organization must meet a *responsiveness test* and an *integral part test*.

Noncharitable Supported Organizations

Certain tax-exempt organizations that are not charitable entities qualify as supported organizations; this means that a charitable organization that is supportive of one or more of these noncharitable entities constitutes a supporting organization. These eligible supported organizations are exempt social welfare organizations [501(c)(4) entities]; labor, agricultural, and horticultural organizations [501(c)(5) entities]; and business leagues, such as trade associations [501(c)(6) entities]. The principal requirement is that these organizations have to satisfy the one-third support test applicable to service provider publicly supported organizations. These organizations frequently meet this support requirement because they have a membership that pays dues.

This rule is principally designed to facilitate public charity status for related foundations and other funds (such as scholarship, award, and research funds) operated by the specified noncharitable organizations. This type of supporting organization can be in an awkward position: It must be charitable in function to be tax exempt, yet be supportive of a noncharitable entity to be a public charity.

Substitutions

The federal tax law is vague as to how a supported organization with respect to a supporting organization can be changed (substituted), without loss of the supporting organization's public charity status. In what may be the only example of this type of substitution to date, the IRS ruled that a tax-exempt entity could retain its status as a supporting organization, notwithstanding a transaction in which a supported organization was substituted. An exempt university caused a related supporting organization to become affiliated with another entity that also functioned to support and benefit the university. This ruling is of limited utility in understanding the bounds of supported organization substitution, however, because, under the facts of the ruling, the functions of the supporting organization remained essentially the same and it continued to indirectly support the university.

An organization that is *operated in connection with* one or more eligible supported organizations can satisfy the specification requirement (discussed earlier in this chapter) even if its articles of organization permit an eligible supported organization that is designated by class or purpose to be substituted for the supported organizations designated by name in its articles but only if the substitution is conditioned on the occurrence of an event that is beyond the control of the supporting organization. This type of event includes, as to a supported organization, loss of tax exemption, substantial failure or abandonment of operations, or dissolution of the entity.

Limitation on Control

As noted, one or more disqualified persons with respect to a supporting organization, other than its officers and the like (technically termed *foundation managers*) cannot (without jeopardizing its public charity status), directly or indirectly, control the organization. An individual who is a disqualified person with respect to a supporting organization does not lose that status because a beneficiary supported organization appoints or designates him or her to be a foundation manager of the supporting organization, to serve as a representative of the supported organization.

A supporting organization is considered *controlled* if the disqualified persons, by aggregating their votes or positions of authority, may require the organization to perform an act that significantly affects its operations or may prevent the supporting organization from performing this type of an act. Generally, control exists if the voting power of these persons is 50% or more of the total voting power of the organization's governing body or if one or more disqualified persons have the right to exercise veto power over the actions of the organization. All pertinent facts and circumstances, including the nature, diversity, and income yield of an organization's holdings, the length of time particular securities or other assets are retained, and the manner of exercising its voting rights with respect to securities in which members of its governing body also have an interest, are taken into consideration in determining whether a disqualified person does in fact indirectly control an organization.

Caution needs to be exercised in this context. The IRS can find indirect control of a supporting organization by disqualified persons by going beyond the foregoing rules. One such instance involved a charitable organization that made distributions to a tax-exempt university. The organization's board of directors was composed of a substantial contributor to the organization; two employees of a business corporation, of which more than 35% of the voting power was owned by the disqualified person; and an individual selected by the university. None of the directors had veto power over the organization's actions. Conceding that disqualified persons did not directly control the organization, the IRS said that "one circumstance to be considered in whether a disqualified person is in a position to influence the decisions of members of the organization's governing body who are not themselves disqualified persons." Thus, the IRS concluded that the two directors who were employees of the disqualified person corporation should be considered the equivalent of disqualified persons for purposes of applying the 50% control rule. This position led to the conclusion that the organization was indirectly controlled by disqualified persons and, therefore, could not be a public charity by virtue of being a qualified supporting organization.

PUBLIC SAFETY TESTING ORGANIZATIONS

Another category of organization that is deemed to be a public charity is an organization that is organized and operated exclusively for testing for public safety. Although these entities are considered public charities, they are not eligible to receive tax-deductible charitable contributions.

IMPORT OF PUBLIC-PRIVATE DICHOTOMY

As a general proposition—and this is from a law standpoint—public charity status is preferable to private foundation status. That is, again, purely from the perspective of the law, there is no advantage to a charitable organization in being a private foundation. (There is nothing inherently wrong in being a private foundation, of course, and about 80,000 of them function quite nicely in that capacity.)

The biggest disadvantage of classification as a private foundation is that a charitable organization is subject to and expected to comply with the private foundation rules concerning mandatory payouts, self-dealing, excess business holdings, jeopardizing investments, and prohibited expenditures (see Chapters 4 through 8). Public charities are generally not caught up in this barrage of restrictions and requirements.

Having said that, however, some of the private foundation rules are being applied in the public charity setting. The excess business holdings rules are applicable to certain supporting organizations (see Chapter 11). At this time, Congress and the IRS are working on mandatory payout requirements for some supporting organizations. Although the self-dealing rules (see Chapter 6) do not apply to public charities, rules as to excess benefit transactions apply in connection with public charities; in several instances, the requirements are the same. Certain basic principles of the law, such as the private inurement and private benefit doctrines (see Chapter 3) are applicable to both categories of charitable organizations.

Another disadvantage to private foundation status is that the charitable giving rules (see Chapter 9) considerably favor public charities. This problem (if there is one) usually is presented at the time a private foundation is initially funded, either because percentage limitations restrict the extent of a charitable contribution deduction or because a deduction for a gift of property is confined to the donor's basis in the property.

SOME STATISTICS

The IRS collects data on private foundations and nonexempt charitable trusts, based on information in these organizations' annual information returns (see Chapter 10). The most recent year for which the IRS has developed these statistics is 2004.

For that year, the total number of returns filed by private foundations was 76,897; nonexempt charitable trusts filed 3,511 returns. The fair market value of foundations' assets for that year was $509.9 billion; the asset value for charitable trusts was about $5.6 billion. Private foundations disbursed $32.1 billion, of which $27.6 billion was in the form of grants; charitable trusts distributed $332 million. Private foundations had $58.7 billion in total revenue in 2004; nonexempt charitable trusts had total revenue in the amount of $502 million. Private foundations had $34 billion in net investment income; the net investment income of nonexempt charitable trusts was $304 million.

Large private foundations—those with $50 million or more in fair market value of total assets at the end of tax year 2004—accounted for the majority of financial activity by the annual return filers. Although they represented less than 2% of the filers (including nonexempt charitable trusts), they held 67% of the aggregate fair market value of total assets. Nearly 60% of all assets were held by the 610 private foundations with assets valued at $100 million or more. Large foundations received 57% of the revenue and distributed 55% of the grants.

For 2004, ten private foundations held nearly one-fifth of private foundations' assets, totaling $97.1 billion. The largest of these foundations held $28.8 billion in assets; the tenth largest of these foundations held $5 billion in assets. The largest private foundation grant-maker distributed $1.3 billion in 2004; the tenth largest grant-maker made grants totaling $210 million.

SUMMARY

This chapter provided basic information as to the distinctions between private foundations and public charities. The types of public charities were discussed, as were the different types of private foundations. Particular emphasis was placed on the various ways a tax-exempt charitable organization can qualify as a publicly supported entity and on the types of supporting organizations. The chapter included a comparative analysis of publicly supported charities and explained the significance of the private foundation–public charity dichotomy. The chapter concluded with a summary of the IRS's statistics concerning private foundations and nonexempt charitable trusts.

2

DISQUALIFIED PERSONS

The purpose of this chapter is to describe the various ways in which an individual or other person can be, with respect to a private foundation, a *disqualified person*. The concept of disqualified persons is critical to an understanding of many of the private foundation rules. There are ten bases on which a person can be considered a disqualified person in relation to a foundation. Specifically, this chapter will:

- Describe the various ways a person can be a *foundation manager*.
- Explain how a person can be regarded as a *substantial contributor*.
- Explain how a *20%-plus owner* can be a disqualified person.
- Explain how *members of a family* can be disqualified persons.
- Explain how a corporation can be a disqualified person.
- Explain how a partnership can be a disqualified person.
- Explain how a trust or an estate can be a disqualified person.
- Explain when a private foundation can be a disqualified person.
- Explain how a government official can be a disqualified person.
- Explain how a person can cease being a disqualified person.
- Explore application of the private benefit doctrine in this context.

BASIC CONCEPTS

A basic concept of the federal tax laws pertaining to private foundations is that of the *disqualified person*. An understanding of the meaning of this term is essential to appreciation of the scope and depth of the rules defining permitted sources for purposes of calculating certain forms of public support (see Chapter 1), controlled organizations (see below), prohibited self-dealing (see Chapter 6), the excess business holding rules (see Chapter 8), and other private foundation rules.

Essentially, a disqualified person is a person (including an individual, corporation, partnership, trust, estate, or other private foundation) standing in one or more close relationships with respect to a private foundation, its trustees, and/or its founders. A disqualified person is basically the same as what is known as an *insider* in the private inurement context and a disqualified person in the intermediate sanctions context (see Chapter 3).

FOUNDATION MANAGERS

The most obvious category of disqualified person is the *foundation manager*, defined to encompass trustees, directors, and officers of private foundations, or individuals having powers or responsibilities similar to those holding one of these three positions. An individual is considered an *officer* of a private foundation if he or she (1) is specifically designated as an officer in the governing instruments of the foundation (usually the bylaws) or (2) regularly exercises general authority to make administrative or policy decisions on behalf of the foundation. Thus, the IRS determined that employees of a bank that was the trustee of a private foundation were foundation managers, because "they [were] free, on a day-to-day basis, to administer the trust and distribute the funds according to their best judgment." A person who has authority to merely make recommendations pertaining to administrative or policy decisions, but lacks the authority to implement them without approval of someone in a superior position, is not a foundation manager. Independent contractors, such as lawyers, accountants, and investment mangers and advisors, acting in that capacity, also are not officers or other managers.

An individual with sufficient authority may be what the IRS terms a *key employee*, which is a person having responsibilities or powers similar to those who are formally denominated trustees, directors, or officers. Pursuant to this concept, the chief management and administrative officials of an organization (such as executive directors and chancellors) are key employees, while the heads of separate departments or smaller units within an organization are not. A chief financial officer and the officer in charge of administration or program operations are key employees if he or she has the authority to control the organization's activities and/or its finances.

Even if an individual lacks the authority to be classified as a foundation manager on an overall basis, he or she can be regarded as a foundation manager with respect to a particular act (or failure to act) over which he or she has the requisite authority.

SUBSTANTIAL CONTRIBUTORS

A category of disqualified person with respect to a private foundation is a substantial contributor to the foundation. The term *substantial contributor* means any person who contributed (including a transfer by bequest) to a private foundation an aggregate amount that is more than the higher of (1) 2% of the total contributions received by the foundation before the close of its tax year in which the contribution is received by the foundation from that person or (2) $5,000. In computing this 2%/$5,000 threshold, all contributions to the foundation since its creation are taken into account.

Here is an example. In 2008, A, an individual, made a first-time gift of $3,000 to the M Foundation (which has a calendar tax year). As of that time, M Foundation had, throughout its existence, received contributions totaling $200,000. Inasmuch as A's gift was less than $5,000 and was also below the 2% floor (2% of $200,000 being $4,000), A did not become a substantial contributor to M because of this gift. A made another gift to M of $3,000 in 2009, when the cumulative total of contributions to that foundation though that year totaled $250,000. A became a substantial contributor to M because of the second gift, which caused her aggregate gift to M to be $6,000 (2% of $250,000 being $5,000).

In determining whether a contributor is a substantial contributor, the totals of the amounts from the contributor and the aggregate total contributions received by the private foundation must be accumulated as of the last day of each tax year. This determination as to aggregate gifts does not mean that a foundation must keep records dating back to ancient history; generally, all contributions made before October 9, 1969, are deemed to have been made on that date. (Undoubtedly, for some readers, 1969 *is* ancient history.) An individual is treated as making all contributions made by his or her spouse. Each contribution of property is valued at its fair market value on the date received. Thus, a private foundation should maintain a running tally of contributions, recording amounts, dates, and sources. An unusual grant exclusion rule (see Chapter 1) is not available in calculating aggregate contributions for purposes of identifying substantial contributors.

A donor becomes a substantial contributor as of the first date on which the private foundation received from him, her, or it an amount that is in excess of the 2%/$5,000 threshold. Thus, foundations are advised to tabulate accumulating totals as contributions are received, lest the foundation inadvertently be involved in an act of self-dealing (see Chapter 6) or otherwise violate one or more of the other rules regulating the operations of private foundations. But the *final* (and controlling) determination as to substantial contributor status is not made until the last day of the tax year, so that contributions made subsequent to the gift(s) of the contributor in question but within the same tax year may operate to keep him, her, or it out of substantial contributor status even though that status was *temporarily* (as it turned out) obtained at an earlier point during the year.

As an example of this point, in 2007, X Corporation gave the Y Foundation (which has a calendar tax year) $3,000. As of the close of 2008, Y Foundation had received $150,000 in contributions from all sources (2% of $150,000 is $3,000). On September 17, 2009, X Corporation gave Y Foundation $3,100. As of September 17, 2009, Y Foundation had received a total of $245,000 in contributions from all sources (2% of $245,000 being $4,900). Between September 18 and December 31, 2009, Y Foundation received $70,000 in contributions from others (2% of $315,000 being $6,300). X Corporation temporarily was a substantial contributor to Y Foundation on September 17, 2009, because X's total gifts of $6,100 were at that time higher than the 2% threshold ($4,900) and $5,000. In the end, however, X is not a substantial contributor to Y, as of December 31, 2009, since the 2% threshold was $6,300.

In the case of a trust, the term *substantial contributor* also means the creator of the trust. The term *person*, in this context, usually includes tax-exempt organizations but does not include governmental units (see Chapter 1). Generally, however, the term *substantial contributor* does not include most charitable organizations that are not private foundations or organizations that are wholly owned by a public charity. This term includes a decedent, even at the point in time preceding the transfer of any property from the estate to the private foundation.

For purposes of the self-dealing rules (see Chapter 6), the term *substantial contributor* does not include any tax-exempt charitable organization, since inclusion of charitable organizations for this purpose would preclude private foundations from making large grants to or otherwise interacting with other private foundations. In computing the public support fraction for purposes of the service provider publicly supported charity rules (see Chapter 1), the term *substantial contributor* includes public charities where the 2%/$5,000 threshold is exceeded, although this type of support may be excluded from the fraction as being an unusual grant (*id.*).

To be a substantial contributor, the person involved must first be a *contributor*. Consequently, where the transfer of money or property to a private foundation is not in the form of a gift or grant, the substantial contributor rules are not applicable. Also, although this discussion of these rules is framed in terms of contributions to private foundations, the rules are also applicable in connection with service provider publicly supported charities (see Chapter 1) and supporting organizations (see Chapters 1 and 11).

20%-PLUS OWNERS

An owner of more than 20% of the total combined voting power of a corporation, the profits interest of a partnership, or the beneficial interest of a trust or unincorporated enterprise, any of which is (during the period of ownership) a substantial contributor to a private foundation, is a disqualified person.

The phrase *combined voting power* includes voting power represented by holdings of voting stock, actual or constructive, but does not include voting rights held only in the capacity as a director or trustee. Thus, for example, an employee stock ownership trust that held 30% of the stock of a corporation that was a substantial contributor to a private foundation, on behalf of the corporation's participating employees who direct the manner in which the trust votes the shares, was held by the IRS to have merely the voting power of a trustee and not the ownership of the stock, and thus to not be a disqualified person with respect to the foundation.

The term *voting power* includes outstanding voting power but does not include voting power obtainable but not obtained, such as voting power obtainable by converting securities or nonvoting stock into voting stock, by exercising warrants or options to obtain voting stock, or voting power that will vest in preferred stockholders only if and when the corporation has failed to pay preferred dividends for a specified period of time or has otherwise failed to meet specified requirements.

For the purpose of determining combined voting power, profits interest, or beneficial interest of an individual, attribution rules must be applied. In respect to combined voting power, stock (or profits or beneficial interests) owned directly or indirectly by or for a corporation, partnership, estate, or trust is considered as being owned proportionately by or for its shareholders, partners, or beneficiaries. Moreover, an individual is considered as owning the stock owned by members of his or her family (discussed later in this chapter). Stockholders that have been counted once (whether by reason of actual or constructive ownership) in application of these rules are not counted a second time.

In an instance involving three national trade associations that elect the directors of a private foundation, the 30 local association members of one of these three associations (which thus was a federation of associations), and another national association controlled by the three associations, the IRS held that the private foundation could make grants to the local associations without engaging in self-dealing, even though the controlled national association was a substantial contributor to the foundation and the federation of associations held more than 20% of the combined voting power of the controlled association, inasmuch as the federation did not have an ownership interest in its local association members and they were not otherwise disqualified persons with respect to the foundation.

The *profits interest* of a partner is that amount equal to his or her distributive share of the income of the partnership as determined in accordance with special federal tax rules. The term *profits interest* includes an interest that is outstanding but not an interest that is obtainable but has not been obtained.

The *beneficial interest* in an unincorporated enterprise (other than a trust or estate) includes any right to receive a distribution of profits of the enterprise or, in the absence of a profit-sharing agreement, any right to receive the assets of the enterprise on its liquidation, except as a creditor or employee. A *right to receive a distribution of profits* includes a right to receive any amount from the profits, other than as a creditor or employee, whether as a sum certain or as a portion of profits realized by the enterprise. In the absence of an agreement fixing the rights of the participants in an enterprise, the fraction of the respective interests of each participant in the enterprise is determined by dividing (1) the amount of all investments or contributions to the capital of the enterprise made or obligated to be made by the participant by (2) the amount of investments or contributions to capital made or obligated to be made by all of them.

For example, partnership S is a substantial contributor to private foundation PF. Trust T, of which G is the sole beneficiary, owns 12% of the profits interest of S. G's spouse, H, owns 10% of the profits interest of S. H is a disqualified person with respect to PF because he is considered to own 22% of the profits interest of S (his 10% interest and the trust's 12% interest). G also is a disqualified person with respect to PF because she too is regarded as owning 22% of the profits interest of S (her 12% beneficial interest in T and the 10% interest she constructively owns by being a member of the family of H).

A person's beneficial interest in a trust is determined in proportion to the actuarial interest of the person in the trust. The term *beneficial interest* includes an interest that is outstanding but not an interest that is obtainable but has not been obtained.

MEMBERS OF FAMILY

The reach of the disqualified person rules is considerably enhanced by inclusion of the family members of disqualified persons in the definition. Thus, a category of disqualified person with respect to a private foundation is a member of the family of an individual who is a foundation manager, a substantial contributor to the foundation, or is a 20%-plus owner of a substantial contributor entity (discussed earlier in this chapter). The phrase *member of the family* means an individual's spouse, ancestors, children, grandchildren, great-grandchildren, and the spouses of children, grandchildren, and great-grandchildren. Consequently, simply by being a member of a particular family, an individual can be a disqualified person with respect to a private foundation.

A legally adopted child of an individual is treated, for purposes of the disqualified persons rules, the same as a child of an individual by blood. A brother or sister of an individual is not, however, considered, for these purposes, a member of a family. Yet, the spouse of a grandchild of an individual is a member of a family.

The determination as to who is a member of a family, for purposes of ascertaining whether he or she is a disqualified person in relation to a private foundation, can be a tricky proposition, particularly if the foundation has been in existence for a long period of time and/or the foundation has a large governing board. Individuals are constantly being born and die, children are adopted, and individuals marry and get divorced. The mix of who is in and who is out of a family can entail a swirl of activities that are difficult to make static at a point in time.

CORPORATIONS

A corporation is a disqualified person with respect to a private foundation if more than 35% of the total combined voting power in the corporation (discussed earlier in this chapter) is owned by foundation managers, substantial contributors to the foundation, 20%-plus owners, or members of the family of any of these individuals. As an illustration (recalling that *voting power* does not include voting rights held only as a trustee), the IRS ruled that stock held in a voting trust, that was related to a bank and held stock of a corporation for a private foundation and other entities, could be excluded in computing this 35% threshold because it was being held by the trust only in a fiduciary capacity, thereby enabling the IRS to conclude that the corporation was not a disqualified person with respect to the foundation and thus that proposed stock redemptions would not be acts of self-dealing.

For example, D is a substantial contributor (see above) to a private foundation, PF. D owns 20% of the outstanding stock of corporation P. E, who is married to D, does not own any stock of P. F, who is E's father, owns 10% of P stock. E is considered to also be a substantial contributor with respect to PF. E is also treated as owning both D's 20% ownership of P and F's 10% ownership of P. E, however, is regarded as not owning any stock of P for these disqualified person rules because D's 20% and F's 10% have already been taken into account once (because of their actual ownership of the stock of P) for these purposes. Consequently, corporation P is not a disqualified person with respect to PF because these individuals combined own only 30% of the stock of P.

In one situation, a corporation made an exchange offer to a private foundation concerning certain shares of the corporation's nonvoting stock. The corporation was once a disqualified person with respect to the private foundation, solely because an individual who was a manager of the foundation owned more than 35% of the total combined voting power of the corporation (see above). Five years before the exchange took place, the foundation manager resigned that position. The IRS ruled that the resignation of the foundation manager terminated the status of the corporation as a disqualified person with respect to the foundation, observing that all aspects of the exchange occurred after the separation from employment of the manager.

PARTNERSHIPS

A partnership is a disqualified person with respect to a private foundation if more than 35% of the profits interest in the partnership (discussed earlier in this chapter) is owned by foundation managers, substantial contributors to the foundation, 20%-plus owners, or members of the family of any of these individuals.

TRUSTS AND ESTATES

A trust or estate is a disqualified person with respect to a private foundation if more than 35% of the beneficial interest in the trust or estate (discussed earlier in this chapter) is owned by foundation managers, substantial contributors to the foundation, 20%-plus owners, or members of the family of any of these individuals.

PRIVATE FOUNDATIONS

A private foundation may be a disqualified person with respect to another private foundation; this can occur, however, only for purposes of the excess business holdings rules (see Chapter 8). For this disqualified person status to arise, the disqualified person private foundation must be effectively controlled, directly or indirectly, by the same person or persons (other than a bank, trust company, or similar organization acting only as a foundation manager [discussed earlier in this chapter]) who control the foundation in question, or must be the recipient of contributions substantially all of which were made, directly or indirectly, by foundation managers, substantial contributors to the foundation, 20%-plus owners, or members of the family of any of these individuals who made, directly or indirectly, substantially all of the contributions to the foundation in question.

One or more persons are considered to have made *substantially all* of the contributions to a private foundation for these purposes if the person(s) have contributed or bequeathed at least 85% of the total contributions and bequests received by the foundation during its entire existence, where each person has contributed or bequeathed at least 2% of the total.

Here is an example: Foundation A has received contributions of $10 million throughout its existence, as follows: $3.5 million from X, $5.1 million from Y (X's father), and $1.4 million from Z (an unrelated person). During its existence, Foundation B has received $10 million in contributions as follows: $5 million from X and $5 million from Q (X's wife). For business holdings purposes, A is a disqualified person with respect to B and B is a disqualified person as to A.

GOVERNMENT OFFICIALS

A government official may be a disqualified person with respect to a private foundation but only for purposes of the self-dealing rules (see Chapter 6). The term *government official* means (1) an elected public official in the U.S. Congress or executive branch; (2) presidential appointees to the U.S. executive or judicial branches; (3) certain higher-compensated or ranking employees in one of these three branches; (4) employees of the House of Representatives or Senate earning at least $15,000 annually; (5) elected or appointed public officials in the executive, legislative, or judicial branch of a state, the District of Columbia, a U.S. possession, or political subdivision or other areas of the foregoing, receiving annual gross compensation of at least $20,00; (6) the personal or executive assistant or secretary to any of the foregoing; or (7) a member of the IRS Oversight Board.

In defining the term *public office*, for purposes of the fifth category of government officials, this term is distinguished from mere employment in the government sector. Although holding a public office is one form of employment by a government, not every position in the employ of a state or other government subdivision constitutes a public office. A determination as to whether a public employee holds a public office depends on the facts and circumstances of the case; the essential element to be considered is whether a significant part of the activities of a public employee is the independent performance of policy-making functions.

Several factors may be considered as indicators that a position in the executive, legislative, or judicial branches of the government of a state, possession of the United States, or political subdivision or other area of any of the foregoing, or of the District of Columbia, constitutes a public office. Among the factors to be considered (in addition to the matter of policy-making functions) are (1) whether the office was created by Congress, a state constitution, or a state legislature, or by a municipality or other governmental body pursuant to authority conferred by Congress, a state constitution, or a state legislature; (2) the powers conferred on the office; and (3) whether the duties to be discharged by the official are defined directly or indirectly by Congress, a state constitution, or a state legislature, or through legislative authority.

For example, a lawyer appointed by a state's attorney general to perform collection services on a part-time basis for the attorney general's office was held by the IRS to not be a government official. Likewise, the IRS ruled that the holder of the office of county attorney is not a government official for these purposes. Similarly, an individual appointed by the president of the United States to serve as director of an entity was ruled to not be a government official, because of her status as a special government employee (based on the number of days of employment). By contrast, a chief administrative officer serving a city's mayor was ruled to be a government official.

This can be an area warranting considerable judgment. In one of the IRS's more astounding rulings, the agency concluded that a state district court judge was not a government official for purposes of these rules. The IRS was moved to reach this conclusion because a state statute provided that district court judges must apply existing law to the facts of each case; by statute, these judges cannot write new law or policy and must apply the law as created by the state's legislature or appellate courts. The IRS held that the judge in this instance "does not exercise significant independent policy-making powers, even though he may independently perform his duties as a government employee." Quite appropriately, soon after this ruling was issued, it was revoked. (It is almost impossible for a judge to write an opinion without creating "new law," irrespective of what a statute may stipulate; the likelihood that a given case will have a precisely applicable precedent is remote. Being human, a judge is not a legal opinion-crunching automaton. This ruling suggested that, absent such a statute, a state district court judge would be a government official for this purpose; it also indicated that state appellate court judges are government officials.)

The rules concerning the fifth category of government officials pertain to an individual's *gross compensation*. This term refers to all receipts attributable to public office that are includible in gross income for federal tax purposes. For example, an elected member of a state legislature may receive a salary of less than $20,000 each year, but also receive an expense allowance that, when added to the salary, results in a total amount of more than $20,000 in annual compensation. Where the expense allowance is a fixed amount given to each legislator irrespective of actual expenses and there is no restriction on its use and no requirement that an accounting of its use be made to the state, the expense allowance is part of the legislator's gross compensation, thereby perhaps causing the legislator to become a disqualified person for these purposes.

A private foundation maintained a director-initiated grant program (enabling its directors to direct grants for charitable purposes that are not processed through the usual staff review system) and a matching gifts program (with respect to gifts by directors and staff). Pursuant to the foundation's policies, these director-initiated grants cannot be made if the director receives a benefit or to fulfill a director's charitable pledge. One of the foundation's directors was a government official. The IRS ruled that this individual's participation in these programs did not entail any payments to the director and that none of these payments constituted compensation to this individual.

The following are illustrations of positions of public employment that do not involve policy-making functions causing individuals to be public officials:

- The chancellor, president, provost, dean, and other officers of a state university who are appointed, elected, or otherwise hired by a state board of regents or equivalent public body and who are subject to the direction and supervision of that body

- Professors, instructors, and other members of the faculty of a state educational institution who are appointed, elected, or otherwise hired by the officers of the institution or by a state board of regents or equivalent public body

- The superintendent of public schools and other public school officials who are appointed, elected, or otherwise hired by a board of education or equivalent public body and who are subject to the direction and supervision of that body

- Public school teachers who are appointed, elected, or otherwise hired by the superintendent of public schools or by a board of education or equivalent public body

- Physicians, nurses, and other professional individuals associated with public hospitals and state boards of health who are appointed, elected, or otherwise hired by the governing board or officers of these hospitals or agencies

- Members of police and fire departments, other than department heads who independently perform policy-making functions as a significant part of their activities

TERMINATION OF DISQUALIFIED PERSON STATUS

The law, in general, is vague as to whether and, if so, how an individual or other person sheds disqualified person status with respect to a private foundation. This determination depends in part on the type of disqualified person status involved. Another factor may be the length of time passing between the attempt to terminate disqualified person status and the transaction that is raising the issue (such as a potential act of self-dealing).

For example, in the case of an individual who is a disqualified person with respect to a private foundation only because he or she is a foundation manager or a government official (see above), it would seem that resignation of or a firing from the position would end the disqualified person classification. Indeed, in the case of a foundation manager, the IRS so ruled—but five years had passed since the individual's resignation from the position and the initiation of the transaction that called into question whether he or she was no longer a disqualified person.

Thereafter, in a striking interpretation of these rules, the IRS concluded that an individual was not a foundation manager (or other type of disqualified person) with respect to a private foundation, in connection with a prospective sale of businesses by the foundation, even though this individual resigned from the foundation's board of directors *the day before* he bid on the assets. (This conclusion averted what otherwise would have been a blatant act of self-dealing [see Chapter 6], should his bid prevail.) He had been an employee of one of the businesses for 25 years and was the chief operating officer of it for many of those years. After he retired, he was persuaded to become reinvolved in the corporate management, as a consultant to a newly formed holding company, because of his knowledge and expertise. He was overseeing the process of selling the businesses on behalf of the foundation; then he decided to become a bidder. Several factors led the IRS to its conclusion that this individual would not exercise undue influence over the sale of the assets, including an open bidding process, evaluation of bids by a bank and an investment firm, supervision of the sale by a court, and the requirement of approval of the transaction by the state's attorney general.

The law is clearest, in this regard, in connection with disqualified person status based on being a substantial contributor (discussed earlier in this chapter). With one exception, once a person becomes a substantial contributor to a private foundation, he, she, or it can never escape that status even though, because of a subsequent increase in funding of the foundation, the contributor might not be so classified if the determination were made at a later date. This exception enables a person's status as a substantial contributor to terminate if, after ten years, the person has no connection with the private foundation. To become disconnected for this purpose, three factors must be present during this ten-year period:

1. The person and any related persons did not make any contributions to the private foundation.

2. Neither the person nor any related person was a foundation manager (discussed later in this chapter) of the private foundation.

3. The aggregate contributions made by the person and any related persons are determined by the IRS "to be insignificant when compared to the aggregate amount of contributions to such foundation by one other person," taking into account appreciation on contributions while held by the private foundation.

For these purposes, the term *related person* means related disqualified persons; in the case of a corporate donor, the term includes the officers and directors of the corporation.

In the case of family members (discussed earlier in this chapter), it is difficult if not impossible to shed disqualified person status. Even death may not end the matter. Consider this example: A husband established a private foundation; he never told his wife about it. He died; she remarried. A child was born of this second marriage. Three generations later, a grandson of this child desires to purchase a parcel of real estate; it so happens that the real property is owned by the foundation. If the grandson purchases the property from the foundation, it would be an act of self-dealing (see Chapter 6), even though the grandson did not know he is a disqualified person with respect to the foundation.

An estate is not a disqualified person with respect to a trust funded by the estate solely because the estate is a continuation of the decedent who was a disqualified person with respect to a private foundation. Where, however, the disqualified person/decedent's children and grandchildren (thus also disqualified persons [discussed earlier in this chapter]) are beneficiaries of trusts funded by the estate and these beneficial interests are more than 35% of the beneficial interest in the estate, the estate is a disqualified person with respect to the foundation.

PRIVATE BENEFIT AND SELF-DEALING

The body of law that concerns *private benefit* is somewhat different from the law encompassed by the doctrine of *private inurement* (see Chapter 3). The private benefit doctrine, an offshoot of the operational test (*id.*) and created largely by the courts, is the more sweeping of the two; it covers a wider range of activities. (For example, in a ruling of questionable validity, the IRS held that the existence of a two-person board of a charity was inherently private benefit.) Most significantly, the private benefit rule does not require involvement of an insider (discussed earlier in this chapter)—this fact alone accounts for its breadth. The law tolerates incidental private benefit. The private benefit doctrine is applicable only to tax-exempt charitable organizations.

The private benefit rule was illustrated by a case involving a nonprofit school, which satisfied all of the federal tax statutory law for exempt status. Individuals were trained there to become political campaign consultants, but the graduates of the school seemed to always end up working for candidates and organizations of the same political party. The school's instructional activities did not constitute political campaign activity (see Chapter 3). The judge in the case, offended by the fact that all of the school's graduates gravitated to this party's candidates and campaigns, decided to deny tax-exempt status to the school. Thus, he ruled that the school could not be exempt because it provided private benefits in the form of assistance to political candidates by the school's alumni.

The private benefit doctrine has, in recent years, emerged as a potent force in the law concerning charitable organizations. The doctrine is not applied only where individuals are benefited. Private benefit can also occur where the beneficiary is a for-profit corporation, as can happen with charitable organizations in joint ventures. Indeed, it is in this context that the doctrine has grown to be so expansive; the very involvement of a for-profit entity in connection with the operations of a charitable organization can trigger application of the doctrine. A federal appellate court wrote: "The critical inquiry is not whether particular contractual payments to a related for-profit organization are reasonable or excessive, but instead whether the entire enterprise is carried on in such a manner that the for-profit organization benefits substantially from the operation of" the nonprofit organization.

In the case that is regarded as being on the outer reaches of all this, several for-profit organizations were found to be exercising "considerable control" over the nonprofit entity in question. The for-profit entities set fees that the nonprofit organization charged the public for training sessions, required the nonprofit organization to carry on certain types of educational activities, and provided management personnel paid for by and responsible to one of the for-profit organizations. Because of these and other facts, a court concluded that the nonprofit organization was "part of a franchise system which is operated for private benefit and ... its affiliation with this system taints it with a substantial commercial purpose." The "ultimate beneficiaries" of the nonprofit organization's activities were found to be the for-profit corporations; the nonprofit organization was portrayed as "simply the instrument to subsidize the for-profit corporations and not vice-versa." The nonprofit organization was held to not be operating primarily for charitable purposes.

Indeed, the IRS, supported to some degree by a court, has aggressively begun finding impermissible private benefit conferred by charitable entities on other types of *tax-exempt* organizations. The court held that an educational foundation affiliated with an exempt trade association could not be tax exempt because its training activities conferred undue private benefit on the association and its members. It is the view of the IRS that foundations established to provide scholarships to participants in beauty pageants cannot qualify for tax exemption by reason of provision of impermissible private benefit to the exempt social welfare organizations (*id.*) that sponsor the pageants.

The private benefit doctrine posits a proverbial trap for the unwary. The private inurement doctrine may not apply because of lack of involvement of an insider. Nonetheless, the private benefit doctrine may be applicable. As is the case with the private inurement doctrine, the sole sanction for transgression of the private benefit doctrine is loss or denial of the organization's tax-exempt status.

Consequently, a private foundation is simultaneously subject to the self-dealing rules and the doctrine of private benefit. Usually, the self-dealing rules take precedence. The private benefit doctrine is rarely invoked in the private foundation setting.

In the sole court case on this point, the court concluded that a transaction was not an act of self-dealing (see Chapter 6) because the individual interacting with a private foundation was not a substantial contributor (see above) and thus not a disqualified person. This outcome, which was a close call for this individual, turned in large part on the court's valuation of the contributed property, enabling the donor to escape $2.7 million in taxes and penalties. Oddly, the IRS never endeavored to utilize the fallback position of revoking the tax-exempt status of the foundation on the basis of private benefit. The transaction involved would have been self-dealing if the individual were a disqualified person; thus, the private benefit element was amply present in these facts.

This, then, is a huge potential trap. A private foundation or a self-dealer (using this term generically) can escape the self-dealing rules by avoiding classification as a disqualified person, only to find that, instead, the private foundation loses its tax-exempt status because of its participation in the transaction on the basis of private benefit (unless that benefit is incidental).

SUMMARY

This chapter provided summaries of the various ways a person can be a disqualified person with respect to a private foundation. The most likely outcomes are that a person is disqualified because he, she, or it is a foundation manager, substantial contributor, 20%-plus owner of an entity, or member of a family. The chapter also discussed how corporations, partnerships, trusts, estates, and even other private foundations, as well as government officials, can be disqualified persons. The chapter explained how a person can shed disqualified person status. The chapter concluded with a discussion as to how the private benefit doctrine can apply in this context, to cause loss of a private foundation's tax-exempt status, in the absence of involvement of a disqualified person.

3

TAX LAW RULES
IN GENERAL

A private foundation is, notwithstanding all of the law requirements unique to foundations imposed on it (see, e.g., Chapters 4 through 8), a tax-exempt charitable organization. As such, it is subject to a plethora of federal tax law rules applicable to all charitable entities, including public charities. Private foundations' management should understand these rules, both from the standpoint of the foundations' organization and operation, and that of the organizations to which they make grants. The principal bodies of these laws are summarized in this chapter. Specifically, this chapter will:

- Discuss the matter of the organization's *form*.
- Summarize the organizational tests.
- Summarize the operational test.
- Discuss the primary purpose test.
- Inventory the various *charitable* purposes and activities.
- Discuss the concept of *recognition* of tax exemption.
- Summarize the doctrine of *private inurement*.
- Briefly integrate the *intermediate sanctions* rules.
- Summarize the federal tax rules concerning *lobbying*.
- Summarize the federal tax rules concerning political campaign activities.

- Discuss the law concerning prohibited tax shelter transactions

- Discuss the law concerning *personal benefit contracts.*

- Summarize the law concerning the excise tax on foundations' net investment income.

- Summarize the law concerning termination of private foundation status.

FORM OF ORGANIZATION

Every tax-exempt organization must have a legal form; this is basically a matter of state law. Tax-exempt, nonprofit organizations generally are of four types: corporation, unincorporated association, trust, and limited liability company. A private foundation will almost always be organized as a nonprofit corporation or trust.

Generically, the document by which a tax-exempt organization is created is known, in the parlance of the federal tax law, as the *articles of organization.* There usually is a separate document containing rules by which the organization conducts its affairs; this document is most often termed *bylaws.* The organization may develop other documents governing its operations, such as various policies and procedures, an employee handbook, a conflict-of-interest policy (although that may be part of the bylaws), and/or a code of ethics.

The types of articles of organization for each of the principal types of tax-exempt, nonprofit organizations are:

- Corporation: articles of incorporation

- Unincorporated association: *constitution*

- Trust: declaration of trust or trust agreement

The contents of a set of articles of organization should include the following:

- The name of the organization

- A statement of its purposes (see below)

- The name(s) and address(es) of its initial directors or trustees

- The name and address of the registered agent (if a corporation)

- The name(s) and address(es) of its incorporator(s) (if a corporation)

- A statement as to whether the entity has members (a private foundation is unlikely to have members)

- A statement as to whether the entity can issue stock (if a corporation)

- Provisions reflecting any other state law requirements

- Provisions reflecting any other federal tax law requirements (e.g., in the case of a private foundation, the foundation rules [Chapters 4 through 8])

- A dissolution clause (discussed later in this chapter)

The bylaws of a nonprofit organization (if any) will usually include provisions with respect to:

- The organization's purposes

- The origins (e.g., election) and duties of its directors

- The origins and duties of its officers

- The role of its members (if any)

- Meetings of members and directors, including dates, notice, quorum, and voting

- The role of executive and other committees

- The role of its chapters (if any)

- The organization's fiscal year

- A conflict-of-interest policy (if not separately stated)

- Reference to (any) affiliated entities

- Restatement of the federal tax law requirements

ORGANIZATIONAL TEST IN GENERAL

In theory, every type of tax-exempt organization must adhere to an *organizational test*. As the name implies, this test looks to the manner in which the entity was organized. Compliance with this test is determined by what is in and is not in the organization's articles of organization. The elements of an organizational test are the most developed in the case of charitable organizations.

Basically, for charitable organizations, the organizational test requires a suitable statement of purposes and mandates a *dissolution clause*. This clause is a provision in the organizing document that dictates where the organization's net income and assets (if any) will be distributed should the organization liquidate or otherwise dissolve. Permissible recipients are one or more other charitable organizations or governmental agencies.

Some tax-exempt charitable organizations have additional operational tests to satisfy. These include private foundations, which generally must incorporate the private foundation rules (Chapters 4 through 8) in their articles of organization. Supporting organizations (see Chapter 1) also have additional requirements as to their articles.

ORGANIZATIONAL TEST FOR FOUNDATIONS

Organizational rules apply to private foundations, in addition to the organizational test applicable to tax-exempt charitable organizations generally. A private foundation cannot be exempt from federal income tax, nor will contributions to it be deductible as charitable gifts, unless its governing instrument includes provisions the effects of which are to require distributions at such time and in such manner as to comply with the payout rules (see Chapter 4) and prohibit the foundation from engaging in any act of self-dealing (see Chapter 6), retaining any excess business holdings (see Chapter 8), making any jeopardizing investments (see Chapter 7), and making any taxable expenditures (see Chapter 5).

The provisions of a foundation's governing instrument must require the foundation to act or refrain from acting so that the foundation, and foundation managers or other disqualified persons with respect to it, will not be liable for any of the private foundation excise tax penalties. The governing instrument of a nonexempt split-interest trust (see Chapter 1) must make comparable provision as respects the applicable private foundation excise taxes.

A foundation's governing instrument is deemed to conform with this organizational requirement if valid provisions of state law have been enacted that require the foundation to act or refrain from acting so as to not subject it to any of the private foundation excise taxes or that deem the required provisions to be contained in the foundation's governing instrument.

OPERATIONAL TEST

Likewise, in theory, every type of tax-exempt organization must adhere to an *operational test*. Again, as the name implies, this test looks to the manner in which the entity is operated, and concerns whether the organization is in fact operated for exempt purposes. The elements of an operational test are the most developed in the case of charitable organizations. Generally, defects in an entity's articles of organization cannot be cured by complete adherence to the operational test.

Charitable organizations, to be tax exempt, must, of course, have charitable purposes and engage in the appropriate activities to advance those purposes. These purposes must, at a minimum, be the organization's primary purposes. There are basically 18 discrete ways an organization can serve charitable purposes (discussed later in this chapter).

PRIMARY PURPOSE TEST

The appropriate category of tax exemption (if any) for a nonprofit organization is dictated by application of the *primary purpose rule*. Also, an organization's primary purpose can change; this development may cause the organization to evolve into a different type of exempt entity (or, in rare cases, to lose exempt status). The law, however, tolerates incidental nonexempt purposes.

The general rule, as stated by the Supreme Court, is that the "presence of a single . . . [nonexempt] purpose, if substantial in nature, will destroy the exemption regardless of the number or importance of truly [exempt] purposes." A federal court of appeals held that nonexempt activity will not result in loss or denial of tax exemption where it is "only incidental and less than substantial" and that a "slight and comparatively unimportant deviation from the narrow furrow of tax approved activity is not fatal." In the words of the IRS, the rules applicable to charitable organizations in general have been "construed as requiring all the resources of the organization [other than an insubstantial part] to be applied to the pursuit of one or more of the [allowable] exempt purposes."

There is no definition of the term *insubstantial* in this context. Thus, application of these rules is an issue of fact to be determined under the facts and circumstances of each case. In some instances, this is a matter of weighing the relative importance of purposes. For example, an organization with some charitable and educational purposes will not qualify for exemption as a charitable organization if its predominate purposes are social and recreational; an organization in this situation will be classified as a social club.

Nonprofit organizations should, therefore, frame their statement of purposes with care. Also, it is prudent to revisit the statement from time to time to be certain that it accurately reflects the entity's contemporary activities and objectives.

CHARITABLE PURPOSES AND ACTIVITIES

The federal tax law recognizes 18 *charitable* (using that term in its most expansive sense) purposes and activities:

1. Relief of the poor
2. Relief of the distressed

3. Promotion of health

4. Lessening the burdens of government

5. Promotion of social welfare

6. Advancement of education

7. Advancement of science

8. Advancement of religion

9. Promotion of the arts

10. Protection of the environment

11. Promotion of patriotism

12. Promotion of sports for youth

13. Prevention of cruelty to children or animals

14. Certain forms of economic development

15. Operation of formal educational institutions (such as schools, colleges, universities, and museums)

16. Operation of scientific organizations, including research entities

17. Operation of religious organizations (such as churches, conventions or associations of churches, and religious orders)

18. Operation of certain cooperative investment entities or charitable risk pools

Any of these purposes and activities can be those of public charities to which private foundations make grants. A private foundation, which must be a charitable organization, must have at least one of the foregoing as its purpose and provide funds for at least one of these types of activities.

RECOGNITION OF TAX EXEMPTION

An organization's tax-exempt status may be *recognized* by the IRS; this is done by issuance of a determination letter or ruling, following the filing by the organization of an application for recognition of exemption. As a general rule, a charitable organization must, to be tax-exempt, have its exemption recognized by the IRS; the application to be filed in this regard is Form 1023. Private foundations and supporting organizations (see Chapter 1) must, to be exempt, have their exemptions so recognized. Churches and certain small organizations are exempt from this requirement.

PRIVATE INUREMENT DOCTRINE

The doctrine of private inurement, which is the essential principle of law distinguishing nonprofit and for-profit organizations, is applicable to nearly all types of tax-exempt organizations. It is most pronounced and developed, however, for charitable organizations, including private foundations. By contrast, for a few types of nonprofit organizations, forms of private benefit are the exempt function.

Charitable Organizations

The federal law of tax exemption for charitable organizations requires that each such entity be organized and operated so that "no part of . . . [its] net earnings . . . inures to the benefit of any private shareholder or individual." Literally, this means that the profits of a charitable organization (and any other type of entity subject to the doctrine) may not be passed along to individuals or other persons in their private capacity, in the way that dividends are paid to shareholders. In actual fact, the private inurement rule, as expanded and amplified by the IRS and the courts, means much more.

The contemporary concept of private inurement is broad and wide ranging. Lawyers for the IRS advised that inurement is "likely to arise where the beneficial benefit represents a transfer of the organization's financial resources to an individual solely by virtue of the individual's relationship with the organization, and without regard to accomplishing exempt purposes." That description is essentially correct for today's private inurement doctrine, but it is a substantial embellishment of the original (and antiquated) statutory rule.

The essence of the private inurement concept is to ensure that a charitable organization is serving public, not private, interests. To be tax exempt, an organization must establish that it is not organized and operated for the benefit of private interests—designated individuals, the creator of the entity or his or her family, shareholders of the organization, persons controlled (directly or indirectly) by private interests, or any persons having a personal and private interest in the activities of the organization.

Insiders

The federal securities laws that govern for-profit business corporations target the notion of the *insider*—someone who has a special and close relationship with a corporation, frequently because he or she is a director, officer, and/or significant shareholder. Thus, for example, the securities laws prohibit insider trading. The private inurement rules, using the odd phrase *private shareholder or individual*, mirror the concept of the insider. In the private foundation setting, the term is *disqualified person* (see Chapter 2).

An insider for private inurement purposes includes an organization's directors, trustees, and officers. It also encompasses key employees, particularly where they have duties or responsibilities normally vested in officers. Further, the family members of insiders and entities controlled by insiders (such as corporations, partnerships, trusts, and estates) are covered. Indeed, the contemporary version of the term *insider* in the exempt organizations context is that it is any person who is in a position to exercise control over a significant portion of the affairs of an organization. It is not necessary that this control, in fact, be exercised.

The inurement doctrine prohibits a transaction between a tax-exempt organization subject to the rule and a person who is an insider, where the latter is able to cause the organization's net earnings to be turned to private purposes as the result of his, her, or its control or influence. The IRS once observed that, as a general rule, an organization's "trustees, officers, members, founders, or contributors may not, by reason of their position, acquire any of its funds." Stating its view another way, the IRS has rather starkly said that the "prohibition of inurement, in its simplest terms, means that a private shareholder or individual cannot pocket the organization's funds."

Standard of Reasonableness

Persons can receive private benefits in many ways; private inurement can take many forms. Still, a charitable organization may incur ordinary and necessary operating expenditures without losing its tax-exempt status. It may pay compensation, rent, interest, and maintenance costs without penalty, because these expenses, even if paid to insiders, further the organization's exempt purposes. The costs, however, must be justifiable and be for reasonable amounts.

The matter of *reasonableness* is one of *fact*, not *law*. The exercise in determining what is reasonable is closely akin to *valuation*. In complex instances, the services of an independent, competent consultant may be warranted. The law that is developing in the intermediate sanctions setting (discussed later in this chapter) is helping to define the parameters of the term *reasonable*.

Compensation

The most common form of private inurement involving nonprofit organizations is excessive and unreasonable compensation. (For private foundations, this concept is mirrored in the self-dealing rules (see Chapter 6). When a charitable organization pays an employee a salary, it is paying a portion of its earnings to an individual in his or her private capacity. Payment of reasonable compensation, however, is allowable; it is not private inurement. Payment of compensation becomes private inurement when the amount is excessive—and is made to an insider. In this context, *compensation* is not confined to payment of a salary or wage; it includes bonuses, commissions, royalties, expense accounts, insurance coverages, deferred compensation, and participation in retirement plans,

Whether compensation paid by a nonprofit organization is reasonable is, as noted, a question of fact, to be decided in the context of each case. Generally, allowable compensation is ascertained by comparing the compensation paid to individuals who have similar responsibilities and expertise, serving organizations of comparable type and size, in the same or similar communities. (Where similar entities are operating in the for-profit sector, compensation paid by them can be included in the evaluation.) Other factors are the need of the organization for a particular individual's services, the amount of time devoted to the job, and whether an independent or captive board approved the compensation.

Thus, individuals (and other persons) serving charitable (and other) tax-exempt organizations are allowed, by the law, fair compensation for their efforts. A federal court observed that the "law places no duty on individuals operating charitable organizations to donate their services; they are entitled to reasonable compensation for their services." Likewise, a congressional committee report contained the observation that "an individual need not necessarily accept reduced compensation merely because he or she renders services to a tax-exempt, as opposed to a taxable, organization."

Three aspects of compensation can make it unreasonable. One is the sheer amount of the compensation, in absolute terms. A federal court, in finding private inurement because of excessive compensation, characterized the salaries as being "substantial" amounts. Other courts, however, tolerate substantial amounts of compensation where the employees' services and skills warrant the level of payment.

The second aspect is extraordinary jumps—or spikes—in the level of compensation. An amount of compensation that might otherwise be reasonable can be suspect if there is a sudden significant increase in pay. A case in point: Two individuals who for years received annual compensation of $20,000 were each awarded a $700,000 bonus; the IRS and two courts found that level of compensation to be unreasonable. Another telling factor is whether the spike in compensation level causes the recipient to enjoy far more compensation than anyone else on the payroll.

The third aspect of compensation that can lead to private inurement is the manner in which the amount is calculated. The IRS may challenge, and courts may agree with the agency, compensation arrangements that are predicated on a percentage of the revenue flow of the tax-exempt organization employer. Case law on this point is inconsistent and unclear but the prevailing view seems to be that private inurement will not be found simply because a commission system is used; the important fact is the reasonableness of the compensation. Private inurement has been found in a compensation arrangement based on a percentage of gross receipts, where an upper limit—a cap—was not placed on total compensation. In another instance, a court focused on the reasonableness of the percentage, not the reasonableness of the resulting compensation. The IRS has recently been rather tolerant of these forms of compensation, particularly in the health care area, where various forms of *gainsharing* have become prevalent.

Prompted by media reports of ostensible excess compensation paid by nonprofit organizations to insiders, the IRS in 2004 launched an enforcement effort to "identify and halt" the practice. The agency initiated contact with what is expected to ultimately be about 2,000 charitable organizations to seek information about the compensation they pay. The IRS terms this undertaking its *Tax Exempt Compensation Enforcement Project*.

Rents and Loans

A charitable organization generally may lease property and pay rent. The private inurement doctrine, however, requires that—where the landlord is an insider—the rental arrangement be beneficial to and suitable for the organization, and that the rental payments be reasonable in amount. Loans between charitable organizations and their insiders are subject to the same standard.

Rental arrangements and terms of a loan involving a charitable organization should be financially advantageous to the organization and in line with its exempt purposes. Where a charity is the borrower and an insider is the lender, the interest charges, amount of security, repayment period, terms of repayment, and other aspects of the loan must be reasonable. The scrutiny will heighten where an insider is borrowing from the charity (assuming state law permits the transaction). If a loan from a charity is not timely repaid, questions of private inurement may be raised. A federal court observed that the "very existence of a private source of loan credit from [a charitable] organization's earnings may itself amount to inurement of benefit."

Some charitable organizations are called on to guarantee the debt of another entity, such as a related nonprofit or even a for-profit organization. The terms of such an arrangement should be carefully reviewed, particularly where an insider is involved. If the loan guarantee does not advance exempt purposes or cannot be characterized as part of a reasonable investment, private inurement may be occurring.

Joint Ventures

Charitable organizations are increasingly involved in partnerships with individuals and/or other joint ventures with individuals or for-profit entities. In a general partnership, all of the partners are subject to liability for the acts committed in the name of the partnership. In a limited partnership, which will have at least one general partner, the limited partners are essentially investors; their liability is confined to the extent of their investment. The general partner(s) in a limited partnership has the responsibility to operate the partnership in a successful manner; this includes efforts to enable the limited partners to achieve an economic return that is worth the commitment of their capital.

In this structure and set of expectations, there is the potential for private inurement. In its worst light, a limited partnership with a charitable organization at the helm can be construed as the running of a business for the benefit of private interests (the limited partners), particularly where the limited partners include or are insiders. This has rarely been the case in the nonprofit organization context. A partnership (general or limited) basically is an entity formed to attract financing—it is a means to an end. In this fashion, a charitable organization is able to secure the funds of others for a legitimate purpose. As long as involvement in the partnership does not deter the charity from advancing its exempt ends and as long as the limited partners' return on their investment is reasonable, there will not be private inurement—notwithstanding the participation of any insiders.

The IRS is having some success in situations where a tax-exempt charitable organization is involved in a joint venture (usually where the venture vehicle is a limited liability company) to the extent that the entirety of the entity is in the venture. If the charitable organization loses control of its resources to (or, as one court put it, "cedes its authority" to) one or more for-profit companies, the charity will lose its tax-exempt status. This may, however, entail application of the private benefit doctrine (see below) rather than the private inurement doctrine.

Sanction

The sanction for violation of the private inurement doctrine is loss or denial of the organization's tax-exempt status. There is no other penalty; there is no sanction imposed on the insider who received the unwarranted benefit.

The private inurement doctrine and the intermediate sanctions rules (discussed later in this chapter) have much in common. The general expectation is that the IRS will first apply intermediate sanctions, and invoke private inurement principles (i.e., pursue revocation of tax exemption) only in egregious cases. Nonetheless, it is certainly possible for the IRS to simultaneously apply both bodies of law, thus penalizing both the insider or insiders who obtained the excess benefit and the tax-exempt organization that provided it. (A somewhat parallel body of law—the private benefit doctrine—is summarized in Chapter 2.)

INTERMEDIATE SANCTIONS

The intermediate sanctions rules are designed to curb and punish abuses in the arena of private inurement using an enforcement mechanism other than revocation of tax-exempt status. These rules are applicable with respect to all tax-exempt public charitable organizations (see Chapter 1) and all exempt social welfare organizations. For this purpose, these two categories of entities are termed *applicable tax-exempt organizations*.

The intermediate sanctions rules do not apply to private foundations. Nonetheless, this body of law is important for private foundations for two reasons: (1) the intermediate sanctions rules apply to the public charities to which foundations make grants, and (2) many components of the intermediate sanctions rules are rested on concepts in the foundation self-dealing rules (see Chapter 6); thus, developments in the law concerning intermediate sanctions are likely to directly impact the law concerning self-dealing.

The heart of this body of tax law is the *excess benefit transaction*. A transaction is considered an excess benefit transaction if an economic benefit is provided by an applicable tax-exempt organization directly or indirectly to, or for the use of, a disqualified person (discussed later in this chapter), if the value of the economic benefit provided exceeds the value of the consideration received by the exempt organization for providing the benefit.

The concept of the excess benefit transaction includes any transaction in which the amount of any economic benefit provided to, or for the use of, a disqualified person is determined in whole or in part by the revenues of one or more activities of the organization, where the transaction is reflected in tax regulations and it results in private inurement.

One of the principal aspects of intermediate sanctions is application of them to instances of unreasonable compensation—where a person's level or type of compensation is deemed to be in excess of the value of the economic benefit derived by the organization from the person's services. In that regard, an economic benefit may not be treated as compensation for the performance of services unless the exempt organization clearly indicated its intent to so treat the benefit. When that intent is not properly evidenced, the provision of the benefit is an *automatic excess benefit transaction*.

A *disqualified person* is any person, member of the family of such an individual, or a controlled entity who was, at any time during the five-year period ending on the date of the transaction, in a position to exercise substantial influence over the affairs of the organization. This term is closely akin to the concept of *disqualified person* in the private foundation context (see Chapter 2).

A disqualified person who inappropriately benefited from an excess benefit transaction is subject to an initial tax equal to 25% of the amount of the excess benefit. (The intent or good faith of the parties is irrelevant to this determination.) Moreover, this person will be required to return the excess benefit amount (generally in cash) to the tax-exempt organization—this is known as *correction*. An *organization manager* (usually a trustee, director, or officer) who participated in an excess benefit transaction, knowing that it was such a transaction, is subject to a tax of 10% of the excess benefit. An additional tax may be imposed on a disqualified person where the initial tax was imposed and the appropriate correction of the excess benefit transaction did not occur. In this situation, the disqualified person is subject to a tax equal to 200% of the excess benefit involved.

A major exception to the intermediate sanctions rules is the *initial contract* exception. These rules do not apply to a fixed payment made by an applicable tax-exempt organization to a disqualified person pursuant to the first contract between the parties. A *fixed payment* is an amount of money or other property specified in the contract involved, or determined by a fixed formula specified in the contract, which is to be paid or transferred in exchange for the provision of specified services or property. An *initial contract* is a binding written contract between an applicable tax-exempt organization and a person who was not a disqualified person immediately prior to entering into the contract.

If a transaction creating a benefit was approved by an independent board of an applicable tax-exempt organization, or an independent committee of the board, a presumption arises that the terms of the transaction are reasonable. This presumption also requires a showing that the board or committee acted on the basis of appropriate data as to comparability and properly documented the transaction. When these three elements are met, the burden of proof shifts to the IRS, which has to overcome (rebut) the presumption to prevail.

In many respects, the concept of the excess benefit transaction will be based on existing law concerning private inurement. The statute, however, expressly states, as noted, that an excess benefit transaction also may include any transaction in which the amount of any economic benefit provided to a disqualified person is determined, at least in part, by the revenue flow of the organization. These transactions are referenced in the legislative history underlying the intermediate sanctions rules as *revenue-sharing transactions*.

The IRS and the courts have determined that a variety of revenue-sharing arrangements do not constitute private inurement. This includes arrangements where the compensation of a person is ascertained, in whole or in part, on the basis of the value of contributions generated, as well as other forms of incentive compensation. The legislative history of the intermediate sanctions rules states that the agency is not bound by these prior determinations when interpreting and applying intermediate sanctions.

As discussed, the sanctions in this context fall on disqualified persons; there is no penalty on applicable tax-exempt organizations. At the same time, the annual information return required to be filed by these organizations (see Chapter 10) poses this question: "Did the organization engage in any . . . excess benefit transaction during the year or did it become aware of an excess benefit transaction from a prior year?" If the answer to this question is "yes," the filing organization is required to attach a statement to the return explaining the transaction or transactions. This disclosure requirement can place the exempt organization in an awkward position, particularly if the disqualified persons involved disagree as to the existence of an excess benefit transaction. Any such statement attached to the return is a public document.

The final tax regulations on this subject having been issued, and IRS enforcement of the intermediate sanctions rules has begun. Private letter rulings and technical advice memoranda are beginning to appear; litigation is under way. This body of law may be expected to be one of the most active components of the overall federal law of nonprofit organizations in the coming years.

LEGISLATIVE ACTIVITIES

Organizations that are tax exempt because they are charitable must, to preserve the exemption, adhere to a variety of requirements (including those summarized above). One of these is that "no substantial part of the activities" of the organization may constitute "carrying on propaganda, or otherwise attempting, to influence legislation." This is known as the *substantial part test*. Another set of rules applicable to public charities is the *expenditure test* (discussed later in this chapter); this test, which applies in lieu of the substantial part test, must be elected.

A charitable organization that has lobbying as a substantial activity is an *action organization*. Excessive lobbying can cause a charitable organization to pay excise taxes. In some instances, too much lobbying results in revocation of tax-exempt status.

Lobbying

Legislative activities can take many forms. Some constitute *direct* lobbying, which occurs when one or more representatives of an organization make contact with a legislator and/or his or her staff, and/or the staff of a legislative committee. Direct lobbying includes office visits, presentation of testimony at hearings, correspondence, publication and dissemination of material, email and other Internet communications, and entertainment.

Grassroots (indirect) lobbying is another form. This type of lobbying occurs when the organization urges the public, or a segment of the public, to contact members of a legislative body or their staffs for the purpose of proposing, supporting, or opposing legislation.

Generally, the federal tax rules concerning lobbying and political campaign activities (discussed later in this chapter) are separate, discrete bodies of law. If, however, a nonprofit organization engages in lobbying, particularly grass-roots lobbying, doing so in the context of a political campaign, so that the advocacy of the issue(s) involved can be tied to the political fortunes of a candidate (such as an incumbent legislator pursuing reelection), the lobbying activity can also be regarded as political campaign activity. Undertakings of this nature are known as *public policy advocacy communications*; they are said to have a *dual character*.

The federal tax law prohibition comprising the substantial part test does not differentiate between direct and indirect lobbying, nor does it distinguish between lobbying that is related to an organization's exempt purposes and lobbying that is not. The function remains lobbying; the various types of it are subject to the proscription. A charitable organization, however, that does not initiate any action with respect to pending legislation but merely responds to a request from a legislative committee to testify is not, solely because of that activity, considered an action organization. Also, a charitable organization can engage in nonpartisan analysis, study, and research and publish the results. Even where some of the plans and policies formulated can be carried out only through legislative enactments, as long as the organization does not advocate the adoption of legislation or legislative action to implement its findings, it escapes classification as an action organization.

There can be a fine line between nonpartisan analysis, study, or research, and lobbying. A charitable organization may evaluate proposed or pending legislation and present an objective analysis of it to the public, as long as it does not participate in the presentation of suggested bills to a legislature and does not engage in any campaign to secure passage of the legislation. If the organization's primary objective can be attained only by legislative action, however, it is an action organization.

Legislation

Because these rules obviously apply to legislative activities—activities undertaken in connection with the championing or opposing of legislation—it is necessary to know what does and does not constitute *legislation*. The term *legislation* refers principally to action by the U.S. Congress, a state legislative body, a local council, or similar governing body, and by the general public in a referendum, initiative, constitutional amendment, or similar procedure.

Legislation generally does not include action by an executive branch of a government, such as the promulgation of rules and regulations, nor does it include action by independent regulatory agencies. Litigation activities, including the filing of amicus curiae briefs, also does not entail action with respect to legislation.

Substantiality

The most important concept under these rules is the meaning of the word *substantial*. The law offers no general formula for computing *substantial* or *insubstantial* legislative undertakings.

There are at least three ways to measure *substantiality* in this context:

1. Determine what percentage of an organization's annual *expenditures* are devoted to efforts to influence legislation.

2. Apply a percentage to legislative *activities*, in relation to total activities.

3. Ascertain whether an organization had a substantial *impact* on or *influence* over a legislative process simply by virtue of its prestige or because of significant information provided during consideration of legislation.

The true measure of substantiality in the lobbying setting remains elusive. In reports accompanying tax legislation over the years, the Senate Finance Committee characterized this state of affairs well. In 1969, the Committee wrote that the "standards as to the permissible level of [legislative] activities under the present law are so vague as to encourage subjective application of the sanction." In 1976, the Committee portrayed the dilemma this way: "many believe that the standards as to the permissible level of [legislative] activities under present law are too vague and thereby tend to encourage subjective and selective enforcement."

Lobbying Taxes

To give the general restriction on lobbying by charities more strength, there is a system of excise taxes on excess lobbying outlays. If a charitable organization loses its tax exemption because of attempts to influence legislation, a tax of 5% of the *lobbying expenditures* is imposed on the organization. This tax, however, does not apply to an organization that is under the expenditure test or that is ineligible to make this election.

A separate 5% tax is applicable to each of the organization's managers (directors, officers, key employees) who agreed to the lobbying expenditures, knowing they were likely to result in revocation of exemption, unless the agreement was not willful and was due to reasonable cause. The burden of proof as to whether a manager knowingly participated in the lobbying expenditure is on the IRS.

The IRS has, in every instance involving a charitable organization's excessive lobbying, the discretion as to whether to revoke tax-exempt status, impose these taxes, or do both.

Expenditure Test

The *expenditure test* regarding permissible lobbying by charitable organizations arose from a desire to clarify the substantial part test. That is, the purpose of this test is to offer charitable entities some reasonable certainty concerning how much lobbying they can undertake without endangering their tax-exempt status. The test is a safe-harbor guideline.

The expenditure test rules provide definitions of terms such as *legislation*, *influencing legislation*, *direct lobbying*, and *grassroots lobbying*. These terms are essentially the same as those used in connection with the substantial part test. In an attempt to define when the legislative process commences (and, therefore, when a lobbying process begins), however, the expenditure test offers a definition of legislative *action*: the "introduction, amendment, enactment, defeat, or repeal of Acts, bills, resolutions, or similar items."

The expenditure test measures permissible and impermissible legislative activities of charitable organizations in terms of sets of declining percentages of total exempt purpose expenditures. (These expenditures do not include fundraising expenses.) The basic permitted level of expenditures for legislative efforts (termed the *lobbying nontaxable amount*) is 20% of the first $500,000 of an organization's expenditures for an exempt purpose (including legislative activities), plus 15% of the next $500,000, 10% of the next $500,000, and 5% of any remaining expenditures. The total amount spent for legislative activities in any year by an electing charitable organization may not exceed $1 million. A separate limitation—amounting to 25% of the foregoing amounts—is imposed on grassroots lobbying expenditures.

A charitable organization that has elected these limitations and exceeds either the general lobbying ceiling amount or the grassroots lobbying ceiling amount becomes subject to an excise tax of 25% of the excess lobbying expenditures. The tax falls on the greater of the two excesses. If an electing organization's lobbying expenditures normally (an average over a four-year period) exceed 150% of either limitation, it will forfeit its tax-exempt status as a charitable organization.

The expenditure test rules contain exceptions for five categories of activities. Consequently, the term *influencing legislation* does not include:

1. Making available the results of nonpartisan analysis, study, or research

2. Providing technical advice or assistance in response to a written request by a governmental body

3. Appearances before, or communications to, any legislative body in connection with a possible decision of that body that might affect the existence of the organization, its powers and duties, its tax-exempt status, or the deductibility of contributions to it

4. Communications between the organization and its bona fide members regarding legislation or proposed legislation that is of direct interest to them, unless the communications directly encourage the members to influence legislation or to urge nonmembers to influence legislation

5. Routine communications with government officials or employees

The third of these exceptions is known as the *self-defense exception*. Sheltered by this exception is all lobbying by a public charity, as long as it can be reasonably rationalized as coming within one or more of the allowable forms of lobbying.

The expenditure test contains a method of aggregating the expenditures of affiliated organizations. The intent of these rules is to forestall the creation of numerous organizations for the purpose of avoiding the expenditure test.

Lobbying by Other Nonprofit Organizations

The federal tax law pertaining to tax-exempt status does not impose lobbying restrictions on nonprofit organizations other than charitable ones. The only constraint is that the organization must pursue its exempt functions as its primary purpose and that any lobbying it may do (other than an insubstantial amount) must further that principal requirement.

Basically, then, entities such as social welfare organizations, labor organizations, business and professional associations, and veterans' organizations may lobby without restriction. Special rules can cause members' dues to not be fully deductible in an instance of lobbying by associations (business leagues). Legislative activities are not normally exempt functions for political organizations.

POLITICAL CAMPAIGN ACTIVITIES

Congress has flatly decreed that charitable organizations may not engage in political campaign activity. In fact, however, these organizations, frequently religious entities, often participate directly and indirectly in political campaigns.

General Rules

The federal tax law states that charitable organizations must "not participate in, or intervene in (including the publishing or distributing of statements), any political campaign on behalf of or in opposition to any candidate for public office." Although this prohibition is framed as an absolute one, minor involvement in politics may not result in loss of tax exemption. As a court observed, a "slight and comparatively unimportant deviation from the narrow furrow of tax approved activity is not fatal."

The concept of an *action organization* is used in the political campaign context. An action organization includes an entity that participates or intervenes, directly or indirectly, in any political campaign on behalf of or in opposition to a candidate for public office; an action organization cannot qualify as a tax-exempt charitable one. Thus, an exempt charitable organization cannot make a contribution to a political campaign, endorse or oppose a candidate, or otherwise support a political candidacy.

Most of the law amplifying the political campaign proscription for charitable organizations is in IRS rulings. These determinations have, over the years, been uniformly rigid in their finding that nearly any activity relating to a political process will prevent charitable organizations from being tax exempt. For example, the evaluation of candidates, the administration of a fair campaign practices code, and even assistance to individuals immediately after they have been elected to public office have been found to be prohibited activities.

In recent years, the IRS has relented somewhat, with the agency ruling that voter education activities are permissible for charitable organizations. As an illustration, a charitable organization can prepare and disseminate a compilation of the voting records of legislators on a variety of subjects, as long as there is no editorial comment and no approval or disapproval of the voting records is implied. A charitable organization may also conduct public forums where there is a fair and impartial treatment of political candidates.

Some charitable organizations have cautiously entered the political milieu as part of the process of advancing education. For example, charitable organizations have been permitted to assemble and donate to libraries the campaign speeches, interviews, and other materials of a candidate for a historically important elective office, and to conduct public forums at which debates and lectures on social, political, and international questions are considered. In performing this type of educational activity, however, charitable organizations are expected to present a balanced view of the pertinent facts. Members of the public must be permitted to form their own opinions and conclusions independent of any presented by the organization.

Taxation of Political Expenditures

Federal law levies taxes in situations where a charitable organization makes a political expenditure. Generally, a *political expenditure* is any amount paid or incurred by a charitable organization in any participation or intervention (including the publication or distribution of statements) in any political campaign, on behalf of or in opposition to any candidate for public office.

In an effort to discourage ostensibly educational organizations from operating in tandem with political campaigns, the term *political expenditure* also applies with respect to an organization "which is formed primarily for purposes of promoting the candidacy (or prospective candidacy) of an individual for public office (or which is effectively controlled by a candidate or prospective candidate and which is availed of primarily for such purposes)."

A political expenditure can trigger an initial tax, payable by the organization, of 10% of the amount of the expenditure. An initial tax of $2\frac{1}{2}$% of the expenditure can also be imposed on each of the organization's managers (such as directors and officers), where these individuals knew it was a political expenditure, unless the agreement to make the expenditure was not willful and was due to reasonable cause. The IRS has the authority to abate these initial taxes where the organization is able to establish that the violation was due to reasonable cause and not to willful neglect, and timely corrects the violation.

An additional tax can be levied on a charitable organization, at a rate of 100% of the political expenditure, where the initial tax was imposed and the expenditure was timely corrected. Such a tax can also be levied on an organization's manager, at a rate of 50% of the expenditure, where the additional tax was imposed on the organization and the manager refused to agree to part or all of the expenditure.

The IRS has, in every instance involving a charitable organization's involvement in political campaign activity, the discretion as to whether to revoke tax-exempt status, impose these taxes, or do both.

Under certain circumstances, the IRS is empowered to commence an action in federal district court to enjoin a charitable organization from making further political expenditures and for other relief to ensure that the assets of the organization are preserved for charitable purposes. If the IRS finds that a charitable organization has flagrantly violated the prohibition against political expenditures, the IRS is required to immediately determine and assess any income and/or excise tax(es) due, by terminating the organization's tax year.

PROHIBITED TAX SHELTER TRANSACTIONS

An excise tax is imposed on most tax-exempt organizations (including private foundations) and/or organization managers that participate in prohibited tax shelter transactions as accommodation parties. This tax can be triggered in three instances:

1. An exempt organization is liable for the tax in the year it becomes a party to the transaction and any subsequent year or years in which it is such a party.

2. An exempt organization is liable for the tax in any year it is a party to a subsequently listed transaction.

3. An exempt organization manager is liable for the tax if the manager caused the organization to be a party to a prohibited tax shelter transaction at any time during a year and knew or had reason to know that the transaction is such a transaction.

A *prohibited tax shelter transaction* is of two types: a listed transaction and a prohibited reportable transaction. A *listed transaction* is a reportable transaction that is the same as, or is substantially similar to, a transaction specifically identified by the IRS as a tax avoidance transaction. A *reportable transaction* is a transaction as to which information is required to be included with a tax return or statement because the transaction is of a type that the IRS determined has a potential for tax avoidance.

A *prohibited reportable transaction* is any confidential or otherwise contractually protected transaction that is a reportable transaction. A *subsequently listed transaction* is a transaction to which a tax-exempt entity is a party and which is determined by the IRS to be a listed transaction at any time after the entity has become a party to the transaction.

Private foundations and their managers are well advised to refrain from participation in a prohibited tax shelter transaction.

PERSONAL BENEFIT CONTRACTS

Charitable split-dollar insurance plans, whereby life insurance was the underpinning for forms of endowment-building investment vehicles for charitable organizations, have been effectively outlawed by the federal tax law. That is, the federal tax law denies an income tax charitable contribution deduction for, and imposes excise tax penalties on, transfers associated with use of these plans.

Specifically, there is no federal charitable contribution deduction for a transfer to or for the use of a charitable organization, if, in connection with the transfer, (1) the organization directly or indirectly pays, or has previously paid, any premium on any personal benefit contract with respect to the transferor; or (2) there is an understanding or expectation that any person will directly or indirectly pay any premium on this type of a contract with respect to the transferor. A *personal benefit contract*, with respect to a transferor, is any life insurance, annuity, or endowment contract, if any direct or indirect beneficiary under the contract is the transferor, any member of the transferor's family, or any other person (other than a charitable organization) designated by the transferor.

Private foundations and their managers are well advised to refrain from participation in a transaction involving a personal benefit contract.

TAX ON INVESTMENT INCOME

A few types of tax-exempt organizations are required to pay tax on their net investment income. One type of exempt organization that must pay a tax of this nature is the private foundation. Other exempt organizations that are required to pay an investment income tax are social clubs, political organizations, and homeowners' associations. Also, under certain circumstances, tax-exempt organizations generally are subject to the unrelated business income tax on investment income to the extent it is derived from debt-financed property (see Chapter 8).

An excise tax of 2% is imposed on the net investment income of U.S. private foundations for each tax year. This tax is imposed on private operating foundations (see Chapter 1) and nonexempt charitable trusts. The excise tax rate on a foundation's net investment income is reduced to 1% for each year during which the foundation's qualifying distributions (see Chapter 4) equal to a distribution amount plus 1% of net investment income. This tax is calculated and paid in connection with the preparation and filing of a foundation's annual information return (see Chapter 10). The tax may have to be paid quarterly in advance in accordance with the corporate estimated tax system. Generally, foreign foundations are taxed at a rate of 4% on their U.S. source investment income. Exempt operating foundations (see Chapter 1) are exempt from this excise tax (the meaning of the word *exempt* in this context).

A private foundation's *net investment income* is the amount by which the sum of its gross investment income and net capital gain exceeds the allowable deductions. Gross investment income includes interest, dividends, rents, royalties, and payments with respect to securities loans. The base of this tax was expanded by reason of legislation enacted in 2007. Allowable deductions include investment management and counseling fees, legal fees, accounting fees, depreciation, and depletion.

TERMINATION OF FOUNDATION STATUS

A private foundation may terminate its existence (dissolve) or terminate its foundation status. As to the former, a foundation may terminate by transferring its assets and net income to one or more charitable organizations, either public charities (see Chapter 1) or private foundations. As to the latter, a foundation may convert to public charity status. These are termed *voluntary terminations*.

A private foundation's private foundation status may be the subject of an *involuntary termination*. This occurs if the organization engages in willful, flagrant, or repeated acts or failures to act that give rise to one or more of the private foundation excise taxes (see Chapters 4 through 8). This concerns at least two acts or failures to act that are voluntary, conscious, and intentional. This type of termination is subject to a termination tax, which is equal to the lower of (1) the amount that the organization substantiates by adequate records or other corroborating evidence as the aggregate tax benefit resulting from the tax-exempt charitable status of the organization or (2) the value of the net assets of the organization.

This *aggregate tax benefit* is the sum of (1) the amount of income tax that would have been imposed on the foundation if it were not a tax-exempt organization (for years beginning after 1912, which was when the constitutional income tax took effect); (2) the amount of the increases in income, estate, and gift taxes that would have been imposed on all substantial contributors to the foundation (see Chapter 2) if the deductions for their gifts (made after February 28, 1913) had been disallowed; (3) any amounts succeeded to from transferor private foundations, and (4) interest on the foregoing increases in tax beginning as of the point in time the organization ceased to be an exempt private foundation. This tax, which is also known as the *third-tier tax* (in relation to the private foundation first-tier and second-tier taxes [see Chapters 4 through 8]), thus is essentially a confiscation of all of the foundation's assets and net income by the federal government.

The IRS has the discretion to abate some or all of this termination tax if the private foundation (1) distributes its net income and assets to one or more public charities that have been in existence for at least 60 calendar months or (2) provides the IRS with effective assurance that its assets will otherwise be used for charitable purposes.

SUMMARY

This chapter provided summaries of the basic federal tax laws applicable to private foundations as tax-exempt charitable organizations, namely, the rules as to form, the organizational and operational tests, the primary purpose test, the various ways an organization can be charitable, the concept of recognition of exemption, private inurement and private benefit, intermediate sanctions, legislative and political campaign activities, prohibited tax shelter transactions, and personal benefit contracts. The chapter concluded with discussions of the law concerning the excise tax on private foundations' net investment income and termination of private foundation status.

4

MANDATORY PAYOUT RULES

The purpose of this chapter is to summarize the mandatory payout rules that are applicable to private foundations. Foundations are required to make at least a minimum amount of qualifying distributions (such as grants) with respect to each year in furtherance of their charitable purposes. Specifically, this chapter will:

- Provide a history of the mandatory payout rules.

- Describe the payout rules.

- Examine the types of assets used in calculating the payout.

- Summarize the allocations needed in the case of dual-use property.

- Summarize the rules for measuring the fair market value of property.

- Describe the distributable amount rules.

- Summarize the concept of *qualifying distributions*.

- Summarize the two sets of rules concerning *set-asides*.

- Describe the requirements as to distributions to foreign recipients.

- Summarize the rules concerning foundation distributions to supporting organizations.

- Describe the various excise taxes.

- Describe the *correction* requirement.

- Describe the tax abatement rules.
- Revisit the third-tier excise tax regime.

SOME HISTORY

The private foundation payout rules, like most of the private foundation rules, date back to 1969. Before then, the rule was that a tax-exempt charitable organization would lose its exempt status if it unreasonably accumulated income. Also, a private foundation could, prior to present law, invest in assets that did not produce income, without having to pay out anything for charitable purposes, even though one or more donors received substantial charitable contribution deductions for funding the foundation.

Congress deemed this situation untenable and thus legislated today's law, which forces a private foundation to transfer, with respect to each of its tax years, some money and/or property to the larger charitable sector in furtherance of charitable, educational, scientific, religious, and/or like programs. Another goal was to induce avoidance of imprudent or private-interest investment practices or, more radically, eliminate foundations that engage in those practices.

The mandatory payout requirement does not forbid a private foundation from making low-yield investments (such as in non-income-producing land). When a private foundation invests in this manner, however, it periodically may have to sell some assets to generate the cash necessary to meet the distribution requirement for charitable purposes (or, in some instances, distribute assets to that end). Obviously, then, unless the value of its investments is increasing, or its income is adequate to satisfy the payout rule, a private foundation must, because of this rule, chip away at its asset base, hastening the day when its imprudent investment approach causes its decline in size and, perhaps ultimately, its demise.

PAYOUT RULES IN GENERAL

Private foundations are required to make, with respect to each year, grants to other charitable organizations and/or otherwise spend a certain amount of money (or distribute property) for charitable purposes. Four of these mandatory payout rules apply in the private foundation context; the applicable one depends on the type of foundation involved. The general mandatory distribution requirement is the subject of this chapter. The distribution rules for private operating foundations and conduit private foundations are discussed in Chapter 1.

A private foundation's mandatory distribution amount principally is a function of the value of its assets that are not held for a charitable use.

The mandatory amount that must be distributed for each year is ascertained by computing the foundation's *distributable amount*, which is equal to the sum of its *minimum investment return* and certain other amounts, reduced by the sum of the foundation's unrelated business income taxes (see Chapter 8) and the excise tax on net investment income (see Chapter 3) for the year. A foundation's *minimum investment return* basically is an amount equal to 5% of the value of its noncharitable assets, reduced by any outstanding debt. That amount must be distributed in the form of one or more *qualifying distributions*. The core concept is that an amount equivalent to a reasonable economic return on a private foundation's investments must be spent, transferred, or used, for each year, for charitable purposes.

This distributable amount must (to avoid tax penalties) be distributed by the end of the foundation's tax year following the year in which the payout amount is determined. Thus, a foundation on the calendar year that determines its payout obligation for 2009 has until December 31, 2010, to make the requisite amount of qualifying distributions. Excess qualifying distributions may be carried forward for up to five years. The first-year payout amount for a new foundation (due by the close of its second tax year) is prorated to take account of any short year; the same approach is taken with respect to a final year (discussed later in this chapter).

This payout rule is often misstated in the popular media and elsewhere. Usually, when this happens, the statement of the rule reads along the lines of the following quote from the *New York Times*: "A private foundation is required to spend 5 percent of its assets each year for charitable purposes." Three errors are embedded in this quotation: (1) the expenditure must be an amount *equal to* 5% of assets (i.e., the assets themselves need not be distributed; otherwise, the foundation would be piecing itself out of existence); (2) a payout is not always required for each tax year of a private foundation; and (3) not all assets of a foundation are involved in applying this rule; only *investment assets* (not investments held for charitable purposes) are in the payout calculation base. Thus, this statement should have read as follows: "A private foundation is required to spend an amount equal to 5% of its investment assets, with respect to each of its years, for charitable purposes." (That phraseology may be too clunky for journalism, but at least it has the virtue of being accurate.)

Even the courts can get this wrong. Here is a quote from a federal court of appeals: A private foundation "must give away at least 5% of its assets annually in order to retain its tax-exempt status." This misstatement of the law contains the three errors just referenced. Plus, the sanction for failing the payout rule is not loss of tax exemption but payment of one or more excise taxes (discussed later in this chapter).

For the most part, a mandatory payout is imposed only on private foundations. There is, however, a distribution requirement applicable to certain supporting organizations that are required to meet an *integral part test* (see Chapter 1). The IRS, however, prodded by Congress, is in the process of developing regulations that will expand the supporting organizations' mandatory payout obligation. Also, much focus these days is on college and university endowment funds, largely because of their size and growth rate. There is some talk in Congress about imposing a mandatory payout on these funds, to generate money to be used to reduce the costs of higher education for low-income students and their families.

DETERMINING PAYOUT PERCENTAGE AMOUNT

The general rule is that a private foundation is required, with respect to each of its tax years, to spend or pay out for charitable and administrative purposes an amount equal to at least 5% of the average fair market value of its investment assets, reduced by the amount of any debt incurred to acquire one or more properties. Often, this payout is made annually, based on the foundation's investment asset value for the preceding year.

The 5% percentage is reduced in the case of a private foundation with a short tax year. If a foundation has a tax year consisting of less than 12 months, this percentage is calculated by dividing the number of days in the short year by 365 and multiplying the resulting number by 5%. For example, consider a private foundation that utilizes the calendar year as its tax year and is created on September 1. Its minimum distribution amount for its first tax year is based on a payout percentage of 1.67% (122 days divided by 365 days × 5%).

As another illustration, a private foundation with the calendar year as its tax year is created on September 1 and receives its first assets on March 1 of the following year. Inasmuch as it does not have any assets for the first 4 months of its existence, this foundation does not have a payout obligation for its first year. As to its next year, the foundation will obviously be in existence for that full year; thus, as to that year its payout percentage is 5%. The average value of its assets for this second year, however, is calculated by considering that it did not have any assets for two months of that year, thereby reducing the asset base to which the percentage is applied.

This partial year allocation of the payout percentage also applies to a private foundation that changes its year-end. For example, a private foundation changes its financial reporting year-end from August 31 to December 31. The payout percentage for the four-month year is 1.67 (discussed earlier in this chapter). That is the amount that must be paid out during the next succeeding full calendar year.

TYPES OF ASSETS USED IN CALCULATION

The calculation of a private foundation's *minimum investment return* depends in part on differentiating investment assets from exempt function assets.

The typical private foundation investment portfolio of stocks, bonds, certificates of deposit, and rental properties forms the basis for calculating the distributable amount. All types of funds—unrestricted, temporarily restricted, permanently restricted, deferred revenue, capital, endowment, and similar types of reserves—are includible in the formula, irrespective of whether income is being produced by the property.

The included assets are reduced by any acquisition indebtedness with respect to them (see below) and a cash reserve for operations presumed to equal 1.5% of total includible assets. Basically, all of a private foundation's assets are included when making this calculation, unless they are specifically excluded. Exclusions are available for future interests or expectancies and exempt function assets (see below). Property used for tax-exempt and investment purposes is termed *dual-use property*; the value of this type of property must be allocated in computing minimum investment return (discussed later in this chapter).

FUTURE INTERESTS OR EXPECTANCIES

Certain assets provide beneficial support to a private foundation, albeit in an indirect fashion. Assets over which the foundation does not have control and in which it essentially does not hold a present interest are not included in the minimum investment return formula. These assets customarily are not included in the financial records or statements of a foundation. These future interests are:

- Charitable remainders and other future interests in property (whether legal or equitable) created by a person other than the foundation. These interests in property are not included in the minimum investment return formula until the intervening interests expire or are otherwise set apart for the foundation. If the foundation is able to take possession of the property at its will or to acquire it readily on giving notice, the property is included in the calculation. Constructive receipt rules apply to use in determining when a cash-basis person receives an item of income.

- Pledges of money or other property to a foundation, irrespective of whether they are legally enforceable.

- Property bequeathed to a foundation while it is held in the decedent's estate. Should the IRS terminate the estate on the ground that the period of administration is unduly prolonged, the assets are treated as assets of the foundation as of the date of the IRS's determination.

- Options to sell property that is not readily marketable, such as a nontransferable right to purchase real estate. Listed options to buy or sell marketable securities or other future obligations that are traded on a stock exchange and have ascertainable value are includible investment assets.

EXEMPT FUNCTION ASSETS

Income, for payout purposes, need not be imputed to property used by (or held by) a private foundation directly in the conduct of its charitable programs. This type of property, known as *exempt function property* (or *exempt function assets*), is not usually held for the production of income (although it can be). The most common types of private foundation assets, excluded from the minimum investment return formula as exempt function assets, are the following:

- Administrative offices, furnishings, equipment, and supplies used by employees in working on the foundation's charitable projects. This property, or this type of property, if used by individuals who manage the investment property of the foundation, however, is treated as investment property. An allocation is required where an item of property is used for both categories of purposes.

- Buildings, equipment, and facilities used directly in foundation projects, such as:

  ○ Historic buildings, libraries, and the furnishings in and other contents of these buildings

  ○ Collections of objects on display for educational purposes, such as works of art or scientific specimens, including artwork loaned to museums, universities, and other charitable institutions

  ○ Research facilities and laboratories, including a limited-access island held vacant to preserve its natural ecosystem, history, and archaeology

  ○ Educational classrooms and print shops

  ○ Property used for a nominal or reduced rent by another charitable organization

  ○ Land of environmental importance being held for ultimate use as a center for environmental and cultural conservation

- Reasonable cash balances, which are considered necessary to carry out a foundation's exempt functions. As noted, 1.5% of the included investment assets is presumed to be a reasonable cash balance, even if a smaller cash balance is actually maintained. If the facts and circumstances indicate that a foundation needs to hold a greater amount of money to cover its expenses and disbursements, it can apply to the IRS for permission to maintain a higher amount (which, if the permission is granted, is excludable).

- An asset acquired by a private foundation for future use may be treated as exempt function property where the foundation has definite plans to commence exempt function use of the property within a limited period of time (usually within one year), even if the property produces some income in the interim. An example of future use property is a building with existing tenants having unexpired leases that a foundation acquires to convert to a community service space for local relief agencies.

- Program-related investments (see Chapter 7). The primary motivation for the making of these investments is not the production of income.

- Functionally related businesses (see Chapter 8). The properties used in conducting these businesses are not included as investment assets because the businesses are related (exempt function) businesses.

A recent ruling from the IRS illustrates the scope and creative use of this exclusion. A private foundation received, by bequest, intellectual property used in connection with television programming and related educational services directed to the promotion of emotional and intellectual development of children. The foundation desired to license the property, on a no-royalty basis, to a public charity in furtherance of its charitable and educational purposes. The public charity agreed to pay any expenses that may be necessary to protect and defend the property. The IRS ruled that the value of this intellectual property may be excluded from the foundation's asset base for purposes of computing its minimum investment return.

DUAL-USE PROPERTY

In many instances, a private foundation owns and uses property for managing and conducting both charitable projects and its investments. In these situations, an allocation between these two uses must be made in constructing the foundation's mandatory payout asset base. An asset that is used 95% or more for one purpose is regarded as used entirely for that purpose.

A typical example of dual-use property owned by a private foundation is an office building housing the foundation. As an illustration, assume an office building with 4,500 square feet, all used by a foundation. Program offices occupy 3,375 square feet of the building (75% of the space); the investment department occupies the remaining 1,125 square feet in the building (25%). In this example, 25% of the building's value is an investment asset. If a foundation is large, this formula may be more complicated, taking into account administration. This occurs where the staff is sophisticated, and separate personnel, accounting, and central supply departments serve the program and investment groups. If property is partly used by a foundation and partly rented, an allocation based on the fair rental value of the respective spaces (rather than square footage) is appropriate.

ASSETS HELD FOR FUTURE USE

It may require a number of years to piece together a project using hard assets such as land, buildings, and equipment. When a private foundation has future plans for the use of property in a charitable activity and obtains an IRS determination that its immediate use of the property is impractical, the asset is excluded from the payout asset base. Definite plans must exist to commence use within a reasonable period of time; the facts and circumstances must prove the intention to devote the property to the exempt use. The concepts for earmarking property of this nature are similar to those pertaining to set-asides (discussed later in this chapter).

Property acquired by a private foundation to be devoted to charitable purposes may be treated as exempt function property as of the time it is acquired, even if it is rented in the interim. The rental status must be for a reasonable and limited period of time, and only while the property is being made ready for its intended exempt use, such as during remodeling or acquisition of adjacent parcels of property. IRS approval in this setting is not required if conversion of the property to a charitable use is accomplished within a year. If, however, the property is rented for more than one year, it is investment property during the following year and thereafter, until it is converted to exempt use.

ACQUISITION INDEBTEDNESS

The formula for calculation of a private foundation's minimum investment return allows a reduction in includible assets by the amount of any acquisition indebtedness with respect to one or more assets. *Acquisition indebtedness* is the unpaid amount of debt incurred by a foundation in acquiring or improving a property. The most common type of acquisition indebtedness incurred by a foundation is a mortgage used to finance acquisition of investment real estate. A margin account created to purchase securities also is a form of acquisition debt, but private foundations seldom borrow on margin because of the prohibition on jeopardizing investments (see Chapter 7).

Some private foundations with significant portfolios of marketable securities enter into securities lending transactions to enhance the return on those investment assets. The foundation lends securities to a financial institution; the borrowing institution, in return, customarily provides the foundation with cash collateral equal to (or perhaps more than) the value of the securities. The foundation retains its right to receive dividends or interest from the securities and invests the cash collateral. This obligation to return collateral security is not an acquisition indebtedness (and income earned in connection with these loans is not unrelated business income [see Chapter 8]).

DETERMINING FAIR MARKET VALUE

In computing its annual distributable amount, a private foundation must, as has been discussed, determine its minimum investment return, which requires computation of the aggregate fair market value of all assets of the foundation, other than those that are excludible from the formula (discussed earlier in this chapter). Different methods, valuation times, and frequencies are provided for various types of investment assets that a private foundation needs to value. Mistakes in valuation of property can cause a foundation to incorrectly determine its required distributable amount. Any commonly acceptable method of valuation may be used, as long as it is reasonable and consistently applied.

Different valuation dates are prescribed for different types of assets:

Cash	Monthly
Marketable securities	Monthly
Real estate	Every five years
Other assets	Annually

Assets valued annually can be valued on any date, as long as the same date is used each year. Likewise, real estate and mineral interest valuation should be done on approximately the same date every fifth year. Cash is valued on a monthly basis by averaging the amount of cash on hand as of the first day of each month and the last day of each month.

Securities for which a market quotation is readily available must be valued monthly, using a reasonable and consistent method. *Securities* include common and preferred stocks, bonds, and mutual fund shares. The monthly security valuation method applies to:

- Stocks listed on the New York Stock Exchange, the American Stock Exchange, or any city or regional exchange in which quotations appear on a daily basis, including foreign securities listed on a recognized foreign national or regional exchange

- Stocks regularly traded in a national or regional over-the-counter market, for which published quotations are available

- Locally traded stocks for which quotations can readily be obtained from established brokerage firms

Blockage discounts up to 10% are permitted to reduce the valuation of securities when a private foundation can show that the quoted market prices do not reflect fair market value for one or more of the following reasons:

- The block of securities is so large in relation to the volume of actual sales on the existing market that it could not be liquidated in a reasonable time without depressing the market.

- Sales of the securities are few or sporadic in nature, and the shares are in a closely held corporation.

- The sale of the securities would result in a forced or distress sale because the securities cannot be offered to the public without first being registered with the Securities and Exchange Commission.

The value of private foundation funds invested in a common trust fund can be based on the fund's valuation reports. Fund participants typically receive periodic valuations of their interests from the fund manager throughout each year and can calculate the average of these valuations. If, for example, the fund issues valuations quarterly, the average of the four reported valuations in a year is the fair market value reportable by the foundation as an investment asset for that year.

A certified appraisal must be prepared every five years for investment real property held by a private foundation. The appraiser must be qualified and independent; as to the latter, the appraiser may not be an employee of or otherwise a disqualified person (see Chapter 2) with respect to the foundation. An appraisal is *certified* when it includes the appraiser's opinion that the value placed on the appraised land was determined in accordance with valuation principles regularly employed in making appraisals of the type of property involved, using all reasonable valuation methods.

More frequent valuations of real property can be made when circumstances dictate, such as when the value of the realty has substantially declined; this starts a new five-year period. The IRS may question an appraisal of real estate, during a five-year period, if the value of the property has materially increased, should the agency conclude that the valuation was outside the range of reasonable values for the particular property.

The valuation date for real estate received by a private foundation by gift, transfer from an estate or trust, or purchase may technically be valued on any date of the year after acquisition of the property. As a practical matter, however, the acquisition date often becomes the date used for investment return valuation purposes, because an appraisal is prepared on that date for the donor or transferor.

Valid mineral interest valuations are based on reserve studies conducted by independent petroleum evaluation engineers. These studies customarily are updated every five years, as is done with the surface real estate and buildings. The IRS has never published any guidance about the valuation of oil property.

A closely held business—whether structured as a corporation, partnership, limited liability company, or other joint venture—can be valued on any day of the year, as long as the practice is annually consistent. Estate tax valuation methods apply. A holding company owning readily marketable securities must value these securities on a monthly basis, rather than annually, if a private foundation and its disqualified persons control the company.

Valuation of computers, other office equipment, and other tangible assets used in managing the investment activities of a private foundation can be determined on the basis of local advertising for used equipment (such as classified advertisements in newspapers) or by obtaining a quotation from a used office furniture dealer.

The value of a whole-life insurance policy is its cash surrender value. Notes and accounts receivable are included in a foundation's payout asset base at their net realizable value or at their face value discounted for any uncollectible portion. (Although logic would dictate that a note receivable, for which a private foundation receives monthly payments that reduce the principal amount of the loan, be valued monthly, the tax regulations mandate annual valuations.) Collectibles, such as gold, gems, and paintings, are valued in accordance with the estate tax valuation rules.

Valuation of *alternative investments*, such as interests in hedge funds and offshore partnerships, for purposes of calculating a private foundation's minimum investment return, is often a challenge. The law basically requires that a consistent method for valuing the property be followed on a monthly or annual basis. Hedge funds and partnerships frequently hold several types of investments, including (1) marketable securities and options that would be valued monthly if held outside a partnership and (2) nonlisted venture capital stocks and loans that are subject to valuation annually. Unless interests in the fund itself are readily marketable, such as is the case with a publicly traded partnership, these investments generally should be valued annually. Some foundations receive valuations more than once a year; there is no guidance as to whether these valuations can be averaged to arrive at an annual valuation.

The average value of an asset held by a private foundation for a portion of a year is calculated by creating a fraction, with the number of days the asset was held by the foundation in the year as the numerator and 365 as the denominator. The value included in the payout asset base is thereby reduced in reflection of the partial-year holding period. For example, if a private foundation acquired an item of real estate, with a value of $100,000, on July 1, the includible asset amount for the acquisition year is $50,000 ($100,000 × 182/365 = $50,000).

A new foundation begins its first year on the date it is created, not the day it first receives assets. Thus, assume the facts of the foregoing example applied to a new foundation, created on March 1 that received the gift of real estate on July 1. The includible asset amount for the acquisition year is $83,300 ($100,000 × 304/365 = 83,300).

DISTRIBUTABLE AMOUNT

A private foundation, other than a private operating foundation (see Chapter 1), is subject to a federal excise tax if it fails to spend or pay out a minimum amount for charitable purposes. It may, without penalty, distribute more than this minimum amount. This required payout amount is termed the *distributable amount*. A private foundation's annual distributable amount is determined by application of a formula.

The distributable amount would seem to be easy to ascertain. For example, a private foundation with $10 million in noncharitable assets would appear to have an annual distributable amount of $500,000 (5% × $10 million). But the law makes these matters somewhat more complex. To simplify this calculation, the following formula is used:

$$A + B - C = D \text{[istributable amount]}$$

A = minimum investment return amount

B = amounts previously included in the payout calculation, but that have become nonqualifying, so they must be included again, such as:

- Student loans or program-related investments (see Chapter 7) repaid to the foundation

- An asset that ceases to become an exempt function asset, where the purchase of it or conversion of it to exempt use was previously included as a qualifying distribution (see below) (The sales proceeds or the fair market value at the time of conversion of the asset is the amount that must be added back.)

- Unused set-aside funds (see below) that are no longer earmarked for a charitable project or that are ineligible for the set-aside because the time period allowed has lapsed

   C = The excise tax on investment income (see Chapter 3) and tax on unrelated business income for the year

An illustration of application of this formula, assuming a standard private foundation with $10 million in noncharitable assets, is as follows:

Value of noncharitable assets for the year	$10,000,000
Less acquisition indebtedness	500,000
	9,500,000
Less cash deemed held for charitable activities	
(1% × $9, 500, 000)	142,500
Net value of noncharitable assets	9, 357,500
Minimum investment return (5% of net value)	467,875
Plus recovery of amounts previously treated as	
qualifying distribution(s)	30,000
Less excise and income tax	22,000
Distributable amount	$475,875

It may be noted that the distributable amount for a private foundation for a year has no relationship to the foundation's actual investment income for that year. Thus, the private foundation in this example may have an 8% return on its investment assets, or $800,000. The law requires expenditure of only the $475,875. The balance of $324,125 may be retained in the foundation's coffers.

An item of controversy and confusion pervades this topic. For years, the IRS took the position that income paid or payable to a private foundation, by a type of trust known as a charitable lead trust, must be added to the distributable amount—despite the fact that the statutory law does not include the requirement. The matter was litigated, with the IRS losing the case (the trial court decision was issued in 1991; the appellate court decision was in 1994). In 2004, the IRS announced that it was going to change the tax regulations to conform with the court opinions; in the interim, the agency stated, private foundations can ignore the original IRS position. To date, however, the IRS has not even issued proposed regulations on the point. Those foundations that complied with the IRS view at the outset had (or have) the opportunity to reduce their distributable amount for one or more prior years or carry the amounts forward to be credited against the payout obligations for future years (discussed later in this chapter).

To avoid an excise tax penalty, the distributable amount must be paid out by a private foundation—by the close of the year immediately following the year for which the amount was determined. For example, a calendar-year foundation must, by December 31, 2009, distribute the amount calculated as due to be paid out for the year ended December 31,

2008. This deadline provides a newly created foundation as much as a two-year period in which to establish its grant systems and earn the income to be distributed. This two-year period of time is, of course, available to private foundations generally.

A private foundation that, subsequent to its first year, has a short tax year (a year of less than 12 months) must pay out its distributable amount prior to the end of the short period. Thus, a foundation that wishes to change its fiscal year should do so with appreciation of the acceleration of the distribution deadline that results. Although the shorter deadline may cause a temporary financial burden, the short year's distributable amount would be based on a reduced percentage prorated according to the number of days in the short year in relation to 365 days. Thus, the amount required to be distributed by the end of the full year following the short year will be a reduced partial-year amount.

QUALIFYING DISTRIBUTIONS

It is commonly said that private foundations make *grants*. They do this, of course, but the technical (and broader) term is *qualifying distributions*. Thus, amounts expended and property transferred by a private foundation to meet the mandatory payout requirement must be in the form of qualifying distributions. The excise tax that is levied on a failure to make the requisite distribution (discussed later in this chapter) is imposed on *undistributed income*, which is the *distributable amount* for the year less qualifying distributions made for the year.

There are some refinements to the concept of the *qualifying distribution*:

- Qualifying distributions must be determined in accordance with the cash receipts and disbursements method of accounting.

- The amount of a qualifying distribution made with property (other than money) is based on the fair market value of the property (discussed earlier in this chapter) on the date of its distribution.

- The distribution requirement can be satisfied only by an actual payout or distribution of property; a mere commitment or pledge of funds or property is inadequate. (An exception to this rule is the *set-aside*.)

For a payment of funds or a distribution of property by a private foundation to constitute a qualifying distribution, two basic tests must be satisfied: (1) the expenditure must be in support of a charitable purpose, and (2) the foundation must relinquish the funds (or property); that is, it cannot retain control over the use of the funds nor restrict them for its own purposes. Not all qualifying distributions are generically grants, however. A *qualifying distribution* can be:

- An amount paid to another person to accomplish one or more charitable purposes (a grant), other than a payment to (1) an organization that is controlled (discussed later in this chapter) by the grantor foundation or by one or more disqualified persons (see Chapter 2) with respect to it or (2) a private foundation that is not a private operating foundation (see Chapter 1) (with an exception for certain redistributions [discussed later in this chapter])

- An amount that is a reasonable and necessary administrative expense

- An amount paid to acquire an asset used or held for use directly in carrying out one or more charitable purposes

- Qualified set-asides

- Program-related investments (see Chapter 7)

Grants made directly to public charities (see Chapter 1), for their general support or for a wide range of specific charitable purposes, comprise by far the majority of qualifying distributions by private foundations. Nonetheless, the fundamental requirement is that these grants be made for charitable *purposes*, not necessarily to charitable *organizations*; support for charitable purposes can conceivably be provided to individuals or any type of organizations (nonprofit or for-profit) anywhere in the world as long as proper procedures are followed (see Chapter 5).

It was noted that a distribution to a controlled organization usually cannot be a qualifying distribution. A grantee organization is *controlled* by a private foundation, or by one or more of its disqualified persons, if the foundation and/or any of these persons can, by aggregating their votes or positions of authority, require the recipient organization to make an expenditure or prevent it from making an expenditure, regardless of the method by which control is exercised or exercisable. This type of control is generally determined on an organizational—or people—level, without regard to conditions imposed on the grantee or any other restriction accompanying the distribution as to the manner in which the distributions are to be used. Consequently, it is when the grantee, not the distribution, is controlled that the grant is not a qualifying distribution. For example, the stipulation that a budgetary procedure be adopted and followed by the grantee as a condition of receiving the financial support is not in *control*.

If a recipient-controlled organization or unrelated private foundation is required to redistribute the funds or property received, the payment is a qualifying distribution. Four elements must be present for this approach to work:

1. The controlled grantee must be a charitable organization.

2. Not later than the close of the first tax year after the controlled grantee's tax year in which the distribution is received, the grantee distributes

an amount equal in value to the full amount of the payment (a pass-through).

3. The grantee may not count the distribution toward satisfaction of its own distribution requirement (if any) but must treat its regranting of the distribution as a payment out of its corpus.

4. The grantor private foundation obtains records or other evidence from the grantee proving that the redistribution was accomplished.

Administrative expenses, including amounts paid to a foundation's personnel and for overhead, expended to accomplish the foundation's charitable purposes constitute qualifying distributions. (This is unfortunate terminology because it suggests that the payment is for management, not program.) Any portion of a foundation's administrative expenses allocable to management of properties held for the production of income, such as investment advisory fees, are not qualifying distributions. Legal, accounting, and state registration and other fees and expenses paid in connection with creation and qualification for tax exemption of a new private foundation are distributions for charitable purposes. Administrative expenses must be reasonable and necessary to accomplish a foundation's exempt purposes to be qualifying distributions.

SET-ASIDES IN GENERAL

Funds set aside for future charitable projects, rather than paid out currently, can be considered qualifying distributions by a private foundation. An amount set aside in a year for a specific charitable project counts toward the payout requirement if (1) payment for the project is to be subsequently made over a period not to exceed 60 months and (2) the rules as to one of two types of set-asides are followed. The funds set aside are credited, for purposes of the qualifying distribution requirements, as if paid in the year the set-aside is established. The amount set aside need not be increased by accumulation of income on the amount. The set-aside is reflected as a liability on the foundation's financial records, indicating that the amount must be paid out of corpus by the end of the set-aside period.

A *specific project* includes situations where relatively long-term expenditures must be made in order to ensure the continuity of a particular undertaking. This concept embraces, as an example, a plan to construct a building to house a tax-exempt activity of a public charity, such as a museum. Likewise, a conversion by a private foundation of newly acquired land, partially to its existing wildlife sanctuary and partially to a park for public use, under a four-year construction contract, pursuant to which payments were not required until the third and fourth years, was ruled by the IRS to be a requisite specific project.

By contrast, a private foundation that made renewable scholarships and fixed-sum research grants that usually ran for three years, proposed to set aside the full amount to be granted to each grantee and make annual payments to them from a set-aside account, rather than take the payments out of its current income; the IRS held that the set-aside approach was inappropriate, because the foundation was simply engaging in ongoing grant-making and there was no specific project. Yet, in a surprising and controversial decision, the IRS thereafter allowed a set-aside for another foundation for a scholarship grant program where the foundation was newly created, students who would benefit from its grants could not be identified during the initial grant period, the request was for a one-time set-aside, the foundation's program does not promise future grants, and the foundation advised its grantees to not expect further funding.

If a private foundation is unable to satisfy either of the set-aside tests for its set-asides, it must distribute its minimum distributable amount by the end of its following tax year to avoid excise tax exposure for failure to make the required minimum distribution.

SET-ASIDE TYPE I: SUITABILITY TEST

There are two types of set-asides. The first type is based on the *suitability test*. This test is satisfied where the basic set-aside requirements are met and where the private foundation is successful in convincing the IRS that the project can be better accomplished by a set-aside than by conventional grant-making. A ruling from the IRS is necessary for this type of set-aside. A private foundation must apply for the ruling before the end of the year in which the amount is to be set aside. The ruling request must include the amount of the intended set-aside, the reasons that the project can be better accomplished by a set-aside, and a detailed description of the project. (The IRS has made it clear that a foundation's desire to retain control of funds so as to receive income from them does not meet the *better accomplished* standard.)

For good cause shown, the period for paying an amount set aside under the suitability test may be extended by the IRS. For example, a private foundation that was permitted a set-aside to construct a youth camp was granted a two-year extension to pay out the funds because a city's building moratorium caused delays in acquiring the necessary property. Other illustrations of IRS-approved set-asides are construction of foundation headquarters where most of the office space is to be rented at below cost to other charitable organizations, redevelopment of a city block as part of rejuvenation of a downtown area, construction of facilities in another country for abandoned and underprivileged children, and the making of guarantees of below-market bank loans to, and loan deposits and interest rate subsidies for, public charities to advance charitable child-care programs.

A private foundation is not penalized if, having obtained a set-aside ruling from the IRS, it thereafter decides instead to engage in general grant-making to further or complete a charitable project, and disregards its ruling.

SET-ASIDE TYPE II: CASH DISTRIBUTION TEST

The second type of private foundation set-aside is based on the *cash distribution test*; this complex approach to charitable funding originated because of reluctance on the part of the IRS to approve set-aside requests, a dilemma that was particularly acute for new foundations that wanted to institute long-term supervised projects in the face of IRS inaction. This test is satisfied where the basic set-aside rules are met, and where (1) the project to which the set-aside relates will not be completed before the end of the tax year of the foundation in which the set-aside is made and (2) the foundation (a) distributes, in cash or its equivalent, the start-up period minimum amount during the foundation's start-up period and (b) distributes, in cash or its equivalent, the full-payment period minimum amount in each tax year of the foundation's full-payment period. A principal virtue—and the reason for creation—of the cash distribution test is that approval from the IRS is not required.

Start-up Period

A private foundation's *start-up period* consists of the four tax years following the tax year in which the organization was created (or became a private foundation). Thus, for example, a private foundation created in 2009, using the calendar year as its tax year, has a start-up period spanning the calendar years 2010–2013.

The *start-up period minimum amount* that must be timely distributed is the sum of:

1. 20% of the private foundation's distributable amount for the first tax year of the start-up period

2. 40% of the foundation's distributable amount for the second tax year of the start-up period

3. 60% of its distributable amount for the third year of the period

4. 80% of its distributable amount for the fourth year of the period

Under certain circumstances, distributions made during the year preceding the foundation's start-up period and/or made within $5\frac{1}{2}$ months following the start-up period are deemed part of the start-up period minimum amount.

For example, a private foundation formed in early 2009, operating on the calendar year, has a start-up period beginning January 1, 2010, and ending December 31, 2013. To meet the cash distribution test for set-aside treatment for set-asides made during the start-up period, this foundation must meet the following requirements:

- Its set-asides must relate to projects that will not be completed before the end of the tax year in which the set-aside is made.

- The set-asides must be distributed within five years of the date on which the amount is set aside.

- The foundation must distribute the required start-up period minimum amount by December 31, 2013.

This foundation's start-up period minimum amount is, in the aggregate, equal to:

- 20% of the foundation's distributable amount for 2010

- 40% of its distributable amount for 2011

- 60% of its distributable amount for 2012

- 80% of its distributable amount for 2013

The requirement that a private foundation distribute the start-up period minimum amount during the start-up period is a requirement that this amount be distributed before the end of the period; it is not a requirement that any portion of this amount be distributed in any particular tax year of the period. Thus, a foundation has until the end of the start-up period to distribute the aggregate start-up period minimum amount.

Thus, with respect to the above example, these amounts do not have to be distributed in the year to which they relate as long as the entire amount is distributed by December 31, 2013. In addition, the amounts set aside and not distributed must be distributed within five years of the date on which they were set aside. For example, this foundation must distribute a set-aside amount made on December 31, 2010, relating to the 2009 distributable amount (required to be distributed no later than December 31, 2010) for the set-aside project no later than December 31, 2015. Because a private foundation is required to distribute a set-aside within five years of the date of the set-aside and not by the end of the fifth year after the date of the set-aside, an amount set aside on June 30, 2010, must be distributed by June 30, 2015.

Full-Payment Period

The years of a private foundation's existence after expiration of the start-up period are termed the *full-payment period*. Therefore, the full-payment period begins in the sixth tax year after the year the foundation is created (or becomes a foundation) and continues with all of its tax years thereafter. For example, as to the preceding illustration of a calendar-year private foundation formed in 2009, if the foundation desires for set-asides made after the close of its start-up period (i.e., for tax years beginning January 1, 2014) to also be treated as set-asides under the cash distribution test, the foundation must continue to distribute the full-payment period amount for each year after its start-up period.

A private foundation's *full-payment period minimum amount* is 100% of the foundation's distributable amount for each tax year during the period. The full-payment period minimum amount must be distributed in each tax year of the period. This is in contrast to the general minimum distributable amount, which may be distributed in a tax year or the immediately succeeding tax year. For purposes of meeting the full-payment period minimum amount, a foundation may take into account payments that are made during the full-payment period with respect to set-asides treated as qualifying distributions in prior years.

If a private foundation fails to distribute the start-up period minimum amount during the start-up period or fails to distribute the full-payment period minimum amount during a tax year of the full-payment period, any set-aside made by the foundation during the start-up period (if the failure relates to that period) or during a subsequent tax year (if the failure relates to the full-payment period) will not be treated as a qualifying distribution (unless the set-aside was approved by the IRS under the suitability test). Any set-aside made after the year of the failure will be regarded as a qualifying distribution only after the IRS approves it pursuant to the suitability test. Thus, these rules would not disqualify a set-aside as a qualifying distribution in a prior period for failure to distribute the full-payment period minimum amount in a subsequent period. A set-aside made in the start-up period would, however, be disallowed as a qualifying distribution if the start-up period minimum amount is not distributed by the end of the start-up period.

IRS Rulings Positions

The design of the start-up period amounts that reflect a 20%, 40%, 60%, and 80% distributable amount for the 4-year period imply that this test applies only to newly created private foundations. The legislative history of this law describes the test as designed for start-up foundations and existing foundations that have recently received a dramatic influx of new assets.

In two rulings, however, the IRS sanctioned the use of the cash distribution set-aside provisions for foundations that had been in existence well beyond their initial start-up period and had not received an influx of funding.

In one of these instances, cash distribution set-asides were allowed in 1986 and 1988 for a private foundation that was formed in 1952. Since the foundation's start-up period had long since passed, it was under the full-payment-period minimum distribution requirements. Based on the facts of the ruling, it was apparent that this foundation had met its distribution requirements for purposes of the standard 5% minimum distribution test. It sought, however, and was allowed to qualify for the 1% excise tax on net investment income, rather than the conventional 2% tax (see Chapter 3). By making use of the cash distribution test for some grants that were not paid by the end of the foundation's tax year, the foundation was able to claim additional set-aside amounts as qualifying distributions for purposes of qualifying for the lesser tax.

In the second ruling, the foundation wanted the ability to use the cash distribution test for multi-installment grants that covered more than one tax year. By claiming set-aside amounts as qualifying distributions prior to actual disbursements of the cash, the foundation was allowed to monitor the multi-year grants and obtain progress reports before the foundation made further distributions to the recipient. Again, the IRS approved use of the cash distribution test for current and *future* tax years for a foundation with years of existence well after the foundation's start-up period expired. Although these two rulings sanctioned use of the cash distribution test by existing foundations, caution is in order in considering this approach.

DISTRIBUTIONS TO FOREIGN RECIPIENTS

A private foundation may make a qualifying distribution to a charitable organization in a country other than the United States, as well as to foreign governments. Additional requirements apply, however, when a foundation is making grants outside the United States. A private foundation that supports charitable activities in foreign lands faces a documentation dilemma. It must obtain information evidencing two important sets of facts:

1. The foundation must be able to prove that its money was expended (or property used) to accomplish one or more charitable purposes, whether it spent the money directly in conduct of a program or made a grant.

2. If funds (or property) were granted to a foreign organization, the foundation must (a) prove that the recipient is not controlled by it and is the equivalent of a U.S. public charity or private operating foundation

(see Chapter 1) or (b) exercise expenditure responsibility with respect to the grant (see Chapter 5).

If a foreign charitable organization has a ruling from the IRS that it is a public charity or private operating foundation (see Chapter 1) for U.S. law purposes (which is unlikely), a private foundation can make a qualifying distribution to the foreign charity in accordance with the rules concerning these distributions generally. Otherwise, a private foundation's distribution to a foreign charity is treated as if made to the equivalent of a U.S. public charity or private operating foundation only if the grantor foundation has made a good faith determination that the grantee is this type of an equivalent.

A *good faith determination* ordinarily is made where the determination is based on a suitable affidavit provided by the prospective grantee or an opinion of legal counsel (of the grantor or grantee) that the prospective grantee qualifies as the equivalent of a U.S. public charity or private operating foundation. This affidavit or opinion must set forth sufficient facts concerning the operations and support of the grantee for the IRS (and the prospective grantor) to determine that the grantee meets the test of public charity or private operating foundation. Based on the facts, the management of a private foundation in this circumstance must make a reasonable judgment that the potential grantee is a charitable organization and then make a good faith determination that the entity is the equivalent of a public charity or private operating foundation under U.S. law.

The IRS developed a procedure enabling U.S. private foundations to make qualifying distributions to foreign charitable organizations, relying solely on an appropriate affidavit. Both this *reasonable judgment* and *good faith determination* may be made on the basis of a currently qualified affidavit prepared by the grantee for the prospective grantor or for another grantor or prospective grantor. This procedure requires that the affidavit be written in English and provide certain information. An affidavit is *currently qualified* where the facts in it are up-to-date, either because they are based on the prospective grantee's most recent complete accounting year or (in the case of an equivalent public charity or private operating foundation where that status is not dependent on public support) if the affidavit is updated at the request of the prospective grantor to reflect the prospective grantee's current information.

DISTRIBUTIONS TO CERTAIN SUPPORTING ORGANIZATIONS

A private foundation may not treat as a qualifying distribution an amount paid to a Type III supporting organization that is not a functionally integrated Type III supporting organization or to any other type of supporting organization (see Chapter 1) if a disqualified person with respect to the foundation (see Chapter 2) directly or indirectly controls the supporting organization or a supported organization of the supporting organization. An amount that does not count as a qualifying distribution under this rule is regarded as a taxable expenditure (see Chapter 5).

A private foundation prospective grantor, acting in good faith, may, in determining whether a grantee is a public charity, rely on information from the IRS's Business Master File or the grantee's current IRS determination letter recognizing the grantee's tax exemption and indicating the grantee's public charity status. In addition, a foundation grantor, acting in good faith, may rely on a written representation from a grantee and certain specified documents in determining the grantee's supporting organization type. In any event, the grantor must verify that the prospective grantee is listed in the IRS's inventory of charitable organizations (Publication 78) or obtain a copy of the grantee's determination letter.

To establish that a grantee is a Type I or II supporting organization, a grantor, acting in good faith, may rely on a written representation signed by a trustee, director, or officer of the grantee that the grantee is one of these types of supporting organizations, provided that:

- The representation describes how the grantee's trustees, directors, and/or officers are selected and references any provision in the governing documents that establish a Type I or II relationship between the grantee and its supported organization(s).

- The grantor collects and reviews copies of the governing documents of the grantee and, if relevant, of the supported organization(s).

To establish that a prospective grantee is a functionally integrated Type III supporting organization, a grantor, acting in good faith, may rely on a written representation signed by a trustee, director, or officer of the grantee that the grantee is a functionally integrated Type III supporting organization, provided that:

- The grantee's representation identifies the one or more supported organizations with which the grantee is functionally integrated.

- The grantor collects and reviews copies of governing documents of the grantee (and, if relevant, of the supported organization[s]) and any other documents that set forth the relationship of the grantee to its supported organization(s), if the relationship is not reflected in the governing documents.

- The grantor reviews a written representation signed by a trustee, director, or officer of each of the supported organizations with which the grantee represents that it is functionally integrated, describing the activities of the grantee and confirming that, but for the involvement of the grantee engaging in activities to perform the functions of, or to carry out the purposes of, the supported organization, the supported organization would normally be engaged in those activities itself (discussed later in this chapter).

As an alternative to the foregoing, a grantor may rely on a reasoned written opinion from legal counsel (of the grantor or grantee) concluding that the grantee is a Type I, Type II, or Type III functionally integrated supporting organization.

A private foundation considering a grant to a Type I, Type II, or Type III functionally integrated supporting organization may need to obtain, from the grantee, a list of the grantee's supported organizations to determine whether any of the supported organizations are controlled (see below) by disqualified persons with respect to the foundation. Likewise, a sponsoring organization considering a grant from a donor-advised fund (see Chapter 11) to one of these types of supporting organizations may need to obtain such a list to determine whether any of the supported organizations is controlled by the fund's donor or donor advisor (and any related parties).

In determining whether a disqualified person with respect to a private foundation *controls* a supporting organization or one of its supported organizations, the standards as to control that are established in the mandatory payout rules apply. Under these standards, an organization is controlled by one or more disqualified persons with respect to a foundation if any of these persons may, by aggregating their votes or positions of authority, require the supporting or supported organization to make an expenditure or prevent the supporting or supported organization from making an expenditure, regardless of the method by which the control is exercised or exercisable.

Private foundation grants to supporting organizations may be considerably reduced as the consequence of these regulatory rules (which came into law in 2006), because of the difficulties and risks associated with compliance with them. Private foundations may simply adopt a policy of not funding supporting organizations. This would be unfortunate in many ways, such as in situations where the supporting organization has fundraising as a principal function. In this regard, an analogy may be made with respect to expenditure responsibility grants (see Chapter 5): Private foundations are permitted to make these types of grants but, because of the intricacies of the rules and the potential for penalties, few do.

IMPOSITION OF EXCISE TAX PENALTIES

The penalties that can be imposed in this context principally are initial and additional taxes, levied on the private foundation involved.

Initial Tax

With respect to each of its tax years, a private foundation is required to spend at least a minimum amount for charitable purposes based on the value of its noncharitable assets (see above). A foundation has the current year and immediately the following year to make the requisite payout for the current year. Private foundations are subject to an excise tax for failure to pay out their distributable amount in a timely fashion and, therefore, had *undistributed income*. An initial tax (also known as a first-tier tax) of 30% of undistributed income is imposed.

The tax is charged for each year or partial year that the deficiency remains uncorrected (discussed later in this chapter). Essentially, the tax calculation starts on the first late date and continues until the IRS issues a notice as to the deficiency (but in whole-year increments). This taxable period also closes on the date of voluntary payment of the tax.

For example, a calendar-year private foundation failed to distribute $100,000 of its distributable amount by December 31, 2008. If this amount is distributed within the first year after the deadline (i.e., by December 31, 2009), a 30% excise tax is due. If this correction takes two years, or is not accomplished until the second year after it was due (on or before January 1, 2010), another 30% tax is due.

Additional Tax

An additional excise tax (also known as a second-tier tax) of 100% is triggered if the foundation fails to make up the deficient distribution(s) with 90 days of receiving, from the IRS, notification of the problem. Payment of these taxes is in addition to, not in lieu of, making the required distributions.

CORRECTION

Not only is this initial tax penalty assessed, a private foundation with undistributed income must correct the deficit with the making of additional qualifying distributions for the year at issue. Certain inadvertent deficiencies can be made up without penalty. Failure to correct a deficiency of this nature can also result in penalties.

To identify a deficiency in connection with a private foundation's distributions, application of the payments must be understood. A foundation's charitable expenditures that are considered qualifying distributions are totaled for each year in which they are paid but they are not necessarily applied with respect to the payment year. A current year's distributable amount is based on the prior year's minimum investment return. Qualifying distributions are applied as follows:

- First, the qualifying distributions are applied to make up any prior year's deficiency in a distributable amount payout requirement.

- Next, the remaining qualifying distributions are applied to the current year's distributable amount (which is essentially the minimum investment return calculated for the prior year).

- Finally, any remaining distributions are taken out of corpus or treated as made out of undistributed income for any year.

Many private foundations accumulate excess qualifying distributions. Some foundations plan to disburse their principal assets and related income over a period of time rather than exist in perpetuity. Other foundations conduct programs that require excess distributions for a period of a few years. Charitable expenditures of foundations paid out in excess of the required amount are carried over to reduce the distributable amount for the five succeeding years.

A private foundation with excess distributions has, as a result, planning opportunities. An obvious potential choice is for the foundation to reduce its current spending until the excess is absorbed (although the realities of existing commitments may thwart that option). Excess distributions can be treated as qualifying distributions for purposes of increasing, to full fair market value, the charitable deduction for a contributor who has made a gift of a noncash asset; the foundation in this circumstance elects to treat as a current distribution out of corpus an amount distributed in a prior tax year, causing the foundation to become, for the year, a conduit foundation (see Chapter 1). A third option is to use excess qualifying distributions in a year to boost the foundation's grant-making so as to qualify for the 1% excise tax on net investment income (see Chapter 3).

If this initial tax is imposed, and if a portion of the undistributed income of the private foundation remains undistributed at the close of the taxable period, a tax equal to 100% of the undistributed amount is, as noted, imposed.

TAX ABATEMENT

When a private foundation fails to make a required annual charitable distribution solely because of an incorrect valuation of assets, the foundation may be excused from the statutory penalty sanction. In the interest of being fair, the tax does not apply and the underdistribution can essentially be corrected if four conditions for abatement are satisfied:

1. Failure to properly value the assets was not willful and was due to reasonable cause.

2. The deficiency is paid out by the foundation as a qualifying distribution within 90 days after receipt of an IRS notice of deficiency.

3. The foundation notifies the IRS of the mistake by submitting information on its annual information return and recalculating its qualifying distributions.

4. The extra distribution made to correct the deficiency is treated as distributed in the year of the deficiency.

To prove that the underdistribution was not *willful* and due to *reasonable cause*, the private foundation must show that it made all reasonable efforts in good faith to correctly value the assets. A consistently followed system for collecting the necessary information satisfies this requirement. A foundation with a portfolio of marketable securities might, for example, retain the month-end copy of stock quotations published in a newspaper to use at year-end. In seeking relief of the penalty for undervaluation of assets that have no readily available value, such as real estate or mineral interests, the foundation must explain the reason(s) as to why the fair market value amount was incorrect. Reliance on an invalid appraisal prepared by a qualified appraiser, having no relationship to the foundation or its disqualified persons, based on full disclosure of information by the foundation, should be considered reasonable.

The IRS has the discretion to abate the first-tier tax—the 30% penalty—for distribution mistakes. Thus, a private foundation that failed to meet the minimum distribution requirement may be excused from the penalty where it can show that it intended to comply with the rules. Abatement may be permitted if the foundation is able to prove that:

- The taxable event (the underdistribution) was due to reasonable cause and not to willful neglect.

- The event was corrected within the correction period for this type of an event.

In a case in which an initial tax is imposed on the undistributed income of a private foundation for a tax year, an *additional tax*, equal to 100%, is imposed on any portion of the income remaining undistributed at the close of the correction period. Where the underdistribution—the *taxable event* – is corrected within the correction period, any additional tax imposed with respect to the event becomes abated.

THIRD-TIER TAX REGIME

As noted, the sanctions underlying the mandatory payout rules include a first-tier and a second-tier tax. The termination tax (see Chapter 3) serves as a third-tier tax. This is the ultimate sanction, applicable where a foundation engaged in willful, flagrant, or repeated acts or failures to act that cause voluntary, conscious, and intentional transgressions of the mandatory payout rules.

SUMMARY

This chapter provided basic information concerning the private foundation mandatory payout rules. It surveyed the history of these rules, described these rules, examined the types of assets used in calculating the payout, summarized the allocations needed in the case of dual-use property, described the distributable amount rules, summarized the concept of the qualifying distribution, summarized the set-aside rules, described the requirements as to distributions to foreign charities, and summarized the intricate rules concerning private foundation distributions to supporting organizations. The chapter concluded by describing the various excise taxes applicable in this context, and the correction and tax abatement rules.

5

PROHIBITED EXPENDITURES RULES

The purpose of this chapter is to summarize the prohibited expenditure rules that are applicable to private foundations. Some of these rules pertain to topics that pertain to tax-exempt charitable organizations generally, yet the rules are more detailed and more stringent when applied to private foundations. Specifically, this chapter will:

- Provide an overview of these rules.
- Discuss these rules as they apply with respect to legislative activities.
- Discuss these rules as they apply with respect to political campaign activities.
- Summarize the rules concerning grants to individuals.
- Describe the rules concerning grants to public charities.
- Describe the rules concerning grants to foreign organizations.
- Summarize the expenditure responsibility rules.
- Describe the rules concerning grants for noncharitable purposes.
- Describe the rules concerning distributions to certain supporting organizations.
- Describe the various excise taxes.
- Describe the tax abatement rules.
- Summarize the third-tier tax regime.

OVERVIEW OF RULES

Private foundations and some, if not all, of their disqualified persons (see Chapter 2) are subject to excise tax penalties, and can lose tax-exempt status, if an amount is paid or incurred for one of the following five categories of *taxable expenditures*:

1. Carrying on of propaganda or otherwise attempting to influence legislation

2. Influencing the outcome of a specific election, or carrying on any voter registration drive (with exceptions)

3. Making a grant to an individual for travel, study, or similar purposes (unless it meets certain conditions)

4. Making a grant to an organization (unless it is a public charity or certain other charitable organizations or expenditure responsibility is exercised)

5. Making a payment for a noncharitable purpose

These prohibitions apply where a private foundation either directly makes the expenditure for the impermissible activity or makes a grant to an organization with the funds targeted for an impermissible expenditure by the grantee.

LEGISLATIVE ACTIVITIES

A private foundation, as a tax-exempt charitable organization, is limited by the federal tax law as to the extent to which it can engage, without endangering its tax exemption, in attempts to influence legislation (see Chapter 3). These undertakings are often referred to as *lobbying activities*. Foundations are also subject to an overlay of additional law in this regard. It is sometimes said that private foundations cannot engage in any legislative activity, but the rules, while tough, are not quite that tight.

General Rules

The general rule is that a private foundation may not pay or incur any amount to carry on propaganda or otherwise attempt to influence legislation. To do so would be to make a taxable expenditure. Thus, although private foundations are subject to the general test of *substantiality*, in connection with lobbying activities, applicable to exempt charitable organizations as a condition of tax exemption, they are also subject to more specific prohibitions.

Two types of lobbying activities are embraced by these prohibitions:

1. An attempt to influence legislation through communication with any member or employee of a legislative body or with any other government official or employee who may participate in the formulation of legislation. This is *direct lobbying*.

2. An attempt to influence any legislation by an effort to affect the opinion of the public or a segment of it. This is *grassroots lobbying*.

An expenditure is an attempt to influence legislation if it is for a direct lobbying communication or a grassroots lobbying communication. A *direct lobbying communication* is an attempt to influence legislation through communication with (1) a member or employee of a legislative body or (2) a government official or employee (other than a member or employee of a legislative body) who may participate in the formulation of the legislation but only if the principal purpose of the communication is to influence legislation. Moreover, to be a direct lobbying communication, it must refer to specific legislation and reflect a view on that legislation.

The term *specific legislation* means:

- Legislation that has been introduced in a legislative body or a specific legislative proposal that the foundation supports or opposes

- In the case of a referendum, ballot initiative, constitutional amendment, or other measure that is placed on a ballot by petitions signed by a required number or percentage of voters, an item that becomes specific legislation when the petition is first circulated among voters for signature

A *grassroots lobbying communication* is an attempt to influence legislation by means of an effort to affect the opinions of the public or a segment of it. To be a grassroots lobbying communication, the communication must refer to specific legislation, reflect a view on the legislation, and encourage the recipient of the communication to take action with respect to the legislation. The phrase *encouraging the recipient to take action* with respect to legislation means that the communication specifically:

- States that the recipient should contact a legislator, staff member, or other government official

- Gives the address, telephone number, or similar information about the individual(s) to be contacted

- Provides some material to facilitate the contact (such as a petition or postcard)

- Identifies one or more legislators who will vote on the legislation as opposing the communication's view of the legislation, being undecided with respect to it, being the recipient's representative in the legislature, or being a member of the committee or subcommittee that will consider the legislation

A private foundation does not make a taxable expenditure when it pays or incurs expenditures in connection with discussions with government officials as long as:

- The subject of the discussions is a program that is jointly funded by the foundation and a governmental body or is a new program that may be so jointly funded.

- The discussions are undertaken for the purpose of exchanging data and information on the subject matter of the program.

- The discussions are not undertaken by foundation managers in order to make any direct attempt to persuade government officials or employees to take particular positions on specific legislative issues.

This prohibition on lobbying does not apply to foundation managers acting in their personal capacity. Even if officials are closely identified with the foundation they have created and/or manage, the rules do not constrain the acts of individuals as such. Certainly, it is prudent for a foundation manager to overtly state that he or she is not acting on behalf of the foundation, and a manager should never use foundation funds or facilities, when promoting a legislative initiative. The IRS promulgated criteria for a member of the clergy to use in differentiating his or her advocacy activities from those of the church involved; foundation managers actively participating in public affairs may extrapolate from this guidance.

Grants to Public Charities that Lobby

A general support grant by a private foundation, to a public charity that engages in lobbying activities, is not a taxable expenditure as long as the grant is not earmarked for use in influencing legislation. The concept of *earmarking* means an agreement, oral or written, that the grant will be used for specific purposes. In this connection, the foundation may rely on budget documents or other sufficient evidence supplied by the prospective grantee—unless the foundation doubts or reasonably should doubt the accuracy or reliability of the documents.

An amount paid or incurred by a recipient of a program-related investment (see Chapter 7) in connection with an appearance before or communication with a legislative body, with respect to legislation or proposed legislation of direct interest to the grantee, is not attributed to the investing foundation, for purposes of the taxable expenditures rules, as long as the foundation did not earmark the funds for legislative activities and the recipient was allowed a business expense deduction for the expense. (A business expense deduction for lobbying costs is available only for lobbying at the local level.)

If a public charity grantee has its tax-exempt status revoked because of excessive legislative activities, the private foundation grantor will not be considered as having made a taxable expenditure if it was unaware of the revocation at the time the grant was made and does not control the grantee. Foundations frequently state in their grant agreements that the grant funds may not be used for legislative purposes. At a minimum, in the case of charitable grantees significantly involved in policy matters, the prudent foundation will retain adequate financial information reflecting the portion (if any) of the public charity's annual expenditures that are devoted to lobbying.

Nonpartisan Study of Social Issues

Sponsoring seminars or conferences, conducting research, and publishing educational material about matters of broad social and economic subjects, such as human rights, war, and peace, are appropriate and permissible activities for a private foundation. These subjects are often the subject matter of legislative efforts, involve public controversy, and raise the possibility that a foundation has conducted prohibited legislative activity. Nonetheless, a foundation is safe when entering this domain, assuming the activities constitute engaging in nonpartisan analysis, study, or research and making available the results of the work to the public, a segment of the public, or government bodies, officials, or employees. Examinations of societal problems are not necessarily direct nor grassroots lobbying communications (discussed earlier in this chapter) even where the problems are those with which a government would be expected to ultimately deal. Expenditures in this context are not taxable ones as long as a communication does not address the merits of a specific legislative proposal or does not directly encourage recipients to take action with respect to an item of legislation.

The phrase *nonpartisan analysis, study, or research* means an independent and objective exposition or study of a particular subject matter. This definition embraces activities that are considered to be *educational* in nature (see Chapter 3). Thus, the analysis can advocate a particular position or viewpoint as long as there is a sufficiently full and fair exposition of the pertinent facts to enable an individual or the public to form an independent opinion or conclusion. (In a sense, this is not an *exception* to the taxable expenditures rules, in that an educational activity is not a lobbying activity to begin with.)

Normally, a publication or a broadcast is evaluated on a presentation-by-presentation basis. If, however, a publication or a broadcast is one of a series prepared or supported by a private foundation and the series in its entirety meets the standards of this exception, an individual publication or broadcast within the series will not result in a taxable expenditure, even if it, alone, does not meet the standards. Whether a broadcast or a publication is part of a *series* ordinarily depends on all of the facts and circumstances of each situation.

As to the *making available* requirement, a private foundation can satisfy this aspect of the exception by distributing reprints of articles and reports, hosting conferences, and disseminating material to the news media and other public forums. These communications, of course, may not be confined to or directed solely toward those who are interested in only one side of an issue. Subsequent use of nonpartisan analysis, study, or research in grassroots lobbying (usually by a public charity grantee) may cause publication of the results to become a grassroots lobbying communication (also known as an *advocacy communication*). A foundation grant is converted to a taxable expenditure under this *subsequent use rule* only where the primary purpose of the foundation in making the grant was for lobbying or where the foundation knew (or should have known) that the public charity's primary purpose in preparing the communication that was funded by the foundation was for use in lobbying.

Technical Advice

Amounts paid or incurred in connection with providing technical advice or assistance to a governmental body, a governmental committee, or a subdivision of either, in response to a written request from that entity (but not merely from a member of it) are not taxable expenditures. The response to the request must be available to every member of the requesting entity. The offering of opinions or recommendations ordinarily is shielded by this exception if they are specifically requested by the entity or are directly related to the requested materials (which is to say that the IRS is not going to impose a prohibited expenditures penalty on a private foundation [or, for that matter, revoke its exempt status] if the foundation has responded to a request from a congressional committee or subcommittee for technical advice).

Self-Defense Exception

A capacious and underutilized exception is available for an amount paid or incurred by a private foundation in connection with an appearance before or communication with a legislative body with respect to a possible decision by that body that might affect the existence of the foundation, its powers and duties, its tax-exempt status, or the deductibility of contributions to it. Pursuant to this *self-defense exception*, a foundation may communicate with anyone (legislature, legislative committees, individual legislators, staff members, or executive branch officials) to any extent, as long as the communication is confined to the prescribed subjects. It is insufficient in this regard, however, that the legislation merely bears on the scope of the foundation's program activities.

POLITICAL CAMPAIGN ACTIVITIES

A private foundation, as a tax-exempt charitable organization, is basically forbidden by the federal tax law to engage, without endangering its tax exemption, in political campaign activities (see Chapter 3). This general rule is an absolute prohibition (as contrasted with the lobbying activities rules, which generally tolerate *insubstantial* legislative efforts).

General Rules

In general, a private foundation may not pay or incur any amount to influence the outcome of a specific public election or carry on, directly or indirectly, a voter registration drive. An outlay of this nature is a taxable expenditure. A grant by a private foundation to a public charity is not a taxable expenditure where the foundation did not earmark the grant (discussed earlier in this chapter) for use in political campaign activity. Thus, if a public charity were to use foundation funds for political purposes, no portion of the grant would be a taxable expenditure.

A private foundation influences the outcome of a specific public election if it participates or intervenes, directly or indirectly, in a political campaign on behalf of or in opposition to a candidate for public office. (This is the rule for charities generally.) The phrase *participation or intervention* in a political campaign includes:

- Publishing or distributing statements or making oral statements on behalf of or in opposition to a candidate for public office

- Paying salaries or expenses of campaign workers

- Conducting or paying the expenses of conducting a voter registration drive limited to the geographic area covered by the campaign (but see below)

- Making a campaign contribution for the benefit of or in opposition to a candidate for public office

Some of these types of activities may also be a violation of federal or state campaign financing laws.

Voter Registration Drives

The taxable expenditures rule as to political campaign activities is inapplicable to an amount paid or incurred by a private foundation (or any other exempt charitable organization), for a voter registration drive, where:

- The foundation's activities are nonpartisan, not confined to a specific election period, and are carried on in at least five states.

- Substantially all (at least 85%) of the foundation's income is expended directly for the active conduct of its exempt functions.

- Substantially all of its support (other than investment income) is received from tax-exempt organizations, the public, governmental units, or any combination of these sources, as long as no more than 25% of this support is received from any one exempt organization and as long as no more than 50% of its support is received from gross investment income, with these computations made on the basis of the most recent five years of the organization.

- Contributions to the organization for voter registration drives are not subject to conditions that they be used only in specified states, possessions of the United States, or political subdivisions or other areas of any of these jurisdictions, or the District of Columbia, or that they may be used in only one specific election period.

GRANTS TO INDIVIDUALS

Private foundations are required to make qualifying distributions (see Chapter 4) for charitable *purposes*; this grant-making is not confined to charitable *organizations*. Thus, a private foundation may make grants to individuals (under certain circumstances) for charitable ends. Foundations' grants to individuals for travel, study, or other similar purposes may be made, however, without incurring penalties, only where they first obtain approval from the IRS for their written procedures for making the grants. A taxable expenditure results if grants of this nature are provided to individuals in the absence of an approved plan. Grants to individuals for other purposes may not require a preapproved plan (discussed later in this chapter).

General Rules

A grant to an individual for travel, study, or other purposes is not a taxable expenditure if the grant, in additional to receipt of prior IRS approval as to its procedures, is awarded on an objective and nondiscriminatory basis, and it is demonstrated to the satisfaction of the IRS that:

- The grant constitutes a scholarship or fellowship grant that is excluded from the recipient's gross income and is to be used for study at an educational institution.

- The grant constitutes a prize or award that is excluded from the recipient's gross income, if the recipient is selected from the public.

- The purpose of the grant is to achieve a specific objective; produce a report or other similar product; or improve or enhance a literary, artistic, musical, scientific, teaching, or similar capacity, skill, or talent of the grantee.

Grants for Travel, Study, or Similar Purposes

Only grants paid to individuals for these three specified purposes are subject to the plan-approval rule. The IRS provided a useful illustration of the concept in a ruling stating three scenarios. In the first scenario, IRS approval of the grant is not required, while approval is necessary in the second and third scenarios.

> *Scenario 1.* A private foundation, organized to promote journalism, annually makes awards to individuals whose work represents the best of investigative reporting concerning the government. Potential recipients are nominated; they cannot apply for the award. The awards are granted in recognition of past achievement; they are not intended to finance any specific activities of the recipients nor impose any conditions on the manner in which the recipients expend the awards.
>
> *Scenario 2.* The annual award recipients are required to take a three-month tour to study government at educational institutions.
>
> *Scenario 3.* These awards must be used to pursue study at an educational institution.

The meaning of grants for *other similar purposes* is not clear. Basically, however, if a private foundation makes a payment to an individual with the expectation or requirement that the recipient perform specific activities that are not directly of benefit to the foundation (discussed later in this chapter), a prior-approval grant occurs. Research grants and payments to allow recipients to compose music or choreograph a ballet are examples of grants for similar purposes. The key is whether the grant recipient is required to perform specific actions or meet certain requirements.

Other Individual Grants

A private foundation need not obtain advance approval from the IRS to make grants to individuals for charitable purposes where the grants are not for one of these three purposes. Thus, a program of payments to indigent individuals for the purchase of food or clothing does not require IRS approval. Similarly, a program to award grants to individuals in recognition of past achievement, such as a competition among students not intended to finance any future activities of the grantees, and where the recipients can expend the grants without conditions, is not a plan needing the approval of the IRS.

Compensation

The term *grants* does not include payments for personal services provided to a private foundation, such as salaries, consultancy fees, and reimbursements of expenses incurred on behalf of the foundation (including travel) paid to individuals (or other persons) working on a foundation's own project. A foundation can, without engaging in grant-making, hire persons to assist it in planning, evaluating, or developing projects and other program activities by consulting, advising, or participating in conferences organized by the foundation. (These payments, nonetheless, are qualifying distributions [see Chapter 4].)

Selection Process

Once a private foundation chooses to make grants that are subject to this approval process, it must adopt a suitable plan. In order for a foundation to establish that its grants to individuals for study, travel, or other purposes will be made on an objective and nondiscriminatory basis, the grants must be awarded in accordance with a program that, if it were a substantial part of the foundation's activities, would be consistent with (1) the basis for the foundation's tax-exempt status, (2) the allowance of deductions for individuals for contributions to it, and (3) the following three requirements, relating to candidates for grants, selection of potential grantees, and the individuals making the selections.

The primary criterion for approval of a plan for making grants to individuals is that the grants be awarded on an *objective and nondiscriminatory basis*. The plan must contain the following elements:

- An objective and nondiscriminatory method of choice, consistent with the foundation's exempt status and purpose of the grant program

- A group from which grantees are selected that is sufficiently broad as to constitute a charitable class

- Criteria used in selecting the recipients, including academic performance, performance on tests designed to measure ability and aptitude, recommendations from instructors, financial need, and/or individuals' potential and personal character (the last of these being conclusions the selection committee might draw from a personal interview)

- A selection committee whose members are not in a position to derive, directly or indirectly, a private benefit if a particular individual is selected

- Grants that are awarded for study at an academic institution, fellowships, prizes or awards, or grants for study or research involving a literary, artistic, musical, scientific, or teaching purpose

- A system to obtain reports in connection with scholarships, fellowships, or research grants

The second of these elements, as noted, requires a sufficiently broad charitable class. This is a relatively easy standard to satisfy when the target group is students; examples are all students in a city or all valedictorians in a state. Also, ethnic minorities usually qualify. Yet, because of the nondiscrimination prong of the standard, caution must be exercised. The IRS, for example, ruled that a scholarship program for students with at least 25% Finnish blood was discriminatory. Yet the IRS upheld a scholarship program for students at a school, based on financial need; the school was an all-boys institution. As to the requirement of breadth, the IRS found that a scholarship program for a group of students attending two named universities failed to constitute a charitable class because of an additional criterion: all of the potential grantees (involving about 600 families) had to have the same surname as the individual who established the program.

Reports and Monitoring

The private foundation, with a program of making grants to individuals, must maintain, and retain for IRS examination, documentation that the grant recipients are chosen in a nondiscriminatory manner and that proper follow-up occurred. The following records must be kept:

- Information used to evaluate the qualification of potential grantees
- Reports of any grantee/director relationships
- Specification of the amount and purpose of each grant
- Grade reports and diversion investigation reports

Scholarships and Fellowships   Generally, with respect to a scholarship or fellowship grant, a private foundation must make arrangements to receive a report of the grantee's work in each academic period. A report, verified by the educational institution, of the grantee's courses taken and grades received in each academic period must be obtained at least once annually. For grantees whose work does not involve classes but the preparation of research papers or projects (such as a doctoral thesis), the foundation should receive an annual report approved by the faculty members supervising the grantee or other school official. On completion of a grantee's study, a final report is required.

Research or Study Grants   With respect to a grant made for travel, study, or other similar purposes, a private foundation must require reports on the use of the funds and the progress made by the grantee toward achieving the purposes of the grant. These reports must be made at least once annually and on completion of the funded undertaking. This final report must describe the grantee's accomplishments as to which the grant was made and contain an accounting of use of the grant funds.

Monitoring   Where the requisite reports or other information (including a failure to submit the reports) indicates that all or a part of a grant is not being used in furtherance of its purposes, the private foundation grantor has a duty to investigate. While conducting its investigation, the foundation must withhold further payments to the extent possible until any delinquent reports have been submitted. In cases in which the foundation determines that any part of a grant has been used for improper purposes and the grantee has not previously diverted grant funds to a use that is not in furtherance of a purpose specified in the grant, the foundation will not be treated as having made a taxable expenditure solely because of the diversion as long as the foundation:

- Is taking all reasonable and appropriate steps either to recover the grant funds or to ensure restoration of the diverted funds and the dedication of other grant funds held by the grantee to the purposes being financed by the grant

- Withholds any further payments to the grantee after the grantor becomes aware that a diversion may have taken place, until it has received the grantee's assurances that diversions will not occur in the future and requires the grantee to take extraordinary precautions to prevent future diversions from occurring

All *reasonable and appropriate steps* may include legal action, but need not include a lawsuit if it would probably not result in recouping of the funds in satisfaction of a judgment.

If a private foundation is treated as having made a taxable expenditure in these circumstances, then—unless the foundation takes the steps described in the first of the preceding items—the amount of the taxable expenditure is the amount that was diverted plus any further payments to the grantee. If, however, the foundation complies with the first requirement but not the second, the amount of the taxable expenditure is the amount of the further payments.

In cases where a grantee has previously diverted funds received from a grantor private foundation and the grantor foundation determines that any part of a grant has again been used for improper purposes, the foundation is not treated as having made a taxable expenditure solely by reason of the diversion as long as the foundation again meets these two requirements.

The same rule as to the appropriateness and necessity of legal action applies in this context. If a private foundation is treated as having made a taxable expenditure in a case to which these rules apply, then—unless the foundation meets the first requirement—the amount of the taxable expenditure is the amount of the diversion plus the amount of any further payments to the grantee. If, however, the foundation complies with the first requirement, but fails to withhold further payments until the second requirement is met, the amount of the taxable expenditure is the amount of the further payments.

Seeking Approval

Grants by a private foundation to individuals for travel, study, or similar purposes must, as noted, be made pursuant to a procedure approved by the IRS in advance. To secure this approval, a foundation must demonstrate to the satisfaction of the IRS that:

- Its grant procedures include an objective and nondiscriminatory selection process.

- The procedures are reasonably calculated to result in performance by grantees of the activities that the grants are intended to finance.

- The foundation plans to obtain reports to determine whether the grantees have performed the activities that the grants are intended to finance.

No single procedure or set of procedures is required. Procedures may vary depending on factors such as the size of the foundation, the amount and purpose of the grants, and whether one or more recipients are involved.

A request for advance approval of a foundation's grant procedures must fully describe the foundation's procedures for awarding grants and for ascertaining that the grants are used for the proper purposes. The approval procedure does not contemplate specific IRS approval of particular grant programs but, instead, a one-time approval of a system of standards, procedures, and follow-up designed to result in grants that meet these rules. Thus, the approval applies to a subsequent grant program as long as the procedures under which it is conducted are not materially different from those described in the request.

This request for advance approval must contain the following:

- A statement describing the selection process, which must be sufficiently detailed to enable the IRS to determine whether the grants are to be made on an objective and nondiscriminatory basis

- A description of the terms and conditions under which the foundation will ordinarily make these grants, which is sufficient to enable the IRS to determine whether the grants awarded under the procedures will meet one of the basic three requirements

- A detailed description of the foundation's procedure for exercising supervision over the grants

- A description of the foundation's procedures for review of grantees' reports, investigation where diversion of grant funds from their proper purposes is indicated, and recovery of diverted grant funds

From time to time, a private foundation may be discovered that is making grants to individuals and has never heard of these rules, and thus is making grants of this nature in the absence of a preapproved procedure. That is the case even though these rules were created nearly 40 years ago.

Obtaining Approval

The IRS frequently does not send written approval of individual grant procedures to successful private foundation applicants. Silence is likely to signify approval. If, by the 45th day after a request for approval of grant procedures has been properly submitted, the foundation has not been notified that the procedures are unacceptable, they may be considered approved as of the date of submission, until any receipt of notice from the IRS that they do not meet the requirements.

A private foundation may find itself in the position of considering its grant-making procedures approved by reason of passage of this 45-day period and making grants to individuals accordingly, then receive notification from the IRS that the procedures do not conform to the requirements. In this situation, a grant made prior to the adverse notice is not a taxable expenditure. Even where the grant is structured in installment payments, payments of installments after receipt of an adverse notice do not result in taxable expenditures, inasmuch as the post-notice payments are considered merely made in satisfaction of the foundation's obligation to continue the grants that were deemed approved. A renewal of a grant made during the prenotification period, however, would be a taxable expenditure, being in the nature of a new grant.

Grant Intermediaries

Private foundations wishing to avoid the administrative burdens and costs of applying for approval of individual grant procedures and disbursing the grants directly have the alternative of funding a grant program, such as a scholarship program, at an independent public charity (discussed later in this chapter). A grant by a foundation to another organization, that the grantee organization uses to make payments to individuals for charitable purposes, is not regarded as a grant by the foundation to one or more individual grantees if (1) the foundation does not control the grantee organization, (2) the foundation does not earmark use of the grant for any named individual, and (3) there is no agreement by which the grantor foundation may cause the selection of an individual by the grantee organization. A grant is not regarded as a grant by the foundation to an individual, even though the foundation has reason to believe that one or more specific individuals will be awarded grants, as long as the grantee organization exercises control over the selection process and makes the selections independently of the foundation.

GRANTS TO PUBLIC CHARITIES

Most private foundations confine their grant-making to public charities (see Chapter 1). This is in large part due to the contours of the federal tax law, which discourages grants to individuals and to entities that are not public charities. This discouragement is primarily in the form of the expenditure responsibility requirements (discussed later in this chapter) and the rules pertaining to grants to individuals. Thus, it is typical for foundations to play it safe, and stay away from grant-making that entails considerable effort at documentation and a much higher risk of tax penalties.

Nonetheless, even though grants to public charities have this mantle of preferred status, the prospective foundation grantor still has the burden of proving that its prospective grantees (or perhaps actual grantees) are in fact public charities. The degree of difficulty in meeting this proof standard varies depending on the type of public charity that is involved. If the potential grantee is a bona fide college or university, hospital, or church, it should not prove too difficult for foundation managers to be assured that the entity is a public charity.

The difficulty in this context (if there is one) is with publicly supported charities (see below) or with supporting organizations (see Chapter 11). Technically, a private foundation can rely on evidence provided by the prospective grantee, such as its determination letter or recent annual information returns, until the IRS publishes a notice of revocation of the organization's tax-exempt or public charity status. But the determination letter may be many years old and/or the data in the annual returns is less than perfect. There are IRS publications to peruse and web sites to search. Ultimately, each foundation must develop its own policies in determining how extensively or deeply it will probe in ascertaining whether a public support fraction is being met. Some entities are obviously publicly supported; sophisticated publicly supported charities will have the necessary financial information readily available. The problems lurk, predictably with the smaller charitable organizations (the ones that probably need the funding the most).

GRANTS TO FOREIGN ORGANIZATIONS

Private foundations making grants to foreign organizations have many potential problems these days. One aspect of this dilemma is making certain that the grant funds are used for charitable purposes. The grant agreement should impose restrictions on the use of the grant that are substantially equivalent to the limitations imposed on foundations, making grants domestically, by the taxable expenditures rules. Another difficulty is ascertaining whether the prospective foreign grantee is the equivalent of a public charity under U.S. law, so as to avoid the expenditure responsibility requirements (discussed later in this chapter). As to the latter, the process is usually easier where the grantee is a school, hospital, or church (see Chapter 4).

The U.S. Department of the Treasury developed "voluntary" best practices for U.S.-based charitable organizations that engage in grant-making or operations in foreign countries. Private foundations, when making foreign grants, should endeavor to comport with these rules, as well as any applicable elements of the USA PATRIOT Act. Also, a private foundation in this circumstance may want to check the Department of State web site periodically to determine if foreign organizations that are potential grantees are denominated terrorist organizations.

EXPENDITURE RESPONSIBILITY

The term *taxable expenditure* includes an amount paid or incurred by a private foundation as a grant (or loan or program-related investment [see Chapter 7]) to an organization that is not a public charity, unless the foundation exercises expenditure responsibility with respect to the grant.

General Rules

The phrase *expenditure responsibility* means what it sounds like it means: that the foundation has the responsibility to exert all reasonable efforts and to establish adequate procedures to:

- See that the grant is spent solely for the charitable purpose or purposes for which it was made.

- Obtain full and complete reports from the grantee on how the funds were spent.

- Submit full and detailed reports to the IRS with respect to the expenditures.

These requirements thus come into play when a private foundation is making a grant to another private foundation (including a private operating foundation but not an exempt operating foundation [see Chapter 1]), an organization that is tax-exempt for reasons other than being a public charity, or a for-profit business. (The rules for grants to individuals carry a variety of responsibilities that are akin to expenditure responsibility.)

Certainly, expenditure responsibility grants are not prohibited as a matter of law. A private foundation is not an insurer of the activities of a grantee. The fundamental requirement is that the grant be for (and be used for) a charitable purpose. Beyond that, a foundation can make a grant to any type of entity it wants as long as it has the requisite oversight procedures in place and files the necessary reports with the IRS. (As discussed, that flexibility may be more theoretical than real, with the foundation sticking to public charity grantees.)

Six Necessary Steps

When a private foundation is contemplating a grant for which it must exercise expenditure responsibility, six steps are required to fulfill the requirements. Each step is required; they must be undertaken sequentially, as follows:

1. Conduct a pregrant inquiry.

2. Enter into a written agreement stating the terms to be followed and establishing a reporting system for the grantee.

3. Follow up by receiving and reviewing reports from the grantee.

4. Investigate any diversion of funds.

5. Annually disclose proper information on the annual information return (see Chapter 10), evidencing compliance with these steps.

6. Retain documentation as to compliance with these requirements for any IRS examination.

Pregrant Inquiry

The first step, then, in an instance of an expenditure responsibility grant is to investigate the potential grantee organization and the project it wants funded. This *pregrant inquiry* is directed toward obtaining sufficient information as to give a reasonable person assurance that the grantee will use the grant for one or more charitable purposes. This inquiry should concern matters such as:

- The identity, history, and experience (if any) of the prospective grantee organization and its managers. The question here is: Is the potential grantee capable of accomplishing the purpose of the contemplated grant?

- The activities of the prospective grantee, based on information from the grantee, the foundation's prior experience with the grantee, and/or from third parties.

The scope of the inquiry is expected to be tailored to the particular facts and circumstances, including the period over which the grant is to be paid, the nature of the project, and the foundation's prior association with the prospective grantee organization. If the putative grantee has received one or more prior expenditure responsibility grants from the foundation and has satisfied the reporting requirements, however, a formal pregrant inquiry is not necessary.

Grant Terms

A trustee, director, or officer of the grant recipient must sign a written agreement that, in addition to stating the charitable purposes to be accomplished, obligates the grantee to:

- Repay any portion of the amount granted that is not used for the charitable purposes of the grant.

- Submit full and complete annual reports on the manner in which the funds are spent and the progress made in accomplishing the grant's purposes.

- Maintain records of the receipts and expenditures, and make its records available to the grantor foundation at reasonable times.

- Not use any of the funds to (1) carry on propaganda or otherwise attempt to influence legislation (discussed earlier in this chapter), (2) influence the outcome of a public election (*id.*), (3) carry on a voter registration drive (*id.*), (4) make a grant to an individual or organization, and (5) undertake any activity for a noncharitable purpose (discussed later in this chapter), to the extent that use of the funds would be a taxable expenditure if made directly by the foundation.

Additional rules apply in the case of program-related investments (see Chapter 7) and grants to foreign organizations (discussed earlier in this chapter and in Chapter 4).

Monitoring System

Since a private foundation is not an insurer of the activity of an organization to which it makes a grant, satisfaction of the expenditure responsibility requirements ordinarily means that the grantor foundation has not, because of the grant, violated the lobbying or political campaign activities rules. A foundation is considered to be exercising expenditure responsibility as long as it exerts the requisite reasonable efforts and establishes the requisite adequate procedures. A court, in concluding that a foundation's grants failed both prongs of the standard, wrote that these rules reflect a "Congressional determination to leave no loophole by imposing strict and detailed conditions to make sure that a private foundation's grants would not be used for proscribed purposes."

Reports from Grantees

In the case of expenditure responsibility grants, other than certain capital endowment grants (discussed later in this chapter), the grantor private foundation must require reports on use of the grant funds, compliance with the terms of the grant, and the progress made by the grantee toward achieving the purposes of the grant. The grantee must make these reports as of the end of its annual accounting period within which the grant or any portion of it was received and all subsequent periods until the grant funds are fully expended or the grant arrangement s otherwise terminated. These reports must be furnished to the grantor within a reasonable period after the close of the grantee's annual accounting period.

Within a reasonable period after the close of its annual accounting period during which use of the grant funds is completed, the grantee must make a final report with respect to all expenditures made from the funds (such as salaries, travel, and supplies) and describe the progress made toward achieving the objectives of the grant. The grantor need not conduct an independent verification of these reports unless it has reason to doubt their accuracy.

If a private foundation makes a grant to another foundation or another organization that is not a public charity, for endowment, for the purchase of capital equipment, or for other capital purposes, the grantor foundation must require reports from the grantee on use of the principal and any income generated by the grant funds. The grantee must make these reports annually for its fiscal year in which the grant was received and the immediately succeeding two years. Only if it is reasonably apparent to the grantor that, before the end of the second succeeding year, neither the principal, the income from the grant funds, nor the equipment purchased with the grant funds has been used for any purpose that would result in liability for a taxable expenditure, the grantor foundation may then allow discontinuance of the reports.

Grantee's Procedures

As a matter of law, a grantee of a private foundation need not segregate grant funds nor separately account for them on its books; the grantor, however, may require either practice. If neither of these practices is followed, grant funds received in a year are deemed to be expended before grants received in a succeeding year. In that event, expenditures of grants received within a year must be prorated among all of the grants.

In accounting for grant expenditures, private foundations may make the necessary computations on a cumulative annual basis (or, where appropriate, as of the date on which the computations are made). These rules are to be applied in a manner consistent with the available records of the grantee and with the grantee's treatment of qualifying distributions. Records of expenditures, as well as copies of the reports submitted to the grantor, must be retained for at least four years after completion of use of the grant funds.

Reliance on Grantee Information

A private foundation exercising expenditure responsibility with respect to its grants may rely on adequate records or other sufficient evidence supplied by the grantee, reflecting, to the extent applicable, the information that the foundation must report to the IRS (discussed later in this chapter). *Other sufficient evidence* includes a statement by an appropriate trustee, director, or officer of the grantee.

Reports to IRS

A private foundation making expenditure responsibility grants must provide specific information, as part of its annual information return (see Chapter 10), for each tax year in which these grant(s) are made. A report of monitoring steps must be provided on subsequent return(s) with respect to each expenditure responsibility grant for which any amount or any report is outstanding at any time during the tax year. With respect to any grant made for endowment or other capital purposes, the grantor must provide the required information in the tax years for which the grantor must require a report from the grantee under the rules concerning capital grants by foundations. Program-related investments (see Chapter 7) must be reported for all of the years the investment is outstanding. If a grantee's report contains the required information, the reporting requirement with respect to that grant may be satisfied by submission, with the foundation's annual return, of the report received from the grantee.

These reports must include the following data with respect to each expenditure responsibility grant:

- Name and address of the grantee
- Date and amount of the grant
- Purpose of the grant
- Amounts expended by the grantee (based on the most recent report from the grantee)
- Whether, to the knowledge of the grantor foundation, the grantee has diverted any funds from the purpose of the grant

- Dates of reports received from the grantee
- Date and results of any verification of the grantee's reports undertaken by or at the direction of the foundation

The IRS is rigid and strict when it comes to timely reporting to it of expenditure responsibility grants. In one instance, a private foundation made an expenditure responsibility grant but neglected to include reference to it on the list of its grants for the year, required to be supplied as part of its annual information return. Subsequently, the foundation discovered this omission and filed an amended annual return. The failure to comply with this reporting requirement caused the grant to be a taxable expenditure (although the foundation was able to correct it).

Document Retention

In addition to the information to be included on a foundation's annual information return, a grantor foundation must make available to the IRS, at the foundation's principal office, a copy of the agreement as to each expenditure responsibility grant, a copy of each report received from each grantee of an expenditure responsibility grant, and a copy of each report made by the grantor's personnel or independent auditors of any audits or other investigations made during the year with respect to an expenditure responsibility grant.

Data in these reports, where the reports are received by a private foundation after the close of its accounting year but before the due date of its annual information return for that year, need not be reported in connection with that return but must be reported on the grantor's information return for the year in which the reports are received from the grantee.

Grantee Diversions

A diversion of expenditure responsibility grant funds (including, in the case of an endowment grant, the income from the funds) by the grantee to a use not in furtherance of a purpose specified in the grant may cause the diverted portion of the grant to be treated as a taxable expenditure by the grantor. The fact that a grantee does not use a portion of the grant funds as indicated in the original budget projection, however, is not treated as a *diversion* if the use to which the funds are committed is consistent with the purpose of the grant, as stated in the grant agreement, and does not violate the terms of the agreement.

In any event, a private foundation that has made an expenditure responsibility grant is not treated as having made a taxable expenditure by reason of a grantee's diversion of funds, if the grantor has complied with one of two requirements (listed next). In cases in which the grantor foundation determines that a part of a grant has been used for improper purposes and the grantee has not previously diverted grant funds, the foundation will not be regarded as having made a taxable expenditure by reason of the diversion, if the foundation can show that it:

1. Is taking all reasonable and appropriate steps either to recover the grant funds or to ensure the restoration of the diverted funds and the dedication of any other grant funds held by the grantee to the purposes being financed by the grant

2. Withholds any further payments to the grantee after it becomes aware that a diversion may have taken place, until it has received the grantee's assurance that future diversions will not occur and requires the grantee to take extraordinary precautions to prevent future diversions

If a foundation is treated as having made a taxable expenditure in this type of circumstance, then, unless the foundation meets the requirements of the first of the above conditions, the amount of the taxable expenditure is the amount of the grant plus the amount of any further payments to the same grantee. If, however, the foundation complies with the requirements of this first condition, but not the requirements of the other, the amount of the taxable expenditure is the amount of the further payments.

In cases where a grantee has previously diverted funds received from a private foundation, and the grantor foundation determines that a portion of a grant has again been used for improper purposes, the foundation will not be treated as having made a taxable expenditure solely by reason of the diversion as long as the foundation can demonstrate that it complied with both of the above two conditions.

If a private foundation is treated as having made a taxable expenditure in this circumstance, then, unless the foundation meets the requirements of the first of these conditions, the amount of the taxable expenditure is the amount of the diversion plus the amount of any further payments to the same grantee. If, however, the foundation complies with the first requirement but fails to withhold further payments until the second requirement is met, the amount of the taxable expenditure is the amount of the further payments.

As to either of these scenarios, the phrase *all reasonable and appropriate steps* includes legal action where appropriate but need not include a lawsuit if the action would in all probability not result in the satisfaction of execution on a judgment.

A failure by a grantee to make the required reports, or the making of inadequate reports, will result in treatment of the expenditure responsibility grant as a taxable expenditure by the grantor unless the grantor has made the grant in accordance with the various expenditure responsibility requirements, has complied with the applicable reporting requirements, makes a reasonable effort to obtain the required report, and withholds all future payments on the grant and on any other grant to the same grantee until the report is furnished. In addition, a grant that is subject to the expenditure responsibility requirements is considered a taxable expenditure of the grantor foundation if the grantor fails to make the requisite pregrant inquiry, fails to make the grant in accordance with a procedure consistent with the various expenditure responsibility requirements, or fails to report to the IRS.

EXPENDITURES FOR NONCHARITABLE PURPOSES

The term *taxable expenditure* includes any amount paid or incurred by a private foundation for a *noncharitable purpose* (see Chapter 3). Ordinarily, only an expenditure by a foundation for an activity that, if it were a substantial part of the organization's total activities, would cause loss of tax exemption is a taxable expenditure. Expenditures that are not treated as taxable expenditures under these rules are (1) payments that constitute qualifying distributions (see Chapter 4), (2) investments to obtain income to be used in furtherance of charitable purposes, (3) reasonable expenses with respect to investments, (4) payment of taxes, (5) expenses that qualify as deductions in the computation of unrelated business taxable income (see Chapter 8), (6) payments that are deductible in connection with the tax on investment income (see Chapter 3), and (7) necessary expenditures to evaluate, acquire, modify, and dispose of program-related investments (see Chapter 7).

Conversely, expenditures for unreasonable administrative expenses— such as excessive compensation, consultants' fees, or other fees for services—are ordinarily taxable expenditures, unless the private foundation can demonstrate that the expenses were paid or incurred in the good faith belief that they were reasonable and that the payment or incurrence of the expenses in the amounts involved was consistent with ordinary business care and prudence. The determination as to whether an expenditure is unreasonable is dependent on the facts and circumstances of each case.

A private foundation may utilize these rules even where an expenditure constitutes an act of self-dealing (see Chapter 6). In one instance, a foundation made a loan to a disqualified person—an act of self-dealing—to generate income to be used solely for the foundation's charitable purposes. The loan was structured using a reasonable rate of interest, was adequately secured, and otherwise was in compliance with prudent investment standards (see Chapter 7). The IRS concluded that the loan was not made for noncharitable purposes and thus was not a taxable expenditure.

DISTRIBUTIONS TO CERTAIN SUPPORTING ORGANIZATIONS

The term *taxable expenditure* includes an amount paid or incurred by a private foundation as a distribution to certain types of supporting organizations (see

Chapter 1), where the amount involved may not be treated as a qualifying distribution (see Chapter 4) and expenditure responsibility is not exercised by the distributing foundation.

IMPOSITION OF EXCISE TAX PENALTIES

The penalties that can be imposed in this context principally are initial and additional taxes, levied on the private foundation involved and/or one or more of its managers.

Initial Taxes

An initial excise tax (also known as a first-tier tax) is imposed on each taxable expenditure of a private foundation; this tax is to be paid by the foundation at the rate of 20% of the amount of each taxable expenditure. This excise tax is also imposed on a foundation manager that agreed to the making of a taxable expenditure by a foundation, equal to 5% of the amount involved, up to a maximum of $10,000. The initial tax on a manager is imposed only where the foundation initial tax is imposed, the manager knows that the expenditure to which he, she, or it agreed is a taxable expenditure, and the agreement is not willful and is due to reasonable cause.

Tax on Managers

The 5% tax with respect to a taxable expenditure applies only to foundation managers (1) who are authorized to approve or to exercise discretion in recommending approval of the expenditure, (2) who agreed to the making of the expenditure by the foundation, and (3) who are members of a group (such as the foundation's governing board) that is so authorized.

The *agreement* of a foundation manager to the making of a taxable expenditure consists of any manifestation of approval of the expenditure that is sufficient to constitute an exercise of the foundation manager's authority to approve, or to exercise discretion in recommending approval of, the making of the expenditure by the foundation, whether or not the manifestation of approval is the final or decisive approval on behalf of the foundation.

A foundation manager is considered to have agreed to an expenditure, knowing that it is a taxable one, only if the manager (1) has actual knowledge of sufficient facts so that, based solely on those facts, the expenditure would be a taxable one; (2) is aware that the expenditure under these circumstances may violate the federal tax law governing taxable expenditures; and (3) negligently fails to make reasonable attempts to ascertain whether the expenditure is a taxable one, or the manager is in fact aware that it is such an expenditure. While the word *knowing* does not mean "having reason to know," evidence tending to show that a foundation manager has reason to know of a particular fact or particular rule is relevant in determining whether he or she had actual knowledge of that fact or rule.

A foundation manager's agreement to a taxable expenditure is *willful* if it is voluntary, conscious, and intentional. A motive to avoid the restrictions of the law or the incurrence of any tax is not necessary to make an agreement willful. A foundation manager's agreement to a taxable expenditure is not willful, however, if the manager does not know that it is a taxable expenditure. A manager's actions are due to *reasonable cause* if the manager has exercised his or her responsibility on behalf of the private foundation with ordinary business care and prudence.

If a foundation manager, after full disclosure of the factual situation to legal counsel (including house counsel), relies on the advice of counsel expressed in a reasoned legal opinion that an expenditure is not a taxable one, even though the expenditure is subsequently held to be a taxable one, the foundation manager's agreement to the expenditure will ordinarily not be considered *knowing* or *willful* and will ordinarily be considered *due to reasonable cause*. This rule also applies with respect to an opinion that proposed reporting procedures concerning an expenditure will satisfy the taxable expenditure rules, even though the procedures are subsequently held to not satisfy the rules, and to grants made with provisions for such reporting procedures that are taxable solely because of such inadequate reporting procedures. A written legal opinion is considered *reasoned* even if it reaches a conclusion that is subsequently determined to be incorrect, as long as the opinion was addressed to the facts and applicable law. By contrast, a written legal opinion is not a reasoned one if it merely recites the facts and expresses a conclusion. The absence of advice of counsel with respect to an expenditure, however, does not alone give rise to an inference that a foundation manager agreed to the making of the expenditure knowingly, willfully, or without reasonable cause.

Additional Tax

An additional excise tax (also known as a second-tier tax) is imposed in any case in which an initial tax is imposed on a private foundation because of a taxable expenditure and the expenditure has not been timely corrected. This additional tax, which is at the rate of 100% of the amount of each taxable expenditure, is to be paid by the foundation. In a case in which an additional tax has been levied on a foundation, an excise tax is imposed on a foundation manager because of a taxable expenditure where the manager refused to agree to part or all of the correction of the expenditure. This additional tax, which is at the rate of 50% of the amount of the taxable expenditure, is to be paid by the manager. Where a taxable event is corrected within the correction period, any additional tax imposed with respect to the event will be abated.

Where more than one foundation manager is liable for an excise tax in the case of a making of a taxable expenditure, all of the managers are jointly and severally liable for the tax. The maximum aggregate amount collectible as an initial tax from all managers with respect to any one taxable expenditure is $10,000; the maximum aggregate amount so collectible as an additional tax is $20,000.

The additional excise taxes are imposed at the end of the *taxable period*, which begins with the date on which the taxable expenditure occurs and ends on the earliest of:

- The date a notice of deficiency with respect to the initial tax is mailed

- The date the initial tax is assessed if a deficiency notice is not mailed

CORRECTION

A taxable expenditure must be corrected (unless the foundation involved wants to watch the IRS confiscate its assets [discussed later in this chapter]). The *correction period* is the period beginning on the date on which the taxable event occurs and ending 90 days after the date of mailing of a notice of deficiency with respect to the additional tax imposed on the event. This period is extended by any length of time during which a deficiency cannot be assessed, and any other period that the IRS determines is reasonable and necessary to bring about correction of the taxable event. In this setting, a *taxable event* is an act or failure to act giving rise to liability for tax under the taxable expenditures rules.

In general, *correction* of a taxable expenditure is accomplished by recovering part or all of the expenditure to the extent a recovery is possible. Where full recovery is not possible, correction entails any additional corrective action that the IRS may prescribe. This additional corrective action is to be determined by the circumstances of each case; this action may include requiring that any unpaid funds due the grantee be withheld, that no further grants be made to the grantee, period reports from the foundation (in addition to any other required reports) with respect to all of its expenditures, improved methods of exercising expenditure responsibility, and improved methods of selecting recipients of individual grants. The private foundation making the expenditure is not under any obligation to attempt to recover the expenditure by legal action if the action would in all probability not result in the satisfaction of execution on a judgment.

If the expenditure is taxable only because of a failure to obtain a full and complete report or because of a failure to make a full and detailed report, correction may be accomplished by obtaining or making the report in question. If the expenditure is taxable only because of a failure to obtain a full and complete report and an investigation indicates that grant funds were not diverted to a use not in furtherance of a purpose of the grant, correction may be accomplished by exerting all reasonable efforts to obtain the report in question and reporting the failure to the IRS, even though the report is not finally obtained.

Where an expenditure is taxable under the rules concerning grants to individuals only because of a failure to obtain advance approval of procedures with respect to these grants, correction may be accomplished by obtaining approval of the grant-making procedures from the IRS and establishing to the satisfaction of the IRS that three facts are in place: (1) grant funds have not been diverted to any use not in furtherance of a purpose of the grant, (2) the grant-making procedures instituted would have been approved if advance approval of the procedures had been properly requested, and (3) where advance approval of grant-making procedures is subsequently required, the approval will be properly requested.

TAX ABATEMENT

The IRS has the discretion to abate this initial tax when a private foundation establishes that the violation was due to reasonable cause and not to willful neglect, and timely corrects the violation. For example, a foundation failed to make the requisite expenditure responsibility reports, a fact that was subsequently uncovered by a new tax advisor; a corrected return was filed and the IRS abated the taxable expenditures initial tax. Likewise, this tax was abated where a foundation, in good faith, relied on what turned out to be incorrect legal advice.

Where the act or failure to act that gave rise to the additional tax is corrected within the correction period, the tax will not be assessed or, if assessed, will be abated or, if collected, will be credited or refunded. The collection period is suspended during the course of any litigation.

A request for abatement is submitted on Form 4720. Details about any corrective action taken and the value of recovered property must be described. If the matter remains uncorrected, an explanation is to be attached. The information provided is the basis on which the IRS will decide as to whether to abate a tax.

THIRD-TIER TAX REGIME

As noted, the sanctions underlying the prohibited expenditures rules include a first-tier and a second-tier tax. The termination tax (see Chapter 3) serves as a third-tier tax. This is the ultimate sanction, with the federal government able to confiscate the value of all federal tax benefits the foundation and its substantial contributors ever received derived from tax exemption and charitable tax deductions, applicable where a foundation engaged in willful, flagrant, or repeated acts or failures to act that cause voluntary, conscious, and intentional transgressions of the prohibited expenditures rules.

SUMMARY

This chapter provides an overview of the prohibited expenditures rules, followed by discussion of these rules as they apply in the contexts of legislative activities, political campaign activities, grants to individuals, grants to public charities, grants to foreign organizations, and grants for noncharitable purposes. The chapter summarizes the expenditure responsibility requirements and the rules for distributions to certain supporting organizations. The chapter concluded by describing the various excise taxes applicable in this context and the tax abatement rules.

6

SELF-DEALING RULES

The purpose of this chapter is to explain the private foundation *self-dealing rules*. This body of law is the most difficult and dangerous of the private foundation rules; potential self-dealing transactions should be approached with great caution. Specifically, this chapter will:

- Provide a basic definition of self-dealing.

- Summarize the various types of acts of self-dealing.

- Explain the rules concerning foundations' payment of compensation and reimbursements.

- Discuss insurance and indemnification coverages.

- Explain the extent to which private foundations and disqualified persons can share space, staff, and expenses.

- Explain indirect self-dealing.

- Discuss early termination of charitable remainder trusts.

- Summarize the various exceptions to the self-dealing rules.

- Explain the issues that arise once self-dealing occurs.

- Describe the various excise taxes.

- Revisit the third-tier tax regime.

BASIC DEFINITION OF *SELF-DEALING*

In essence, all direct and indirect financial transactions between a private foundation and its disqualified persons (see Chapter 2) are prohibited. Indeed, there are exceptions to the self-dealing prohibition. Nonetheless, these rules can be draconian. This is in part the case because, generally, an individual's intent is irrelevant in this context and it is immaterial if a self-dealing transaction results in a benefit to the foundation. An *indirect act* of self-dealing is a transaction between a disqualified person and an organization controlled by a private foundation.

There are six types of acts of self-dealing (all discussed below):

1. Sale, exchange, or leasing of property

2. Lending of money or other extensions of credit

3. Furnishing of goods, services, or facilities

4. Payment of compensation or payment or reimbursement of expenses

5. Transfer to, or use by or for the benefit of, a disqualified person of any income or assets of the private foundation

6. Payment to a government official

These transactions are not forbidden, in the sense of a rule of law, but are underlain with such harsh tax penalties that the self-dealing rules are, as a practical matter, prohibitions.

SALES OR EXCHANGES OF PROPERTY

The sale or exchange of property between a private foundation and a disqualified person with respect to the foundation generally constitutes an act of self-dealing. As noted, these rules are sweeping. Thus, the sale of incidental supplies by a disqualified person to a foundation or the sale of stock by a disqualified person to a foundation for a bargain price are acts of self-dealing, irrespective of the amount paid. A private foundation's purchase of a mortgage held by its bank trustee/disqualified person was self-dealing, even though the rate was much more favorable than was otherwise available. An installment sale involving a foundation and a disqualified person is self-dealing, as a sale of property or an extension of credit (discussed later in this chapter).

The transfer of real or personal property by a disqualified person to a private foundation is a sale or exchange for these purposes if the foundation assumed a mortgage or similar lien that was placed on the property prior to the transfer, or takes the property subject to a mortgage or similar lien that a disqualified person placed on the property within the one-year period ending on the date of the transfer. A *similar lien* includes deeds of trust and vendors' liens, but does not include any other lien if it is insignificant in relation to the fair market value of the property transferred.

The fact that an intermediary person or agent handles a transaction does not facilitate circumvention of the self-dealing rules. Self-dealing thus occurs when a disqualified person buys private foundation property from an agent through whom the foundation is selling property. In a case involving an art object consigned by a foundation to a commercial art auction house, the purchase of the artwork by a disqualified person with respect to the foundation was ruled by the IRS to constitute self-dealing. Similarly, the leasing of property to a disqualified person by a management company was held to be self-dealing, inasmuch as a private foundation controlled the manager.

A transfer of property, such as the distribution of shares of stock in payment of an interest-free loan, is a sale or exchange. A transfer of real estate equal to the amount of a disqualified person's loan was held to be self-dealing. (In this instance, an effort was made to correct an act of self-dealing, but the exchange was ruled to be a second act of self-dealing.) Conversely, a transfer of real estate in satisfaction of a pledge to pay cash or readily marketable securities was held to not amount to a sale or exchange, because the pledge was not legally enforceable and a pledge is not a form of debt.

As an example of the niceties in this area, the IRS ruled that a split-dollar life insurance arrangement, involving a private foundation and its chief executive officer (and thus a disqualified person with respect to the foundation), that was included as part of a compensation program did not entail self-dealing. The premiums to be paid by the foundation and its executive are sent directly to the insurance company. The IRS ruled that these payments did not amount to an exchange of property between the parties. The arrangement permitted the executive to assign his rights under the agreement to another party, such as an irrevocable life insurance trust. The IRS also ruled that an assignment by this executive of his rights under the insurance arrangement, and the assignee's exercise of the rights and assumptions of obligations pursuant to the agreement, would not involve a sale, exchange, or other transfer of property between the executive and the private foundation.

Likewise, the partition of unproductive property held as tenants-in-common with a disqualified person did not constitute self-dealing with a private foundation. A partition of this nature is not a prohibited sale or exchange. The foundation received the undivided interest in the property as a gift from the disqualified person. (A contribution to a private foundation by a disqualified person with respect to it is not an act of self-dealing.) Local law prohibited a nonprofit corporation from holding unproductive property; the foundation wanted to make the property marketable by creating a divided interest.

LEASING OF PROPERTY

The leasing of property between a private foundation and a disqualified person with respect to it generally constitutes self-dealing. The leasing of property by a disqualified person to a private foundation without charge, however, is not an act of self-dealing. A lease is considered to be *without charge* even though a private foundation pays its portion of janitorial services, utilities, or other maintenance costs, as long as the payment of this type of expense is not made directly or indirectly to a disqualified person.

A self-dealing issue can arise in connection with works of art. For example, a private foundation operating a museum may borrow, without cost, an art object from a disqualified person for display. In this circumstance, the foundation can pay maintenance and insurance costs directly to the service providers, even though the consequence may be that the foundation is paying some of the disqualified person's costs of owning the art object while the artwork is on display, because of the benefits of the display accruing to the public. By contrast, placement of a private foundation's art in its creator's home, away from public view, would be self-dealing. Displays of art on the creator's property that is accessible by the public has been permitted but only because the foundation's collection was displayed throughout a city, primarily on public lands, as part of a comprehensive outdoor museum program.

FURNISHING OF PROPERTY

Generally, self-dealing includes any direct or indirect furnishing of goods, services, or facilities between a private foundation and disqualified persons with respect to it. An exception, however, allows the furnishing, without charge, of a disqualified person's goods, services, or facilities to a private foundation as long as they are used exclusively for charitable purposes. The permitted furnishing is *without charge*, even though the foundation pays for transportation, insurance, maintenance, and other costs it incurs in obtaining or using the property, as long as the payment is not made directly or indirectly to a disqualified person.

Another exception permits a private foundation to furnish a disqualified person with exempt functions goods, services, or facilities that the foundation regularly provides to the public, such as a park, museum, or library. This type of furnishing is not self-dealing if the conditions and charges made to the public are at least on as favorable a basis as the goods or services are made available for the disqualified person's use. This exception is intended to apply with respect to functionally related facilities (see Chapter 8) that a substantial number of persons, other than disqualified persons, use. For example, a director of a private foundation that operates a museum can, without engaging in self-dealing, pay the usual price for admission to the museum and make a purchase in the museum gift shop. (These rules are strict but rarely absurd.)

A private foundation is allowed to furnish goods, services, or facilities to its managers in recognition of their services as employees. The value of the goods or the like must be reasonable and the furnishing necessary to the performance of their tasks in carrying out the charitable purposes of the foundation. Whether or not reportable as taxable income, the value of goods or facilities provided must not, when added to other amounts provided to a manager, cause him or her to receive excessive compensation.

CO-OWNED PROPERTY

Mere co-ownership of an item of property by a private foundation and a disqualified person with respect to it is not self-dealing. Therefore, a foundation can receive and hold a gift or bequest, from a disqualified person, of an undivided interest in property. The difficulty is that only the foundation can *use* the property, inasmuch as the use of foundation income or assets by a disqualified person is self-dealing (see below). Nonetheless, this type of shared ownership can provide some advantage to persons holding this type of an interest.

In one instance, a husband and wife owned an expensive art collection that they bequeathed to a museum they created, which was organized as a private foundation. When the husband died, the museum and the surviving spouse became joint tenants holding an undivided interest in each object in the collection. The IRS did not permit her to display even a small portion of the co-owned artwork in her home or otherwise use any of the art. The museum, however, was allowed to pay for insurance on the entire collection.

An individual made a gift to a private foundation of an undivided interest in real estate, with the donor planning to thereafter sell the property. The donor relinquished all rights to use the realty but retained the right to inspect it. Expenses were shared proportionately between the donor and the foundation. When this property was sold, the proceeds were appropriately divided. The IRS ruled that self-dealing did not occur as a result of the gift, the co-ownership of the property, or the sale of the property (to an independent party).

The IRS permits types of passive investments that could, pursuant to a literal reading of the rules, be considered self-dealing. For example, in one case, the IRS labeled a co-ownership of real property, by a private foundation and disqualified persons, an "investment relationship." The parties each received their ownership interest by gift, held the property as tenants-in-common, and had separate interests in a long-term lease of the property. Because there was no sale, lease, or transfer of the property among the foundation and these persons, the IRS concluded there was no self-dealing. As to the lease, the foundation received its share of the rent directly, thereby "precluding its interest in the lease from being used by a disqualified person."

An alternative to the holding of property as co-owners—becoming partners—has been sanctioned by the IRS in the private founda-tion/disqualified person context. That is, the holding and use of separate interests in a partnership is not considered the use of jointly owned property. Caution should nonetheless be used in structuring these arrangements, to assure that the terms of the partnership agreement permit each partner to have exclusive control or use of their respective interests and do not create any common or shared interests.

LOANS AND OTHER EXTENSIONS OF CREDIT

The lending of money or other extension of credit, directly or indirectly, between a private foundation and a disqualified person generally constitutes self-dealing. The fact that the rate of interest is greater than the foundation would otherwise receive is irrelevant. A circuitous route taken, so that the first borrower is not a disqualified person, cannot redeem the matter if indebtedness payable to or from a private foundation results. For example, if a foundation sells property to an unrelated party, who borrowed to buy it and who thereafter sells the property to a party related to the foundation, where this disqualified person assumes liability for the mortgage or takes the property subject to a mortgage payable to the foundation, self-dealing occurs with the second of the sales.

A loan by a private foundation to an individual, as part of a compensation package being negotiated, made before he or she became a foundation manager (and thus a disqualified person) is not self-dealing, since the disqualified person status arose only following completion of the negotiations. Where the loan principal remains outstanding once the individual became a disqualified person, however, self-dealing occurs. Indeed, a separate act of self-dealing takes place in each year the indebtedness remains.

As should be clear by now, the self-dealing rules are tough and tricky. Consider the disqualified person who contributed to a private foundation a life insurance policy subject to a policy loan. The decision by the IRS that this was self-dealing rested on the notion that a life insurance policy loan is sometimes characterized as an advance of the policy's proceeds, with the loan and the interest on it considered charges against the property, rather than amounts that must be paid to the insurer. The IRS concluded that the effect of the transfer was essentially the same as the transfer of property subject to a lien, in that the transfer of the policy relieved the donor of the obligation to repay the loan, pay interest on the loan as it accrues, or suffer diminution in the value of the policy. The IRS noted that the amount of the loan was significant in relation to the value of the property, although any loan amount (other than a trivial sum) would seem to entail self-dealing.

A transfer of indebted real or personal property to a private foundation by a disqualified person is considered an impermissible assumption of debt if the person placed the loan on the property within a ten-year period ending on the date of the transfer. The date on which the loan was made, not when the loan or line of credit was approved, is the date from which this ten-year rule is measured. It is normally the date a lien is actually placed on the property, even though the loan is part of a multiphase financing plan started more than ten years before the transfer.

The lending of money or other extension of credit, without interest or other charge (disregarding the imputed interest rules) by a disqualified person to a private foundation is permitted if the proceeds of the loan are used exclusively in carrying out the foundation's charitable activities. Thus, the making of a promise, pledge, or similar arrangement to a private foundation by a disqualified person, whether evidenced by an oral or written agreement, a promissory note, or other instrument of indebtedness, to the extent motivated by charitable intent and unsupported by consideration, is not an extension of credit before the date of maturity.

The payment of expenses on behalf of a private foundation by a disqualified person can be considered an interest-free loan to the foundation. If expense advances are treated as loans without charge and are paid in connection with its charitable activities, a foundation can reimburse the expenses, by "repaying" the "loan." Limited advances and reimbursement of expenses are permitted for foundation managers (discussed later in this chapter). The tax regulations concerning the facility-sharing exception, however, prohibit a foundation's payment of costs it incurs in using the property to a disqualified person. Despite this potential conflict, the IRS takes a practical approach and permits reimbursement in circumstances where the transaction clearly allows a foundation to better accomplish its exempt purposes.

This exception is voided where a private foundation repays or cancels a debt by transferring property other than money (such as securities) to a disqualified person in repayment of a loan. The view of the IRS is that this type of transfer, when coupled with the making of the loan, is a sale or exchange of property between the foundation and the disqualified person constituting self-dealing.

Never-ending surprises are rampant in the world of self-dealing. One of the most entertaining examples is the case of an individual, a disqualified person who controlled a private foundation, who made an interest-free loan to a tax-exempt school to enable it to complete construction, purchase furniture and other materials, and hire staff. This individual, the president of the school, wanted his loan repaid. The foundation made a grant to the school in the precise amount of this debt, with the *understanding* that the school would use the funds to repay the loan. Blatant self-dealing, right? Nope. The IRS ruled that the making of this grant was not self-dealing because the grant was "unrestricted" and the school "may" repay the loan. The disqualified person was said to have "no control" over the school (despite being its president) to compel it to repay his loan; the school was characterized by the IRS as being "under no [legal] requirement to use the grant to repay" the disqualified person lender. (The grant was used to pay off the loan.)

PAYMENT OF COMPENSATION

The payment of compensation, including payment or reimbursement of expenses, by a private foundation to a disqualified person generally constitutes an act of self-dealing. This rule, on its face, would seem to preclude a foundation from hiring a disqualified person as an employee (or independent contractor) or from ongoing compensation to key employees (inasmuch as they are foundation managers and thus disqualified persons [see Chapter 2]). An obviously extremely important and frequently used exception to this general rule, however, allows payment of compensation to a disqualified person for services rendered in carrying out foundation affairs. For this capacious exception to be available, the compensation must be for personal services, the compensation must be reasonable (see Chapter 3), the compensation must be necessary for advancement of the foundation's exempt purposes, and the individual being compensated must not be a government official (see Chapter 2).

The term *personal services* is not defined by statute or the tax regulations; the boundaries of this element of the exception are not precisely drawn. This *personal services exception* is, according to the IRS, a "special rule" that should be "strictly construed," because, if not, the "fabric woven by Congress to generally prohibit insider transactions [involving private foundations] would unravel." This exception is available irrespective of whether the person who receives the compensation (or expense payment or reimbursement) is an individual; thus, personal services can be provided by a corporation, partnership, limited liability company, or other type of service provider.

The tax regulations contain examples of application of this exception, revealing that it embraces services provided by lawyers (who wrote the regulations), accountants, and investment counselor and managers, as well as certain services provided by banks. The sole court decision on the point held that the services sheltered by the exception are confined to those that are "essentially professional and managerial in nature." (The case involved the provision by a disqualified person company of janitorial services to a private foundation; the services were ruled to be neither professional nor managerial.)

Favorable IRS rulings have been extended to services provided for cash and debt management, other forms of investment management, and other types of financial and management services. (These rulings indicate that the exception is available for services that are *either* professional or managerial in nature.) The IRS distinguishes personal services from *operational* services, such as maintenance, repair, cleaning, and landscaping services. The exception covers the services of an *agent* for a foundation but not the services of a *dealer* for a foundation (a person buying from a foundation and selling to third parties). A person who manages real estate for a private foundation is engaged in personal services; a person who is a real estate broker for a foundation is not.

Foundations and disqualified persons should be cautious in relying on this exception. In one instance, a disqualified person company that manufactures microscopes sold a batch of them to a private foundation engaged in scientific research. The price paid for the microscopes was below-market and thus reasonable; the foundation used the microscopes in furtherance of its charitable purposes. Nonetheless, the payments for these microscopes were acts of self-dealing because they were not compensation for the performance of personal services.

A topic that is infrequently discussed in the law is the matter of compensation paid to members of the board of trustees or directors of a private foundation for their services as such. This is a common practice; the assumption seems to be that services of this nature constitute *personal services*. An IRS ruling concerned compensation paid to foundation trustees who performed services normally provided by officers and outside professionals, as well as services in fields such as investments, personnel, and grant-making. (Trustees of this nature are sometimes referred to as *executive trustees*.) Noting that these trustees' fees were less than those charged by financial institutions for similar services, the IRS ruled that the fees were reasonable and that the payment of them was not self-dealing. This ruling apparently assumed—it did not hold—that the services provided by the trustees were personal services.

The term *compensation* in this setting generally means a salary or wage, any bonuses, fringe benefits, retirement benefits, and the like. Occasionally, however, other economic benefits are treated as compensation for purposes of the self-dealing rules. For example, the IRS ruled that a split-dollar life insurance arrangement established by a foundation for the benefit of a key employee was a form of compensation of the employee. Under certain circumstances, the value of an indemnification by a private foundation of a foundation manager or the payment by a foundation of the premiums for an insurance policy for a foundation manager, must be treated as compensation to avoid self-dealing (discussed later in this chapter). By contrast, when the self-dealing rules are explicit in prohibiting a particular type of transaction between private foundations and disqualified persons, the rules cannot be sidestepped by treating the value of the economic benefit provided as part of the disqualified person's total (and presumably reasonable) compensation.

ADVANCES AND EXPENSE REIMBURSEMENTS

Advances that are reasonable in relation to the duties and expense requirements of a foundation manager are permitted. According to the tax regulations, cash advances should not ordinarily exceed $500. When a foundation chooses to exceed this $500 threshold, appropriate documentation should be gathered. To mitigate an amount needed as an advance, a foundation can directly purchase items such as airline tickets. In instances of extended travel time or trips to places where carrying cash is inadvisable, a foundation may allow disqualified persons to use a credit card. Personal use of this type of credit card should be discouraged.

Expenses for travel and meals incurred in connection with the conduct of private foundation programs and its other affairs can be paid or reimbursed. A foundation with directors and personnel in different locations, for example, can pay for the cost of travel to attend a meeting in one of the locations. The expenses of site visits to potential grantees can be paid. When a foundation pays expenses of this nature on behalf of its disqualified persons, a written policy should be developed describing the terms of reimbursement and required documentation. Complete reports documenting the expenditures, along with descriptions of the nature of the work performed, meetings held, or other foundation business that necessitated the travel, should be compiled.

BANK FEES

Banks and trust companies frequently serve as trustees for private foundations; in this capacity, they often face the prospects of self-dealing transactions. To help alleviate the possibility of unavoidable self-dealing, the law provides that certain banking functions that a bank performs for all of its customers can be performed for private foundations for which it serves as trustee without constituting self-dealing. Assuming a fair interest rate for the use of the funds by the bank, a private foundation can pay the institution reasonable compensation. The general banking services that are permitted are:

- The provision of checking accounts, as long as the bank does not charge interest on any overdrafts. Payment of overdraft charges not in excess of the bank's cost of processing an overdraft is, however, acceptable.

- The provision of savings accounts, as long as the foundation may withdraw its funds on no more than 30 days' notice without subjecting itself to a loss of interest on its money for the time the money was on deposit.

- Safekeeping activities.

Transactions outside the scope of these relationships may be problematic. Thus, if a private foundation were to leave funds, which were not earning interest, in a disqualified person bank, self-dealing would generally occur. A bank trustee's purchase of securities owned by independent parties for a foundation's account is not, of course, self-dealing but purchase of the bank's own mortgage loans for the account would be self-dealing.

The purchase of certificates of deposit by a foundation from a disqualified person bank is impermissible if the certificates provide for a reduced rate of interest if they are not held to the full maturity date.

INDEMNIFICATION AND INSURANCE

It is common for a private foundation to provide officers' and directors' liability insurance to, or to indemnify, foundation managers in connection with civil proceedings arising from the managers' performance of services for the foundation. Generally, these practices do not entail self-dealing. Moreover, the amounts expended by a foundation for insurance or indemnification generally are not included in the compensation of the disqualified persons for purposes of determining whether the compensation is reasonable.

Indemnification payments and insurance coverage are divided into two categories: noncompensatory and compensatory. This body of law is a component of the general statutory scheme by which transfers to, or use by or for the benefit of, a disqualified person of the income or assets of a private foundation generally constitute self-dealing (discussed in the next section).

Noncompensatory Indemnification and Insurance

Self-dealing does not occur, as a general rule, when a private foundation indemnifies a foundation manager with respect to the manager's defense in any civil judicial or administrative proceeding arising out of the manager's performance of services (or failure to perform services) on behalf of the foundation. This indemnification may be against all expenses (other than taxes, including any of the private foundation taxes, penalties, or expenses of correction) and can include payment of lawyers' fees, judgments, and settlement expenditures. The following two conditions must exist for the indemnification to not be considered self-dealing:

1. The manager must reasonably incur the expenses in connection with the proceeding.

2. The manager must not have acted willfully or without reasonable cause with respect to the act (or failure to act) that led to the proceeding or liability for a private foundation tax.

Likewise, the self-dealing rules do not apply to the payment of premiums for insurance to cover or reimburse a foundation for this type of indemnification payment. These payments are viewed as expenses for the foundation's operations, rather than compensation for the manager's services.

Compensatory Indemnification and Insurance

The indemnification of a foundation manager against payment of a penalty tax, and the associated defense, is considered to be part of the manager's compensation. This type of payment by a private foundation is an act of self-dealing, unless, when the payment is added to other compensation paid to the manager, the total compensation is reasonable. A *compensatory expense* of this nature includes payment of any of the following:

- A penalty, tax (including a private foundation tax), or expense of correction that is owed by a foundation manager

- An expense not reasonably incurred by a manager in connection with a civil judicial or administrative proceeding arising out of the manager's performance of services on behalf of the foundation

- An expense resulting from an act or failure to act with respect to which the manager has acted willfully and without reasonable cause

Likewise, the payment by a private foundation of the premiums for an insurance policy providing liability insurance to a foundation manager for any of these categories of expenses is an act of self-dealing, unless, when the premiums are added to the other compensation paid to the manager, the total compensation is reasonable. These payments are viewed as being exclusively for the benefit of the manager, not the private foundation involved.

A private foundation did not engage in an act of self-dealing if the foundation purchased an insurance policy to provide its managers both noncompensatory and compensatory coverage, as long as the insurance premium is allocated between the two coverages, and each manager's portion of the premium that is attributable to the compensatory coverage is included in the manager's compensation for purposes of determining reasonable compensation.

The term *indemnification* includes not only reimbursement by a private foundation for expenses that a foundation manager has already incurred or anticipates incurring, but also direct payment by the foundation of the expenses as they arise.

USES OF INCOME OR ASSETS

The transfer to, or use by or for the benefit of, a disqualified person of the income or assets of a private foundation generally constitutes self-dealing. This prohibition is, in the words of the IRS, "extremely broad" and thus entails traps; it is in this context that self-dealing can inadvertently occur.

For example, disqualified persons with respect to a private foundation had assets in an investment company that had a collateralization obligation used to satisfy margin requirements. The foundation also had assets placed with the company. The company took the foundation's assets into account to enable the disqualified persons to comply with their collateralization requirement. The IRS concluded that this arrangement constituted self-dealing, in that the foundation's assets were used for the benefit of the disqualified persons. (Indeed, the IRS was so upset with this application of foundation assets it revoked the tax-exempt status of the foundation.)

Securities Transactions

The purchase or sale of securities by a private foundation is an act of self-dealing, if the purchase or sale is made in an attempt to manipulate the price of the securities to the advantage of a disqualified person with respect to the foundation. For example, securities may be sold in a secondary public offering (where the offering would not take place but for the involvement of a private foundation); self-dealing would occur if one or more disqualified persons also participated in the securities transaction. By contrast, a public offering of stock undertaken to enable a private foundation to sell its shares is not self-dealing if disqualified persons are excluded from the transaction.

Payment of Charitable Pledges

Self-dealing in the form of use of a private foundation's assets for the benefit of a disqualified person occurs if the foundation makes a grant to a charitable organization that satisfies the disqualified person's legally enforceable pledge to make a charitable contribution to that organization. This type of pledge is considered a debt, with the foundation grant constituting relief of the debtor's (pledgor's) legal obligation to the charity.

This can be a harsh rule. For example, several corporations established a private foundation to serve as a conduit for their charitable contributions. Part of the foundation's initial funding was made on the condition that the foundation use the funds to pay charitable pledges previously committed to by the corporations. The IRS took the position that payment of these pledges by the foundation would be self-dealing. The funds in this case came from the corporations (as substantial contributors [see Chapter 2]), which, of course, could have paid the pledges directly; a respectable argument was that any benefit to the corporations was incidental (discussed later in this chapter) because of the mere conduit function of the foundation. Nonetheless, as a matter of law, once the funds are transferred to the foundation—under any circumstances—they are assets of the foundation that cannot be used for the benefit of disqualified persons.

Memberships

A private foundation engages in an act of self-dealing when it pays membership dues or fees on behalf of a disqualified person and thereby relieves him or her of that obligation. The benefit to the person, in this context, is direct and economic in nature; it is not incidental (discussed later in this chapter). In one instance, a foundation paid its trustee's church dues, thereby enabling him to maintain his membership in and otherwise participate in the religious activities of the congregation. The dues payment was ruled to constitute self-dealing, with the IRS concluding that the foundation's payment of the dues "result[ed] in a direct economic benefit to the disqualified person because that person would have been expected to pay the membership dues had they not been paid by the foundation."

Benefit Tickets

The matter of the purchase of tickets to charitable fundraising events constantly confounds private foundations. Foundations want to support charities in their community; one way to do that is to financially support these organizations in connection with their special events, such as dinners, award banquets, entertainment events, and the like. The problem is that individuals, once the tickets are bought, usually are expected to attend the event; these individuals are often (if not always) disqualified persons with respect to the foundation (such as foundation managers and their spouses).

Self-dealing was found by the IRS when a joint purchase of benefit tickets was made by sharing the cost of the tickets. A private foundation paid the deductible (charitable contribution) cost of the tickets; the disqualified person paid for the portion of the tickets price allocable to the fair market value of the event. Self-dealing occurred because the benefits were more than incidental (see below). To be able to attend the benefit, foundation representatives would have been required to individually pay the full ticket price. Thus, they reaped direct economic benefit to the extent that the foundation paid for a part of the tickets price.

This is a most difficult matter. There are, of course, two different types of fundraising events. Some are exciting and sought-after entertainment opportunities; others are tedious, with the attendees wishing fervently they were elsewhere (award events top this category). No matter the type of event, however, it cannot occur without patrons. The seats around the tables need to be filled; humans are needed to provide the applause for the distribution of certificates and the end of speeches. Representatives of private foundations often play these roles.

As a practical matter, if private foundation representatives truly want to attend a fundraising event (such as because of the nature of the entertainment or the popularity of the speaker), payment for the tickets by the foundation is probably self-dealing. Conversely, if the representatives do not want to attend the event and are doing so only out of obligation, payment by the foundation for the tickets likely is not self-dealing. This is the *fun factor* versus the *rubber chicken* rule (not formally a part of the law).

For the Benefit of Transactions

It is in this context that most of the traps lurk. It is relatively easy to spot self-dealing where a benefit is provided by a private foundation *to* a disqualified person. Likewise, self-dealing can be readily seen where a disqualified person is *using* the assets of a foundation for private benefit. But, because self-dealing can occur where a benefit is provided by a foundation to a person who is *not* a disqualified person, the *for the benefit of* rule can cause problems. Again, self-dealing can occur where a foundation engages in a transaction that causes the income or assets of the foundation to be utilized for the benefit of one or more disqualified persons.

Consider this scenario: A lawyer is the sole trustee of a private foundation. A significant client (not a disqualified person with respect to the foundation) of the lawyer's law firm needed a loan, could not get one conventionally, and asked the lawyer for assistance. The lawyer caused the foundation to make the loan, pursuant to terms (such as rate of interest and security) that were amply reasonable. This lending transaction was self-dealing. Why? Because the ability of the lawyer to generate this loan *enhanced the lawyer's reputation* in the view of the client; this use of foundation resources provided an economic benefit to the disqualified person lawyer.

Here is an example where an *increase in goodwill* was the forbidden benefit. A bank that extended credit to large corporations and tax-exempt organizations, and in the process sold notes, engaged in self-dealing when it caused some of the notes to be purchased by private foundations for which it acted as trustee. The IRS regarded the foundations' purchase of the notes as a substantial activity that enhanced the reputation of the bank as a credit provider and significantly increased its goodwill. The provision of these benefits to the bank was self-dealing. In another instance, the use of a foundation's resources to provide *marketing opportunities* for a disqualified person was found to be self-dealing.

Consequently, it is not enough to analyze a transaction involving a private foundation to determine if one or more disqualified persons were directly provided a benefit. The analysis needs to continue to see if some economic advantage was provided to one or more third parties that threw off a benefit to a disqualified person. Sometimes even the IRS misses this one. In one instance, the IRS ruled that a benefit was not provided *to* a disqualified person and thus that the transaction was not self-dealing, without also analyzing whether one or more benefits were nonetheless provided to disqualified persons because of advantages conferred on others (even though the IRS wrote that the disqualified persons received an "intangible public benefit," which presumably is akin to enhanced reputation and increased goodwill).

Incidental or Tenuous Benefits

The fact that a disqualified person receives an incidental or tenuous benefit from the use by a private foundation of its income or assets will not, by itself, result in an act of self-dealing. The IRS ruled that an incidental or tenuous benefit occurs when the general reputation or prestige of a disqualified person is enhanced by public acknowledgment of a contribution, when a disqualified person receives some other relatively minor benefit, or when a disqualified person merely participates in a wholly incidental degree in the fruits of a charitable program that is of broad public interest.

SHARING SPACE, PEOPLE, EXPENSES

Many private foundations are operated in tandem with their creators, such as families or corporations. Usually, at least until a foundation accumulates a certain volume of assets with consequential grant-making activity, rental of a separate office and engagement of separate staff is beyond the foundation's reasonable financial capacity (and, in any event, detracts from direct charitable activity). Not surprisingly, when foundations are administered alongside disqualified persons, there is considerable potential for self-dealing.

Determining What Foundations Can Pay

The law is not clear as to when a private foundation can pay for its portion of expenses in a sharing situation involving disqualified persons. This type of relationship is chilled by the rule that prohibits the "furnishing of goods, services, or facilities" between (to or from) a foundation and a disqualified person. The types of property covered by this rule include office space, automobiles, secretarial assistance, meals, libraries, laboratories, and parking lots.

When these strict prohibitions were imposed in 1969, Congress provided a transitional period, until 1980, during which then-existing contractual sharing arrangements could be maintained without self-dealing taking place. Thereafter, however, as the cost of the absolute ban on sharing proved unreasonable in a variety of circumstances, the IRS by means of private letter rulings relaxed what would otherwise have been an impenetrable barrier to arrangements in which a foundation and its creators, funders, and/or administrators share the expenses of space, staff, and the like.

OFFICE SPACE, EQUIPMENT, AND PERSONNEL

Many private foundations have obtained IRS approval for shared office space and personnel. The key is to avoid arrangements where disqualified persons receive any economic subsidy or other benefit. As to office space, for example, a foundation and a disqualified person can have separate offices, yet a common reception area, as long as there are separate leases. (A disqualified person cannot be a lessor to a foundation.) A foundation and a disqualified person can jointly purchase office equipment and hire employees; self-dealing is avoided where time records are kept to ascertain each party's share of the costs and foundation payments are not made to disqualified persons.

Some disqualified persons have family management corporations that render accounting, tax, and management services. In one instance, a corporation of this nature operated on a cost-recovery basis to serve the business needs of "family assets held in trusts, foundations, and partnerships." Although this arrangement is obviously one involving sharing, the IRS ruled that payment of a fee by foundations based on actual costs was reasonable compensation for services rendered and thus not self-dealing.

Group Insurance

Group insurance policies present similar dilemmas. Corporations and other conglomerate groups funding private foundations have been allowed to include their private foundation employees in common insurance policies (such as health insurance). The foundation pays directly for the premiums allocable to its employees or reimburses the company. Direct and separate payments are strongly preferred by the IRS but, if that is impossible, the agency may tolerate reimbursements. The rationale for this tolerance is found in the rule that provides that the lending of money by a disqualified person to a foundation is not self-dealing if the loan is without interest or other charge and the proceeds of the loan are used exclusively for the foundation's charitable purposes.

Public Facilities

A private foundation that operates a museum, maintains a wildlife preserve, produces an educational journal, or engages in comparable programs faces the statutory decree that it not furnish goods, services, or facilities to its disqualified persons. Applied literally, this prohibition prevents disqualified persons from visiting the sites, purchasing the journal, and similar entanglements with the foundation's programs. This, of course, would be an absurd outcome.

A private foundation's furnishing, to a disqualified person, of goods, services, or facilities normally open or available to the public, however, falls within an exception to the general self-dealing rules. This exception is available where:

- The property involved is functionally related to the exercise or performance by the foundation of its charitable purpose.

- The number of persons (other than disqualified persons) who use the facility is sufficiently substantial to indicate that members of the public are the primary users.

- The terms for disqualified person usage are not more favorable than the terms under which the public acquires or uses the property.

PAYMENTS TO GOVERNMENT OFFICIALS

In general, a payment by a private foundation to a government official (see Chapter 2) is prohibited. Such a payment is not self-dealing, however, where the purpose of the payment is to employ a government official for a period after termination of his or her government service and the official is terminating service within a 90-day period.

Certain de minimis payments to government officials are permitted:

- A prize or award that is not includible in gross income, if the government official receiving the prize or award is selected from the public and where the prize or award is paid over to a charitable organization

- A scholarship or fellowship that is excludable from gross income and that is to be utilized for study at a qualified educational institution and used only for tuition, fees, and books

- Certain types of pension plans and annuity payments

- A contribution of property (other than money), or of a service or facility, if the aggregate value of the contribution(s) is no more than $25 in a calendar year

- Government employee training programs

- Reimbursement of the cost of travel, including meals and lodging, within the United States for attendance at a charitable function, not to exceed 125% of the prevailing per diem rate

INDIRECT SELF-DEALING

An act of self-dealing may be direct or indirect. An *indirect* act of self-dealing generally occurs in the form of a transaction between a disqualified person and an organization that is controlled by a private foundation. For this purpose, an organization is *controlled* by a foundation if the foundation or one or more of its foundation managers may, by aggregating their votes or positions of authority, require the organization to engage in a transaction which, if engaged in with the foundation, would constitute self-dealing. An organization is considered to be controlled by a foundation, or by a foundation and disqualified persons, if such persons are in fact able to control the foundation (even if their aggregate voting power is less than 50% of the total voting power of the organization's governing body) or if one or more of such persons has the right to exercise veto power over the actions of the organization that are relevant to any potential acts of self-dealing.

The term *indirect self-dealing* does not include a transaction between a disqualified person and an organization controlled by a private foundation, where the foundation's assets may be affected by the transaction, when:

- The transaction arises in the normal and customary course of a retail business engaged in with the public.

- The transaction is at least as favorable to the controlled organization as an arm's-length transaction with an unrelated person.

- The total of the amounts involved in the transaction with respect to any disqualified person in any tax year does not exceed $5,000.

PROPERTY HELD BY FIDUCIARIES

A trustee or executor of an estate may determine that property given or bequeathed to a private foundation, such as an undivided interest in property, is not suitable to be held by the foundation. At times, the best solution in this situation, concerning disposition of the property, would result, under the general rules, in self-dealing. Nonetheless, the law provides considerable leeway to the trust or estate representatives to allocate or sell assets among beneficiaries, inasmuch as the property involved has yet to become owned by the foundation. This exception to the self-dealing rules is known as the *estate administration exception*.

Transactions during administration of an estate, regarding a private foundation's interest or expectancy in property (whether or not encumbered) held by the estate (regardless of when title vests), with disqualified persons are not acts of self-dealing where:

- The executor, administrator, or trustee has the authority to either sell the property or allocate it to another beneficiary, or is required to sell the property pursuant to the terms of the trust instrument or will.

- A probate court with jurisdiction over the estate approves the transaction.

- The transaction occurs before the estate or trust is terminated.

- The estate or trust receives an amount that is at least equal to the fair market value of its interest or expectancy in the property at the time of the transaction.

- The foundation receives an interest at least as liquid as the one given up, an exempt function asset, or an amount of money equal to that required under an option binding on the estate or trust.

EARLY TERMINATIONS OF CHARITABLE REMAINDER TRUSTS

A charitable remainder trust (see Chapter 9) may be terminated sooner than is provided in the trust instrument. There are several reasons for the premature termination of this type of trust, most likely a desire to transfer the trust assets earlier to the remainder interest beneficiary or an income beneficiary's dissatisfaction with the level of income payments. These trusts are treated as private foundations for purposes of the self-dealing (and certain other foundation) rules.

There is no formal procedure for early termination of these trusts. (By contrast, the law is quite formal as to the process by which private foundations may be terminated [see Chapter 3].) Informally, the IRS scrutinizes these proposed terminations. The agency's principal concern is that the premature termination will result in greater allocation of the trust's assets to the income beneficiary, and thus to the detriment of the remainder interest beneficiary (a charitable organization), than would be the case if the termination instead occurred at the time prescribed in the trust instrument.

In appropriate circumstances, nonetheless, the IRS will permit an early termination of a charitable remainder trust. The elements the agency reviews are whether:

1. The trustee will be distributing to the income and remainder interest beneficiaries lump sums equal to the present value of their respective interests as of the termination date.

2. The income and remainder interests are vested.

3. All income beneficiaries are of full legal capacity.

4. All of the beneficiaries favor early termination of the trust.

5. Any of the income beneficiaries have a medical condition that is expected to result in a shortening of life.

6. The trust instrument prohibits early termination of the trust.

7. State law or regulatory authorities permits early termination of the trust.

The law is not yet clear as to whether an early termination of a charitable remainder trust, where the remainder interest beneficiary is a private foundation, constitutes self-dealing.

EXCEPTIONS TO RULES

A transaction between a private foundation and a corporation that is a disqualified person with respect to the foundation is not an act of self-dealing if the transaction is engaged in pursuant to a liquidation, merger, redemption, recapitalization, or other corporate adjustment, organization, or reorganization. For this exception to apply, however, all of the securities of the same class as that held (prior to the transaction) by the foundation must be subject to the same terms; the terms must provide for receipt by the foundation of no less than fair market value.

A transaction between a private foundation and a disqualified person is not self-dealing if (1) the transaction is a purchase or sale of securities by the foundation through a stockbroker, where normal trading procedures on a stock exchange or recognized over-the-counter market are followed; (2) neither the buyer nor the seller of the securities, nor the agent of either, knows the identity of the other party involved; and (3) the sale is made in the ordinary course of business and does not involve a block of securities larger than the average trading volume of the stock over the previous four weeks.

A variety of other statutory exceptions eliminate some of the absoluteness from the six prohibitions and bring some reasonableness to these rules. The basic concept common to these exceptions is that they permit certain transactions that provide a benefit to a private foundation without producing any unwarranted gain to a disqualified person. Thus, the following types of transactions (some of which are noted above) are permitted:

- Payment of reasonable compensation, and payment or reimbursement of expenses, by a private foundation to a disqualified person with respect to it (discussed earlier in this chapter).

- Transfer of indebted real or personal property to a foundation by a disqualified person by sale where the foundation assumes a mortgage or similar debt, or if it takes the property by gift subject to a debt placed on the property by a disqualified person before the ten-year period ending on the date of the transfer.

- A loan by a disqualified person to a foundation where it is without interest or other charge and the loan proceeds are used exclusively by the foundation for its charitable purposes.

- Offering a no-rent lease or the furnishing of free use of a disqualified person's goods, services, or facilities to a foundation, where the property or services are used exclusively by the foundation for its charitable purposes.

- Furnishing a disqualified person with exempt-function goods, facilities, or services that the foundation regularly provides to the public, where the conditions and charges for the transaction are the same as those for the public.

- Certain scholarship, travel, and pension payments to elected or appointed federal and state government officials.

Further, the tax regulations provide additional exceptions in this context. For example, in a significant exception, transactions during the administration of an estate or revocable trust in which a private foundation has an interest or expectancy are not forms of self-dealing, where certain requirements are satisfied (discussed later in this chapter).

Also, a transaction between a private foundation and a disqualified person is not an act of self-dealing if:

- The transaction is a purchase or sale of securities by a private foundation through a stockbroker, where normal trading procedures on a stock exchange or recognized over-the-counter market are followed.

- Neither the buyer nor the seller of the securities nor the agent of either knows the identity of the other party involved.

- The sale is made in the ordinary course of business.

- The sale does not involve a block of securities larger than the average daily trading volume of that stock over the previous four weeks.

A private foundation converting to classification as a public charity (see Chapter 3) is not treated as a private foundation for self-dealing purposes during its 60-month termination period. Therefore, transactions that are prohibited for private foundations are allowed during the conversion period.

IMPOSITION OF EXCISE TAX PENALITIES

The penalties that can be imposed in this context principally are initial and additional taxes, levied on the self-dealer(s) involved and/or one or more of the foundation managers.

Initial Taxes

Two types of initial excise taxes (also known as first-tier taxes) are imposed on each act of self-dealing between a private foundation and (directly or indirectly) a disqualified person. The foundation involved does not pay any self-dealing taxes. The self-dealer, that is, the disqualified person participating in the act (other than a foundation manager acting only in that capacity), pays an initial tax of 10% on the amount involved with respect to the act of self-dealing for each year (or part of a year) in the taxable period. The self-dealer is taxed even if he, she, or it was unaware that a self-dealing rule was violated.

Tax on Managers

Foundation managers that participate in an act of self-dealing are subject to a tax at the rate of 5% of the taxable amount. This tax is imposed, however, only where (1) the initial tax on the self-dealer is imposed, (2) the foundation manager knew that the act was an act of self-dealing, and (3) the participation by the foundation manager was willful and not due to reasonable cause. A self-dealer also acting as a foundation manager can be subject to both taxes.

For purposes of this tax, a foundation manager is treated as *participating* in an act of self-dealing in any case in which the person engages or takes part in the transaction by himself, herself, or itself, or directs a person to do so. In this context, the term *participation* includes silence or inaction on the part of a foundation manager where he or she is under a duty to speak or act, as well as any affirmative action by the manager. A foundation manager is not considered to have participated in an act of self-dealing, however, where he or she has opposed the act in a manner consistent with the fulfillment of his or her responsibilities to the private foundation.

Participation by a foundation manager is deemed *willful* if it is voluntary, conscious, and intentional. A motive to avoid the restrictions of the law or the incurrence of any tax is not necessary to make the participation willful. Participation by a foundation manager is not willful, however, if he or she does not know that the transaction in which he or she participated is an act of self-dealing.

A foundation manager's participation is due to *reasonable cause* if he or she has exercised his or her responsibility on behalf of the foundation with ordinary business care and prudence. A manager having a reasonable cause (that might excuse imposition of the tax) would be one found to be attentive to the affairs of the foundation, to be aware of the private foundation rules sanctions, and to remain sufficiently informed of the foundation's activities to prevent any violation of the sanctions.

The term *knowing* does not mean "having reason to know." Evidence tending to show that an individual has reason to know of a particular fact or particular rule, however, is relevant in determining whether he or she had actual knowledge of that fact or rule. For example, evidence tending to show that an individual has reason to know of sufficient facts so that, based solely on those facts, a transaction would be an act of self-dealing is relevant in determining whether he or she has actual knowledge of those facts.

An individual is considered to have participated in a transaction *knowing* that it is an act of self-dealing only if he or she:

- Has actual knowledge of sufficient facts so that, based solely on those facts, the transaction would be an act of self-dealing

- Is aware that the act under these circumstances may violate the self-dealing rules

- Negligently fails to make reasonable attempts to ascertain whether the transaction is an act of self-dealing, or he or she is in fact aware that it is this type of act

In the case of a government official, a tax can be imposed only if the official, as a disqualified person, participated in the act of self-dealing knowing that it was this type of act. Otherwise, the tax is imposed on a disqualified person even though the person did not have knowledge at the time of the act that it constituted self-dealing.

The *taxable period* is, with respect to an act of self-dealing, the period beginning with the date on which the act of self-dealing occurred and ending on the earliest of the date:

- Of mailing of a notice of deficiency with respect to the initial tax

- On which the tax is assessed

- On which correction of the act of self-dealing (see above) is completed

If a transaction between a private foundation and a disqualified person concerns the leasing of property, the lending of money or other extension of credit, other use of money or property, or payment of compensation, the transaction will generally be treated as giving rise to an act of self-dealing on the day the transaction occurs, plus an act of self-dealing on the first day of each applicable calendar year after that date.

If joint participation in a transaction by two or more disqualified persons constitutes self-dealing (such as a joint sale of property to a private foundation), the transaction is generally treated as a separate act of self-dealing with respect to each disqualified person. Should more than one person be liable for one of these initial excise taxes, all of them are jointly and severally liable for the tax with respect to the act of self-dealing involved, up to a maximum of $20,000 for all.

This self-dealing tax is imposed annually (at the 10% rate), rather than merely with respect to the year in which the self-dealing took place. For example, if a private foundation made a multiyear loan to a disqualified person, there would be an act of self-dealing with respect to each year there was an outstanding principal balance on the loan.

Additional Tax

Where the initial tax is imposed and the self-dealing is not corrected in a timely fashion (see above), an additional tax (also known as a second-tier tax) of 200% of the amount involved is imposed on the self-dealer. A foundation manager who refuses to agree to a correction faces a penalty tax of 50% of the amount involved. Again, if more than one foundation manager is liable for one of these taxes, all of them are jointly and severally liable for the tax with respect to the act of self-dealing involved (maximum of $20,000).

Amount Involved

The tax penalties imposed in connection with a self-dealing transaction are based on the *amount involved*, which is the "greater of the amount of money and the fair market value of the other property given or the amount of money and the fair market value of the other property received."

Compensation   In the case of compensation paid for personal services to persons other than governmental officials, the amount involved is the portion of the total compensation that is in excess of the reasonable amount.

Loans   In the case of a loan, the amount involved is the greater of the amount paid for the use of the funds (interest actually paid) or the fair market value of the use (prevailing market rate) for the period of time the money was lent.

Use of Property   Where a transaction entails the use of money or other property, the amount involved is the greater of the amount paid for the use or the fair market value of the use for the period for which the money or other property is used.

Date of Valuation

To calculate the first-tier tax initially imposed on a sale, exchange, or lease of property (discussed later in this chapter), in a private foundation self-dealing transaction, the amount involved is determined as of the date on which the self-dealing occurred. An act of self-dealing *occurs* on the date on which all of the terms and conditions of the transaction and the liabilities of the parties have been fixed. If the self-dealing goes uncorrected and the second-tier (additional) tax is calculated, the valuation is equal to the highest value during the period of time the self-dealing continued uncorrected.

Advice of Counsel

If a foundation manager, after full disclosure of the factual situation to legal counsel (including house counsel), relies on the advice of that counsel expressed in a reasoned written legal opinion that an act is not an act of self-dealing—even if that act is subsequently held to be self-dealing—the individual's participation in the act will ordinarily not be considered knowing or willful and will ordinarily be considered due to reasonable cause. This document provided by legal counsel is not required to be a formal opinion letter; rather, it can be a letter or memorandum containing the views of counsel on the point or points involved.

A written legal opinion is considered *reasoned*, even if it reaches a conclusion that is subsequently determined to be incorrect, as long as the opinion addresses itself to the facts and applicable law. A written legal opinion is not reasoned, however, if it does no more than recite the facts and express a conclusion. The absence of advice of counsel with respect to an act does not, by itself, give rise to any inference that a person participated in the act knowingly, willfully, or without reasonable cause.

CORRECTION

The federal tax law prohibition on self-dealing involving private foundations is (as is the case with the other private foundation rules) enforced by a regime of excise taxes (and other sanctions) that are, in fact, penalties for what Congress has characterized as wrongful conduct. A court described these sanctions as follows: "The language of the [Tax Reform] Act [of 1969], its legislative history, the graduated levels of the sanctions imposed, and the almost confiscatory level of the exactions assessed, convince us that the exactions in question were intended to curb the described conduct through pecuniary punishment."

Once it has been determined that self-dealing has occurred, the steps involved in repairing the damage are undoing (correcting) the transaction, determining the amount attributable to the self-dealing, deciding who has to pay an excise tax, the filing of an excise tax return (Form 4720), and advancing any claim of reasonable cause to reduce or avoid any additional tax. This is a self-enforcement system; the parties should not merely await some form of IRS action.

To undo a self-dealing transaction, the transaction must be corrected (rescinded) to the extent possible, such as return of property in an instance of a sale. The term *correction* means undoing the transaction to the extent possible but, in any case, placing the private foundation in a financial position not worse than that in which it would be if the disqualified person(s) were dealing under the highest fiduciary standards. Specific rules govern sales by or to a foundation, loans, uses of property, and compensation arrangements.

Sales by Foundation   In the case of a sale of property by a private foundation to a disqualified person, undoing the transaction includes rescission of the sale. If the purchaser still holds the property, the foundation must take back the property. The foundation then repays the purchaser the sales price or an amount equal to the fair market value of the property at the time of the correction, whichever is less. Any income earned by the disqualified person/buyer from the property in excess of the foundation's earnings on the money (from investment of the sales proceeds) during the self-dealing period should be restored to the foundation. If the property has been sold, the foundation is to receive the greater of the original proceeds that it received or what the disqualified person received on the resale.

Sales to Foundation   In the case of a sale of property to a private foundation by a disqualified person, rescission of the sale is required. Fair market value and resale considerations similar to those just referenced are taken into account, to assure that the foundation is restored to the financial position in which it would have been had it not purchased the property.

Loans   Where a loan has been made, correction of the self-dealing entails repayment of the loan principal.

Uses of Property   Whether the property is being used by a private foundation or a disqualified person, the impermissible use must be stopped. If the rent paid by a foundation exceeds fair rental value, an imputed rent amount must be repaid to the foundation. Different correction rules apply, depending on whether a foundation or a disqualified person rented the property.

Excessive Compensation   When excessive (or unreasonable) compensation has been paid by a private foundation to a disqualified person, the excess amount must be repaid to the foundation. Termination of the employment or independent contractor arrangement, however, is not required.

Caution: Additional Self-Dealing   Caution should be exercised when attempting to correct an act of self-dealing; if the correction is not properly undertaken, the effort may be another act of self-dealing. This nearly occurred when a disqualified person, in attempting to correct a self-dealing act in the form of a loan to him from a private foundation, proposed transfer to the foundation of a parcel of real estate with a fair market value equal to the amount of the loan. The IRS held that (1) the transfer would constitute self-dealing because, since the self-dealer's indebtedness to the foundation would be canceled, the transaction would be a sale of the property by the disqualified person to the foundation, which would be self-dealing (see above), and (2) the minimum standards for an authentic correction would not be met because it would be less advantageous to the foundation to receive the property than to have the loan repaid in cash because of the potential difficulty and cost for the foundation to convert the property to cash and thus restore its position. Nonetheless, a transfer of property may be an acceptable means of correcting a self-dealing loan transaction where the property has substantial value and can be readily converted into an amount of money in excess of the debt amount.

TAX ABATEMENT

The IRS generally has the authority to abate the private foundation initial taxes where reasonable cause can be shown, as well as in the absence of willful neglect (see Chapters 4, 5, 7, and 8). This authority does not, however, extend to the self-dealing taxes.

Nonetheless, in one instance, the IRS found acts of self-dealing on audit of a private foundation, yet worked with foundation management to revise the organization's operations so as to correct the activities that gave rise to the transgression. The IRS used its general authority to grant relief to do so retroactively for the benefit of the foundation (because ongoing tax-exempt status was also at issue) and its management on the self-dealing issues.

THIRD-TIER TAX REGIME

As noted, the sanctions underlying the prohibited expenditures rules include a first-tier and a second-tier tax. The termination tax (see Chapter 3) serves as a third-tier tax. This is the ultimate sanction, with the federal government able to confiscate the value of all federal tax benefits the foundation and its substantial contributors ever received derived from tax exemption and charitable tax deductions, applicable where a foundation engaged in willful, flagrant, or repeated acts or failures to act that cause voluntary, conscious, and intentional transgressions of the self-dealing rules.

SUMMARY

This chapter provided basic information concerning the private foundation self-dealing rules. A basic definition of the concept of self-dealing was provided, followed by a summary of the various types of acts of self-dealing. The chapter explained the rules concerning foundation's payment of compensation and reimbursements, discussed insurance and indemnification coverages, and explained the extent to which foundations and disqualified persons can share space, staff, and expenses. The chapter explained the rules as to indirect self-dealing, early termination of charitable remainder trusts, and the various exceptions to the self-dealing rules. The chapter concluded by analyzing the issues that arise once self-dealing occurs and summarized the various excise tax penalties involved.

7

INVESTMENT RULES

The purpose of this chapter is to explain the federal tax rules concerning investments by private foundations. Foundations are the only type of tax-exempt organization that is subject to tax laws pertaining to their investment practices; investments that jeopardize a foundation's corpus—known as *jeopardizing investments*—are not permitted. Specifically, this chapter will:

- Explain and summarize the private foundation investment rules.
- Define the concept of *jeopardy*.
- Summarize the rules applicable to donated assets.
- Explain the *prudent investor* standards.
- Summarize the rules concerning *program-related investments*.
- Describe the various excise taxes.
- Describe the tax abatement rules.
- Revisit the third-tier tax regime.

PURPOSE OF RULES

The purpose of the jeopardizing investment rules is to shield private foundations' assets from a high degree of risk, so as to maximize capital and resulting income available for charitable endeavors. The underlying notion is that, if a foundation's assets are used in a way that jeopardizes their use for charitable purposes, the tax policy underlying tax exemption and the charitable contribution deduction is frustrated. This body of federal law generally parallels that of state law, where the trustees and directors of foundations have a fiduciary responsibility to safeguard a charitable entity's assets on behalf of its charitable constituency by following prudent investor standards (discussed later in this chapter).

Under the law prior to the enactment of the jeopardizing investments rules (in 1969), a private foundation manager could invest a foundation's assets in warrants, commodity futures, options, and the like, or purchase assets on margin, or otherwise expose the corpus of the foundation to a significant risk of loss without being subject to any sanction. A court, however, held (before enactment of the tax rules) that the consistent practice of making reckless investments constituted operation of a foundation for a substantial nonexempt purpose, thereby endangering its tax-exempt status.

The legislative history of these rules makes it clear that the determination as to whether an investment jeopardizes the carrying out of a private foundation's charitable purposes is to be made at the time of the investment, in accordance with the prudent trustee approach, and not on the basis of hindsight.

GENERAL RULES

A private foundation cannot invest any amount (income or principal) in a manner that would jeopardize the carrying out of any of its tax-exempt purposes. The federal tax statute, however, is silent as to what type or types of investments are jeopardizing investments. (A carve-out from this general rule is the program-related investment [discussed later in this chapter].) The tax regulations, nonetheless, endeavor to shrink the magnitude of this statutory silence by providing that an investment is considered to jeopardize the carrying out of an exempt purpose of a foundation if it is determined that a foundation manager, in making the investment, failed to exercise ordinary business care and prudence, under the facts and circumstances prevailing at the time the investment was made, in providing for the short- and long-term financial needs of the foundation to carry out its exempt purposes.

A determination as to whether the making of a particular investment jeopardizes the tax-exempt purposes of a private foundation is to be made on an investment-by-investment basis, in each case taking into account the entirety of the foundation's portfolio. It is considered prudent for a foundation's managers to consider the expected economic return (income and appreciation in value of the capital), the risks of rising and falling price levels, and the need for diversification within the investment portfolio. As to this third criterion, a foundation manager should consider the type of security involved, the type of industry, the maturity of the company, the degree of risk, and the potential for return. To avoid imposition of a penalty tax (see below), however, a careful analysis of potential investments must be made and good business judgment must be exercised.

Once it has been ascertained that an investment does not jeopardize the carrying out of a private foundation's tax-exempt purposes, the investment is never considered to jeopardize the carrying out of exempt purposes, even though, as a consequence of the investment, the foundation subsequently realizes a loss.

An investment that jeopardizes the carrying out of a private foundation's charitable purposes is considered to be removed from jeopardy when the foundation sells or otherwise disposes of the investment and the proceeds from the disposition are applied in a manner not involving investments that jeopardize the carrying out of the foundation's exempt purposes.

DEFINING *JEOPARDY*

No category of investments is treated as a per se violation of these rules. The types or methods of investment that are closely scrutinized to determine whether foundation managers have met the requisite standard of care and prudence, however, include trading in securities on margin; trading in commodity futures; investments in oil and gas syndications; the purchase of puts, calls, and straddles; the purchase of warrants; and selling short. The financial markets have changed dramatically since the writing of the tax regulations on this subject (in 1970); the regulations have not been updated to take into account contemporary investment practices. Modern investment concepts are rested on the *prudent investor rule*, which recognizes that return on investment is related to risk, that risk includes the risk of deterioration of real return owing to inflation, and that the risk/return relationship must be taken into account in managing trust assets.

It is hard to believe but in the more than 35 years during which these rules have been in effect, the IRS has made a public determination as to whether an investment constitutes a jeopardizing investment on *one* occasion (in 1980). This occurred when the IRS considered a situation involving the contribution to a private foundation of a whole-life insurance policy. The policy was subject to a loan. The donor (the insured) at the time of the gift had a ten-year life expectancy. The foundation did not surrender the policy for its cash value but continued to pay the annual premiums and the interest due on the policy and the loan. Finding that the premium and interest payments were such that, by the end of eight years, the foundation would have expended a greater amount in making these payments than it could receive as a return on the investment (namely, the insurance proceeds it would receive following the death of the insured), the IRS concluded that the foundation's managers, "by investing at the projected rate of return prevailing at the time of the investment, failed to exercise ordinary business care and prudence in providing for the long-term and short-term financial needs of the foundation in carrying out its exempt purposes." Therefore, under these circumstances, the IRS held that each payment made by this foundation for a policy premium and interest on the policy loan was a jeopardizing investment.

There is only one court opinion on this subject; it is not particularly enlightening because the facts reflect obvious poor judgment in investing by a private foundation. In this case, the manager of a private foundation invested the *entire* corpus of the foundation in a Bahamian bank without any inquiry into the integrity of that financial institution. Therefore, unknown to the manager was the fact that the bank's license to do business had been revoked, as had its charter. Interest payments to the foundation were irregular. The IRS concluded, and the court agreed, that the investment in the bank was a jeopardizing one.

There are only a few IRS private letter rulings on jeopardizing investing involving private foundations. One of them involved the purchase by a foundation of gold stocks to protect a portfolio as a hedge against inflation. The IRS held that this was not a jeopardizing investment, despite a net loss of $7,000 on a $14,400 investment. The foundation bought the shares over a three-year period; it made money on one block and lost money on two others. The IRS ruling noted that the foundation, as to its entire portfolio, realized $31,000 in gains and $23,000 in dividends during the same period; the portfolio performance as a whole was found to enable the foundation to carry out its charitable purposes.

A "managed commodity trading program" was found by the IRS to provide diversity to a private foundation's marketable securities portfolio and not entail a jeopardizing investment. Inasmuch as commodity futures have little or no correlation to the stock market, the added diversity was viewed as providing less risk for the foundation's overall investment. The foundation, in this instance, proposed to invest 10% of its portfolio in this fashion.

The IRS considered a situation where a private foundation wanted to accept a contribution of a working interest in an oil and gas exploration and development venture. The foundation was subject to calls for capital; it was obligated to pay the expenses of ongoing maintenance and exploration. There was no public market for sale of this interest; any liquidation of it would have entailed sale to the other investors in the project at a substantial discount. Noting that the project had been highly profitable and that the foundation's share of the venture was 1%, the IRS ruled that the interest of the foundation in the venture would not constitute a jeopardizing investment.

A private foundation's involvement in a limited partnership trading in the futures and forward markets was held by the IRS's lawyers to not be a jeopardizing investment. The foundation invested a "significant amount" of its assets in this partnership. The examining agent contended that the foundation could have received a better return with less risk in one or more other investment vehicles. Nonetheless, IRS legal counsel concluded that the foundation managers took reasonable measures and exercised ordinary business care and prudence prior to investing in the partnership, on the basis of these facts:

- The foundation managers were actively involved in establishing the partnership and selecting four advisors to make allocations of foundation assets to counterbalance the investment.

- Special conditions were negotiated that allowed the foundation to withdraw its funds at any time on written notice prior to the end of the normal term of the partnership.

- Two legal opinions concluding that the establishment of the partnership and the foundation's investment in it was not a jeopardizing investment were secured by the foundation prior to making the investment.

- There was no relationship among the foundation, its managers, or the investment advisors that would have been furthered by the investment.

This determination by the IRS is significant. Although the foundation clearly placed a substantial portion of its assets in a high-risk investment, the IRS's lawyers said that neither of these elements were "necessarily dispositive" of the issue as to whether a jeopardizing investment was present. Diversification was said to be "one factor" to be considered. This statement may be the most important of all: "[M]erely because the end result is not as beneficial to the financial interests of a private foundation as another investment might have been is not grounds in itself for finding that a jeopardizing investment was made."

An IRS ruling concerned a reorganization of a hospital system. Within the system was a supporting organization (see Chapter 1) that had three for-profit subsidiaries, each of which was a risky venture. As a result of the reorganization, the supporting organization became a private foundation. The IRS sidestepped the issue as to whether the foundation's continued ownership of these ventures constituted jeopardizing investments, by ruling that the rules did not apply because, when the subsidiaries were created, their parent was a public charity. (In any event, the stock in the three corporations had to be sold because of the excess business holdings rules [see Chapter 8].)

The IRS ruled that "approval of an investment procedure governing investments to be made in the future is not possible." This position reflects the fact that advance approval of investment procedures by the IRS would constitute a determination prior to the investment, would not be on an investment-by-investment basis, and would unavoidably preclude application of the "prudent trustee" approach. The IRS will, however, rule as to a currently proposed investment.

If a private foundation changes the form or terms of an investment, it is considered to have entered into a new investment on the date of the change. Thus, a determination as to whether the change in the investment causes the investment to be a jeopardizing one is made as of that time.

DONATED ASSETS

The jeopardizing investment rules do not apply to investments made by a person who subsequently contributed them to a private foundation. Also, these rules are inapplicable to an investment that is acquired by a foundation solely as a result of a corporate reorganization. If a foundation, however, furnishes any consideration to a person in connection with these types of transfers, the foundation is treated as having made an investment in the amount of the consideration.

In one instance, an estate (where the decedent was the founder of the private foundation involved) proposed to gratuitously transfer assets to the foundation. The IRS ruled that, inasmuch as the foundation, in acquiring these assets, was not incurring any obligation to use its resources in the future in connection with maintenance of the gifted assets and thus would be "in a position in which it only [stood] to gain and [had] nothing to lose," the jeopardy investment rules were not triggered.

The various private foundation rules are not exclusive. For example, if a foundation purchased an active business enterprise in the form of a sole proprietorship, it may well incur tax penalties under the excess business holdings rules (see Chapter 8) as well as be penalized pursuant to the jeopardizing investment rules.

PRUDENT INVESTMENT STANDARDS

The jeopardizing investment rules do not exempt or relieve any person from compliance with any federal or state law imposing any obligation, duty, responsibility, or other standard of conduct with respect to the operation or administration of an entity to which these rules applies. Likewise, state law cannot exempt or relieve any person from any obligation, duty, responsibility, or other standard of conduct imposed by the jeopardizing investment rules. In selecting prudent investments, foundation managers must take into consideration their need to satisfy the foundation rules, including the mandatory payout rules (see Chapter 4).

Investment Principles In General

The managers of a private foundation can be guided by the *prudent investor* rules in evaluating proposed investments, whether from the standpoint of the general rules as to fiduciary responsibility (see Chapter 12) or the jeopardizing investment rules. An investment policy that follows the prudent investor rules should—theoretically—prevent the making of a jeopardizing investment. These standards, initially developed by the American Bar Association (ABA) in connection with the administration of trusts, provide that "a trustee is under a duty to the beneficiaries to invest and manage the funds of a trust as a prudent investor would, in light of the purposes, terms, distribution requirements, and other circumstances of the trust." The *business judgment* rule requires essentially the same standard for nonprofit corporations and trustees in regard to the management of endowment funds and restricted gifts or bequests.

The prudent investor rules are codified and have been adopted as statutory law by many states. The Uniform Prudent Investor Act (UPIA), which is applicable in connection with trusts, was finalized in 1995. The Uniform Management of Institutional Funds Act (UMIFA), completed in 1972, applies to incorporated and unincorporated charitable organizations and certain government organizations. The UMIFA has been adopted (in various forms) by 47 states and the District of Columbia. Under the UPIA and UMIFA, trustees and directors are permitted to delegate their responsibilities in connection with investment activity to professional managers. The UPIA directs trustees to periodically review the entire portfolio; it does not require diversification. The UMIFA endorsed the total return concept (discussed later in this chapter) and encourages diversification into a sufficient range of assets to achieve a balance as to risk. The prudent-trustee approach in the tax regulations, which suggest an investment-by-investment approach, is not entirely consistent (nor entirely inconsistent) with the prudent-investor rule and the standards of the UMIFA. IRS rulings (particularly the private ones) acknowledge the prudence of diversification of investments and the need to consider each investment's relationship to the whole in achieving this objective. (On one of these occasions, the IRS observed: "Generally, diversification is a prudent strategy for management of investment assets.") Foundation managers should acknowledge the inconsistency between the federal tax law and state law in these regards, and take both sets of rules into account in meeting their obligation to prudently invest the foundation's funds.

The UMIFA is in the process of being replaced by the Uniform Prudent Management of Institutional Funds Act (UPMIFA). The UPMIFA, prepared in 2006, has been adopted (in various forms) by 14 states and the District of Columbia; more enactments may be anticipated. The highlights of the UPMIFA include greater investment freedom portfolio managers have in the selection of assets for the portfolio, prudent management of costs in relationship to the assets, express authorization of the total return principle, an optional rule by which expenditures in excess of 7% of total return (see Chapter 4) are presumed imprudent, procedures for releasing restrictions on small institutional funds (less than $25,000) held for a long period of time (at least 20 years), and application of this law to funds in any entity form.

The prudent person rule, first set forth by a court in 1830 (and thus then referenced as the *prudent man* rule), directed trustees to "observe how men of prudence, discretion, and intelligence manage their own affairs, not in regard to speculation, but in regard to the permanent disposition of their funds, considering the probable income, as well as the probable safety of the capital to be invested." In an effort to modernize this rule, the ABA guidance cautioned that the facts and circumstances of each investor must be considered in selecting appropriate investments. Therefore, a private foundation's financial managers should be familiar with basic contemporary investment concepts and strategies, while, as noted, taking into account the unique emphases of the private foundation rules.

Unless the trustees or directors of a private foundation possess the expertise and have the time to manage the foundation's investments with the requisite care, skill, and caution, they have a duty to delegate the investment process to competent managers and advisors. Fees charged by professional investment managers may be modest when viewed in relation to the prospects of enhanced yield over time and protection against excise taxation for one or more jeopardizing investments.

Evaluating Investment Alternatives

Always striving to avoid a jeopardy investment, the financial managers of a private foundation should constantly evaluate the portion of the foundation's funds that can suitably be invested in a permanent fashion. Depending on the answers to the following questions, the managers might prudently keep only a part of the foundation's assets in cash-type interest-bearing accounts. Alternatively, the foundation may be fully (or nearly fully) invested in equities, bonds, real estate, and "alternative investments." The questions that form the basis for investment decisions are these:

1. *What rate of return should the private foundation reasonably expect on its investments?* Unlike investors generally (some of whom might seek maximum capital appreciation), a foundation must take into consideration the mandatory distribution rules, which basically require that a foundation pay out (in money or other assets) an amount equal to 5% of the fair market value of its investment assets (see Chapter 4). Thus, without regard to other factors, such as a goal of expanding programs or enabling principal to keep pace with inflation, a foundation tries to achieve at least a 5% current (nominal) return on its investments.

2. *Should the foundation use a total return investment policy?* The answer to this question, for a private foundation, is related to its answer to the previous question. A foundation investing for *total return* defines its income to include dividends, rent, interest, and other current

payments, plus increase in the value of its assets or minus a decline in the value. A foundation in this position would expect to fund its grants with dividends, interest, and capital gains. Since the total return approach typically embodies capital gains, this policy can have a modest advantage in relation to the payout rules if the foundation distributes one or more items of appreciated property rather than sell property to generate funds to make cash distributions.

3. *For what length of time can the funds be invested?* The foundation's need for liquidity should be projected for a number of years. To choose prudent investments, the foundation must know when, or if, the funds might be required to meet its annual distribution requirement, purchase a needed asset, or satisfy some other financial obligation or program goal. For a foundation with significant illiquid investment assets, such as real estate, this question is particularly pertinent. The value of the investment real estate is included in the minimum investment return asset base, for purposes of calculating the 5% payout, even if the property is not currently yielding income. In this situation, it is highly desirable (or, quite likely, necessary) that the foundation's other investment assets generate a return that is sufficiently above the minimum investment percentage.

4. *Can the foundation afford a loss on its principal?* The answer to this question reflects the level of risk that the foundation perceives to be prudent. The rate of return from interest, dividends, and/or increase in assets' value is related to the possibility that the original investment can be lost. The higher the risk of loss, the higher the expected return (discussed later in this chapter). The possibility that an investment might decline in value (instead of increase, as anticipated) is not necessarily evidence that the investment is a jeopardizing one. The issue here is primarily to evaluate the foundation's ability to meet its financial obligations (including those imposed by law).

5. *How secure are the foundation's funding sources?* Although many private foundations are endowed, some foundations are dependent (partially or fully) on new funding to support the conduct of their programs. Each foundation must evaluate the stability of its funding sources to project the level of contingency, or emergency, reserves it may require. For example, a foundation that sponsors ongoing programs receives annual funding from members of the family of its creators, with that funding dependent on their income level and allowable charitable contribution deductions. Assume that this foundation commonly makes annual disbursements that are well in excess of the required amount and, in some years, in excess of its current annual funding. This foundation would prudently maintain its funds in investments with a low risk of loss in principal value (in that funds may be needed at a time when the asset value is low).

6. *Is the foundation's staff capable of overseeing the investments?* Special talents and training are required to successfully manage a fully diversified investment portfolio. This question has two components. As evidenced by stock market fluctuations over the years, no one knows when or whether stock values will go up or down. A foundation's managers should evaluate their knowledge and experience, and consider engaging outside professional asset managers. In a questioning by the IRS about an investment that resulted in a loss, the fact that the foundation used the services of a qualified independent investment advisor or manager would go a long way in sidestepping a tax penalty.

7. *How will economic conditions impact the investment?* Fixed-money investments, such as certificates of deposit and U.S. Treasury obligations, fluctuate in value in relation to the prevailing interest rate and overall economic factors, but have a determinable value if held to maturity. Conversely, the value of common stocks, real estate, and tangibles rise or fall in relation to a multitude of factors, including a company's earnings, investor moods, and inflationary or deflationary conditions. A foundation's economic advisors should anticipate or successfully predict coming economic conditions to properly diversify its investments.

Alternative Investments

Many private foundations (and other tax-exempt organizations) are choosing to place some of their investment assets in *alternative investments*, such as hedge funds and offshore partnerships. These investments trigger a multitude of tax and other law considerations that are not present in connection with an investment constituting a portfolio of marketable (U.S.) securities. Foundation managers should be aware of the host of tax law issues inherent in these alternative investment vehicles and ventures. Here are the principal questions to ask.

Form of Investment Entity

- Is the investment entity a partnership or a limited liability company taxable as a partnership (where income passes through, retaining its character as interest, dividend, other ordinary income or capital gain)?

- Is the investment entity a subchapter S corporation (where all income is taxable to a private foundation as unrelated business income [see Chapter 8])?

- Is the investment entity a standard corporation (where it is taxed on the income generated)?

- Is the investment entity an offshore company that does not report any U.S. taxable income?

Character of Income

- Is the foundation's share of distributable income comprised of passive income (interest, dividends, rents, and royalties, that may escape unrelated business taxation but be subject to the foundation excise tax on net investment income [see Chapter 3])?

- If ordinary taxable income is distributed, are there any deductible (including allocable) expenses, such as investment management, legal, and accounting fees?

- Is current income or gains from options, futures, derivatives, currency transactions, and types of alternative investment income taxable?

- Does the venture operate an active business and/or have indebtedness (potential for creation of unrelated business income)?

- Does the partnership or limited liability company (LLC) agreement provide protection against unrelated business income for tax-exempt partners?

- Does the venture operate outside the U.S. (causing special law to become applicable)?

Fiduciary Responsibility/Jeopardizing Investment

- Does the private foundation engage independent investment advisors?

- Were the investments purchased under a plan to diversify the foundation's investments in adherence to prudent investor rules?

- What portion of the foundation's overall investment assets is in one or more alternative investments?

- Was an opinion of legal counsel obtained, concluding that the investment(s) would not be jeopardizing?

- Is the investment readily marketable? (If not, there is greater risk.)

- Does a lock-in feature (meaning that funds cannot be withdrawn from the venture) mean that the value of the investment should be discounted?

Tax Basis/Gain on Disposition

- Does the capital account (reported by the venture on Form K-1) reflect the foundation's tax basis? Is a system in place to record changes in the tax basis?

- Does the venture book increases and decreases in value into the capital accounts?

- Do special rules concerning allocations of deductions apply?

- Does the investment entity have assets that are debt financed (as to unrelated debt-financed income)?

- Will gain on sale of the investment asset be taxable due to an acquisition indebtedness?

Valuation Issues

- Does the investment manager provide periodic valuation information for calculation of average values (for minimum investment return purposes (see Chapter 4) and financial reporting purposes (see Chapter 10).

- Do terms of the investment limit sale or withdrawal so that a discount in value is appropriate?

- Must the investment be valued monthly or annually?

Excess Business Holdings (See Chapter 8)

- Does the foundation own more than 2% of the venture?

- What percentage of the venture do disqualified persons with respect to the foundation (see Chapter 2) own?

- Is more than 95% of the income produced by the investment passive in nature?

Tax Filing Requirements In General

- Must the income from the investment be reported and taxed on Form 990-T (see Chapter 10)?

- Was a Form K-1 received for a partnership investment that reports the unrelated business income character of distributions?

- If more than $100,000 was transferred to a foreign corporation or partnership, has the foundation determined the forms to be filed (discussed later in this chapter)?

- Must the foundation make deposits of estimated income tax?

Filing Requirements Where Investment Entity Is Foreign Corporation

- Was more than $100,000 transferred to the corporation within a 12-month period? (If the answer is "yes," the filing of IRS Form 926 may be required.)

- Does the investment represent at least a 10% ownership in the corporation? (If the answer is "yes," the filing of IRS Forms 926 and 5471 may be required.)

- During the tax year, was the investment interest reduced from more than 10% to less than 1%? (If the answer is "yes," Form 5471 may be required.)

- Did the foundation own 50% or more of the corporation for at least 30 consecutive days during the tax year? (If the answer is "yes," Form 5471 may be required.) (Also see Chapter 8.)

- Is the entity a passive foreign investment company? (If the answer is "yes," IRS Form 8621 may be required.)

Filing Requirements Where Investment Entity Is Foreign Partnership

- Was more than $100,000 transferred to the partnership within a 12-month period? (If the answer is "yes," the filing of IRS Form 8865 may be required.)

- Does the investment in the partnership represent ownership of at least 10%? (If the answer is "yes," the filing of Form 8865 may be required.)

- During the tax year, did the partnership interest increase or decrease by at least 10%? (If the answer is "yes," the filing of IRS Form 8865 may be required.)

- Is the investment entity a foreign disregarded entity? (If the answer is "yes," the filing of IRS Form 8858 may be required.)

- Does the foundation have a financial interest in or signatory authority over foreign financial accounts, the aggregate value of which exceeds $10,000? (If the answer is "yes," the filing of Form 90–22.1 may be required.)

- Does the foundation hold more than a 50% interest in a partnership that has legal title to foreign financial accounts, the aggregate value of which exceeds $10,000? (If the answer is "yes," the filing of Form 90–22.1 may be required.)

Facing the Unknown

In seeking answers to the seven questions concerning the evaluation of investment alternatives, a healthy dose of skepticism and an appreciation of the uncertainty that abounds in the realm of investing is important for foundation managers to have so as to avoid (or try to avoid) a jeopardizing investment. The financial markets in which a foundation must choose to place its funds are influenced daily by forces (including international ones) that are obviously beyond its control. Who knows whether a stock's value will go up or down, a global stock fund will sustain its yield, or the U.S. dollar will go up or down in relation to a foreign currency?

Diversification is an important technique designed to help face the unknown. It essentially reflects this fundamental maxim: "Don't put all your eggs in one basket." A prudently balanced investment portfolio contains a variety of financial instruments—stocks, bonds, real estate, and the like. The mix of investment types assumes that some go up, some go down, and in the long run the averages will provide a desirable stream of income. It is not prudent to maintain all of the funds invested in fixed-money or interest-bearing securities, or all in equities. The types of investments available to private foundations (and everyone else) are as follows:

Fixed money value (principal dollar amount fixed)
>   Interest-bearing checking account
>
>   Money market account
>
>   Certificate of deposit
>
>   Treasury bills
>
>   Series EE bonds
>
>   Fixed annuities

Variable money value (principal value fluctuates with prevailing interest rates but interest rate on investment is usually fixed)
>   Treasury notes and bonds
>
>   Mortgage-backed bonds
>
>   Corporate bonds
>
>   Municipal bonds
>
>   Annuities or universal life insurance policies
>
>   Derivatives of the above variable securities

Equity investments (principal value and dividend rate varies)
>   Common stock
>
>   Preferred stock
>
>   Convertible bonds

Real estate
>   Commercial real estate (office, store, hotel, or factory buildings)
>
>   Residential real estate (single-family or multiperson apartment or condominium buildings)

Undeveloped land

Agricultural land

Tangibles (the first three of these are also *collectibles*)
Gold and silver

Antiques

Works of art

Minerals

Commodities (such as oil)

Alternative investments
Venture capital funds

Hedge funds

Offshore entities

Distressed securities

Emerging market securities

A classically diversified investment portfolio contains some investments in nearly all of these categories. The portion of the total investments held in each category is largely dependent on the private foundation's tolerance of risk. Here are the traditional investment ratios:

	Conservative	**Moderate**	**Risky**
Cash and bonds	80%	40%	30%
Equities	20	55	60
Real estate	0	5	5
Hedge funds/venture capital	0	0	5
Total investments	100%	100%	100%

If the board of a foundation, with $1 million to invest permanently, adopted the historically conservative approach to investing, the foundation would be invested $300,000 in short-term cash and bonds, $500,000 in long-term bonds, and $200,000 in common stocks, with no investments in real estate, gold, or commodities.

The investments within each category might be further diversified. A fixed-money portfolio, for example, may have debt instruments with staggered maturity dates and credit ratings, since fixed-return investments can also fluctuate in value and thus have inherent risk of loss. The $300,000 in the preceding example might include $100,000 of 5-year bonds, $100,000 of 7-year bonds, and $100,000 of 30-year bonds. Similarly, a portfolio of common stocks may include stock of companies in different lines of business, such as automobile manufacturing, pharmaceuticals, computer software, and banking.

Risk versus Return

A private foundation should carefully identify the funds that are suitable for each category of investment type (again, taking into consideration its unique circumstances, such as the mandatory payout and the excise tax on net investment income). The possibility of a higher yield or overall return provided by common stocks is not always worth the level of risk inherent in that type of investment. Thus, a private foundation investing funds that have been set aside for a multiyear charitable project (see Chapter 4) should be seeking a comfortable rate of interest but avoid investing the funds in technology stocks.

The relationship of risk to investment return is commonly understood. The less the uncertainty, the lower the yield; as uncertainty about risk of loss increases, so too (at least in theory) does the yield. The reason a six-month certificate of deposit pays a relatively low interest rate is that (absent a bank collapse or some banking system crisis) no risk is taken by the investor. Likewise, the reason that college and university (and other charitable institutions') endowment funds are enjoying annual earnings in excess of 20% is their heavy investment in hedge funds and other alternative investments.

PROGRAM-RELATED INVESTMENTS

As discussed, the federal tax law imposes a prudent investor requirement on private foundations but it provides an exception from that requirement for purchases of business assets (such as stock) or loans to businesses or individuals that further a charitable purpose of the foundation. The acquisition of these assets or the making of these loans is known as a program-related investment.

A program-related investment, by a private foundation, is not—by statute—a jeopardizing investment. A *program-related investment* is an investment by a foundation, the primary purpose of which is to accomplish one or more charitable purposes. Also, the production of income or the appreciation of property may not be a significant purpose of the investment. The tax regulations added a third characteristic of this type of an investment, in that no purpose of the investment may be the furthering of substantial legislative or any political campaign activities (see Chapter 3). Conspicuously absent from the elements of the program-related investment are the proscriptions on private inurement and private benefit (*id.*), simply because persons connected with the investment vehicle unavoidably benefit from the investment, albeit as a by-product of achievement of a larger—charitable—purpose.

An investment is considered as made primarily to accomplish one or more charitable purposes if it significantly furthers the accomplishment of a private foundation's tax-exempt activities and if the investment would not have been made but for the relationship between the investment and the conduct of the activities. An investment in a functionally related business (see Chapter 8) is regarded as an investment made primarily to accomplish charitable purposes.

In determining whether a significant purpose of an investment is the production of income or the appreciation of property, it is relevant to determine whether for-profit investors would be likely to make the investment on the same terms as the foundation's proposed investment. The fact that an investment produces significant income or capital appreciation is not, in the absence of other factors, conclusive evidence of this type of significant purpose.

The term *program-related investment* is potentially confusing. A more apt term might be *program-related expenditure*. This type of outlay is not an *investment*, in the conventional use of that word, which is intended or expected to return to the private foundation the capital that is transferred plus a market rate of financial return on those expenditures. Rather, expenditures of this type are an alternative to an outright grant, such as the making of a loan to an individual for educational purposes instead of making a scholarship grant. Reasons why a foundation may buy a business asset or make a loan to a business, rather than making a grant to a charitable organization (or a governmental body), include an effort to avoid a wasting of funds and/or the hope of (someday) receiving back the capital is extended. Central to the concept of a program-related investment is the fact that the recipient of the investment does not need to be a tax-exempt charitable organization.

Examples of program-related investments provided in the tax regulations focus on investments in "small business enterprises." The charitable objective, from the foundation's standpoint, is the provision of employment for disadvantaged individuals (notwithstanding the concomitant provision of economic advancement for those who are the owners of the enterprise). Another charitable outcome in this context is, by providing a market for the sale of goods, the economic development of depressed areas.

The IRS has issued a considerable number of rulings as to what constitutes a program-related investment (almost all of which were favorable to the private foundations involved). A review of these rulings reveals that the IRS has routinely and consistently approved purchases of business assets, as well as loans to businesses, as program-related investments. Likewise, the IRS has regularly recognized economic development of a disadvantaged area as a justification for the purchase of a business interest by a private foundation. Also, the IRS has issued a raft of rulings endorsing, as program-related investments, expenditures for business assets because the investment reduced the burdens of a governmental body; these businesses include the operation of a convention center, theater, hotel, or parking lot, as well as the purchase of professional sports teams.

Specific illustrations of program-related investments include:

- An investment by a foundation in a fund established to invest in businesses in low-income communities. The businesses were owned or controlled by members of disadvantaged groups, who had not been able to obtain conventional financing on reasonable terms. This fund was expected to provide an economic return, albeit lower than that from a typical private investment fund. The primary purpose of the investment was to advance these charitable ends: enhance social welfare, fight prejudice and discrimination, and promote the economic self-sufficiency of low-income communities.

- An investment by a foundation in a for-profit reinsurance company that was established to address increasing medical malpractice insurance premiums in a state, which was leading to an exodus of physicians. The investment was made for the charitable purpose of promoting the health of the community by enabling physicians to, on a financially feasible basis, locate or continue to practice in the state and thus ameliorate the adverse health consequences resulting from the lack of medical providers.

- An investment by a foundation, to assist a city in revitalizing its downtown, for the purpose of funding the construction of apartment buildings and the renovation of existing buildings, and the making of loans to public charities which in turn made loans to for-profit developers. The charitable purpose served was combating community deterioration.

- Low-interest loans by a foundation to blind individuals to enable them to establish themselves in business.

- An investment by a foundation to provide housing in a deteriorating city for low-income individuals, with special assistance for the elderly and handicapped.

- An investment by a foundation to rehabilitate a building in a deteriorating neighborhood, formerly used for warehousing and manufacturing purposes and to be used for retail and office use, to stimulate the economy in a depressed area.

- A loan by a foundation to a limited partnership for the construction of a hotel in a blighted and deteriorated downtown area, to aid in the rehabilitation of the area.

- A loan by a foundation to rehabilitate an inner-city area by creating residential units for low- and moderate-income individuals, and for commercial space, for the purpose of eliminating community deterioration, and reduce crime and juvenile delinquency.

- A loan by a foundation to a minority-owned bank that engaged in making real estate and commercial loans to minorities to prevent the bank from failing.

- An investment by a foundation in a for-profit financial intermediary formed to finance and promote development of environmentally oriented businesses, in fulfillment of the foundation's purpose of supporting biodiversity and environmental sustainability.

- A loan by a foundation to for-profit developers to purchase environmentally sensitive undeveloped land in areas subject to development pressure, for the purpose of preserving environmentally significant land.

Program-related investments can be made with public charities and other nonprofit organizations. Here are some illustrations:

- An investment by a foundation in an organization to enable it to develop a performing arts theater, in furtherance of the recipient's educational and cultural purposes

- An investment by a foundation in a museum in an economically depressed area, in part to revive the area

- A loan by a foundation to a public charity for redevelopment and rehabilitation of a blighted area by consolidating small deteriorated properties, and for clearing land and preparing it for resale to developers and other businesses

- A loan by a foundation to a public charity to establish a fund for use by local charities, to alleviate cash-flow problems experienced by them

- A loan by a foundation to a public charity to assist it in restoring a historically significant building, to be used for charitable purposes

- A loan by a foundation to a tax-exempt school to enable it to renovate its facilities

- A loan by a foundation to a nonprofit cooperative that could not obtain commercial financing on economically feasible terms, to facilitate the provision of communications services to the cooperative's member nonprofit organizations

- A deposit by a foundation into a loan program operated by a public charity that provides grants and loans to neighborhood-based organizations that provide affordable housing and essential social services to the poor in economically depressed areas

- Loans by a foundation to public charities for construction projects in disadvantaged areas to revitalize inner-city areas suffering from blight and decay

- A loan by a foundation to a public charity, that addressed issues concerning the environment and utilization of global resources, to be used for the creation of an endowment fund

- A loan by a foundation to a public charity that will construct and equip a research center

- A purchase by a foundation of no-interest bonds from a public charity that provided ten-year, no-interest, first-mortgage loans to low-income families

- A purchase by a foundation of stock in a professional baseball team, pursuant to a plan undertaken by a local government, in an effort to cause the team to remain in the area, where the government could not continue to endeavor to retain the team due to inadequate funding and other restrictions (lessening the burdens of government)

- Deposits by a foundation into banks to guarantee loans to public charities to finance construction of child-care facilities

- Loans and investments by a foundation to promote economic development in a foreign country that had a low standard of living, energy and food shortages, and natural disasters

- Investment in and operation, by a foundation, of a farm in a foreign country, previously conducted as a for-profit operation by the founder of the foundation, which became operated after his death as an exempt demonstration project

- Investments by a foundation in an angel investment fund for businesses owned by members of disadvantaged groups in low-income communities

Once it has been determined that an investment by a private foundation constitutes a program-related investment, it does not cease to qualify as such an investment, as long as any changes in the form or terms of the investment are made primarily for charitable purposes and not for any significant purpose involving the production of income or the appreciation in property. A change made in the form or terms of a program-related investment for the prudent protection of a foundation's investment ordinarily will not cause the investment to cease to qualify as a program-related one. A program-related investment may cease to be this type of investment because of a critical change in circumstances, such as where it is serving an illegal purpose or a private purpose of one or more of the foundation's managers. An investment that stops being a program-related one because of a critical change in circumstances will not subject the foundation to a jeopardizing investment penalty before the 30th day after the date on which the foundation, or any of its managers, has actual knowledge of the critical change.

A program-related investment constitutes a qualifying distribution for a private foundation (see Chapter 4). Expenditure responsibility (see Chapter 5) must be exercised by a private foundation for program-related investments.

IMPOSITION OF EXCISE TAX PENALTIES

If a private foundation invests an amount in a manner that jeopardizes the carrying out of any of its charitable purposes, a consequence can be imposition of one or more penalty excise taxes. The penalties that can be imposed in this context principally are initial and additional taxes, levied on the private foundation involved.

Initial Taxes

An initial tax (also known as a first-tier tax) is imposed on a private foundation on the making of a jeopardy investment, at the rate of 10% of the amount so invested, for each tax year or part of a year during the taxable period. This tax must be paid by the foundation.

In any case in which this initial tax is imposed on a private foundation, a tax is imposed on the participation of a foundation manager in the making of the investment, where the manager knew that the investment is jeopardizing the carrying out of any of the foundation's charitable purposes. This tax is equal to 10% of the amount so invested for each tax year, or part of a year, of the foundation in the taxable period. With respect to any one jeopardizing investment, the maximum amount of this tax per person is $10,000. Managers found guilty under these rules are jointly and severally liable for the tax(es). This tax, which must be paid by any participating foundation manager, is not imposed where the participation is not willful and is due to reasonable cause.

When a Manager *Knows*

A foundation manager is considered to have participated in the making of an investment, *knowing* that it is a jeopardizing one, only if the manager:

- Has actual knowledge of sufficient facts so that, based solely on those facts, the investment would be a jeopardizing one

- Is aware that the investment under these circumstances may violate the federal tax law rules governing jeopardizing investments

- Negligently fails to make reasonable attempts to ascertain whether the investment is a jeopardizing one or is in fact aware that it is a jeopardizing investment

The word *knowing* does not mean *having reason to know*. Evidence tending to show that a foundation manager has reason to know of a particular fact or particular, however, is relevant in determining whether the manager had actual knowledge of the fact or rule. Evidence tending to show that a foundation manager has reason to know of sufficient facts so that, based solely on the facts, an investment would be (or is) a jeopardizing one is relevant in determining whether the manager has actual knowledge of the facts. Thus, the pertinent facts and circumstances are examined to find out why the manager did not know of the relevant facts or law. To be excused from the potential tax liability, the foundation manager essentially must be ignorant of the pertinent facts or law.

For example, the board of trustees of a private foundation consists of ten members, three of whom comprise a finance committee. The written investment policy of the foundation provides that the board approves investment decisions proposed by the finance committee, based on the advice of independent investment advisor. The members of the foundation's board who are not on the finance committee should not be assumed to have knowledge of or otherwise be aware of details discussed in the committee's meetings.

A foundation manager's participation in the making of a jeopardizing investment is *willful* if it is voluntary, conscious, and intentional. A motive to avoid the restrictions of the law or the incurrence of a tax is not necessary to make this type of participation willful. A foundation manager's participation in a jeopardizing investment is not willful if the manager does not know that it is a jeopardizing investment.

A foundation manager's actions are due to *reasonable cause* if the manager has exercised his or her responsibility on behalf of the foundation with ordinary business care and prudence. The *participation* of any foundation manager in the making of an investment consists of any manifestation of approval of the investment. Clearly, a vote as a board member to approve an investment is participation. Board members who do not attend meetings of the board but sanction investment decisions may be derelict as to their fiduciary responsibility but their inability to participate in the investment decision and resulting lack of knowledge may shield them from these tax penalties. If members of the board of directors of a private foundation receive a board information packet revealing the investment under consideration, they are deemed to have the requisite knowledge; however, the tax penalties apply only if they somehow participate in the decision to approve the investment. Ignorance is tax penalty bliss.

Reliance on Legal Counsel

If a foundation manager, after full disclosure of the factual situation to legal counsel, including house counsel, relies on the advice of that counsel, expressed in a reasoned legal opinion that an investment would not jeopardize the carrying out of any of the private foundation's charitable purposes, the foundation manager's participation in the investment will ordinarily not be considered knowing or willful, and will ordinarily be considered due to reasonable cause. This is the case even where the investment is subsequently determined to be a jeopardizing one. A lawyer is not qualified to opine on the appropriateness of an investment as such. Thus, a legal opinion must address a situation where, as a matter of law, the investment is excepted from classification as a jeopardizing investment, such as because the investment is a recognized form of prudent investment or it is a program-related investment. A lawyer might seek an opinion of a qualified investment advisor and incorporate that in his or her reasoned opinion.

A written legal opinion is considered *reasoned*, even if it reaches a conclusion that is subsequently determined to be incorrect, as long as the opinion addresses the facts and applicable law. A written legal opinion will not be considered reasoned if it does nothing more than recite the facts and state a conclusion. The absence of advice of legal counsel with respect to an investment, however, does not, by itself, give rise to an inference that a foundation manager participated in the investment knowingly, willfully, or without reasonable cause.

Likewise, if a foundation manager, after full disclosure of the facts to a qualified investment counsel, relies on the advice of that counsel, the foundation manager's participation in failing to provide for the long- and short-term financial needs of the foundation will ordinarily not be considered knowing or willful, and will ordinarily be considered due to reasonable cause. For this rule to apply, the advice must have been derived in a manner consistent with generally accepted practices of individuals who are qualified investment counsel and expressed in writing that a particular investment will provide for these financial needs of the foundation. Again, this is the case even where the investment is subsequently determined to be a jeopardizing one.

Additional Taxes

An additional tax (also known as a second-tier tax) is imposed on a private foundation in a case in which the initial tax is imposed and the investment is not removed from jeopardy during the taxable period. The *taxable period* is the period beginning with the date on which the amount is invested in a jeopardizing manner and ending on the earliest of the following dates:

- The date on which the IRS mails a notice of deficiency with respect to the initial tax imposed on the foundation

- The date on which the initial tax is assessed

- The date on which the amount invested is removed from jeopardy

This additional tax, which is to be paid by the foundation, is at the rate of 25% of the amount of the investment. Where this tax is imposed and a foundation manager refuses to agree to part or all of the removal of the investment from jeopardy, a tax is imposed on the manager at the rate of 5% of the amount of the investment. With respect to any one investment, the maximum amount of this tax per person is $20,000. Where, however, more than one foundation manager is liable for an additional tax with respect to a jeopardizing investment, all of the foundation's managers are jointly and severally liable for the tax.

CORRECTION

A jeopardizing investment must be corrected (unless the foundation involved wants to watch the IRS confiscate its assets [see below]). The *correction period* is the period beginning on the date on which the taxable event occurs and ending 90 days after the date of mailing of a notice of deficiency with respect to the additional tax imposed in connection with the event, extended by any period in which a deficiency cannot be assessed and any other period that the IRS determines is reasonable and necessary to bring about correction of the jeopardizing investment. This period is suspended during the course of any litigation. In this setting, a *taxable event* is an act or failure to act giving rise to liability for tax under the jeopardizing investment rules. This event occurs on the date a jeopardizing investment takes place. *Correction* means removal of the investment from jeopardy.

An investment that jeopardizes the carrying out of charitable purposes is considered to be removed from jeopardy when the investment is sold or otherwise disposed of, and the proceeds from the disposition are not invested in a manner that jeopardizes the carrying out of the foundation's

exempt purposes. Correction of a jeopardizing investment may be difficult (if not impossible)—there is no court opinion or IRS ruling on the
point—because the asset is not marketable. An effort to maximize funds
from the investment may be of help in avoiding the additional tax.

A change by a private foundation in the form or terms of a jeopardizing investment results in the removal of the investment from jeopardy
if, after the change, the investment no longer jeopardizes the carrying out
of the foundation's charitable purposes. The making of one jeopardizing
investment by a foundation and a subsequent change by the foundation of the investment for another jeopardizing investment is generally
treated as only one jeopardizing investment. A jeopardizing investment
cannot be removed from jeopardy by a transfer from a foundation to
another foundation that is related to the transferor foundation, unless the
investment is a program-related investment made by the transferee foundation.

TAX ABATEMENT

The IRS has the discretion to abate this initial tax when a private foundation
establishes that the violation was due to reasonable cause and not to willful
neglect, and timely corrects the violation.

Where the act or failure to act that gave rise to the additional tax is
corrected within the correction period, the tax will not be assessed, or if
assessed will be abated, or if collected will be credited or refunded. The
collection period is suspended during the course of any litigation.

A request for abatement is submitted on Form 4720. Details about
any corrective action taken and the value of recovered property must
be described. If the matter remains uncorrected, an explanation is to be
attached. The information provided is the basis on which the IRS will decide
whether to abate a tax.

THIRD-TIER EXCISE TAX REGIME

As noted, the sanctions underlying the jeopardizing investments rules
include a first-tier and a second-tier tax. The termination tax (see Chapter 3)
serves as a third-tier tax. This is the ultimate sanction, with the federal government able to confiscate the value of all federal tax benefits the foundation
and its substantial contributors ever received derived from tax exemption
and charitable tax deductions, applicable where a foundation engaged in
willful, flagrant, or repeated acts or failures to act that cause voluntary,
conscious, and intentional transgressions of the jeopardizing investments
rules.

SUMMARY

This chapter provided a summary of the private foundation investment rules, including a summary of the prudent investor standards in general. The chapter explained the concept of jeopardizing investments, summarized the rules applicable to contributed assets, and summarized the program-related investments rules. The chapter concluded by describing the various excise tax penalties applicable in this context and the tax abatement rules, as well as the third-tier tax regime.

8

BUSINESS HOLDINGS RULES

The purpose of this chapter is to explain the federal tax rules concerning the holding of business interests and the conduct of business by private foundations. There are two aspects of this matter. Foundations are the only type of tax-exempt organization that is subject to tax laws pertaining to their ability to own stock and otherwise hold forms of business interests; this body of law concerns *excess business holdings*. Another element of the law applies to tax-exempt organizations generally (and thus to private foundations): the *unrelated business rules*. Specifically, this chapter will:

- Provide a summary of the excess business holding rules.
- Define the phrase *business enterprise*.
- Discuss the concept of the *passive business*.
- Explore the investment partnership rules.
- Summarize the applicable percentage limitations.
- Discuss permitted and excess holdings.
- Summarize the rules concerning *functionally related businesses*.
- Describe the various excise taxes.
- Describe the tax abatement rules.
- Revisit the third-tier tax regime.
- Summarize the unrelated business law rules.

- Discuss regularly carried on businesses.

- Discuss the concepts of *related* and *unrelated* businesses.

- Explain the exceptions from the unrelated business tax scheme.

- Explain how the unrelated business rules apply in the private foundation setting.

GENERAL RULES

A private foundation's ability to own a business—one that is not conducted as a charitable function—is limited by rules concerning *excess business holdings*. The basic rule is that the combined ownership of a foundation and those who are disqualified persons with respect to it (see Chapter 2), of a business enterprise in any form—corporation, limited liability company, partnership, joint venture, sole proprietorship, or other type of unincorporated entity—may not exceed 20 percent. The law enables foundations to, without penalty, receive and dispose of excess holdings when the enterprise or business interests were acquired by the foundation by means of a contribution or inheritance.

These rules came into being (in 1969) out of concern that foundations were being used as holding companies of commercial enterprises, with owners of the businesses obtaining a charitable contribution deduction (see Chapter 9) for transfer of ownership from one entity they controlled (the business) to another entity they controlled (the foundation). A collateral worry was that these business enterprises did not produce much income to be used for charitable purposes. (The mandatory payout rules [see Chapter 4] are directed at the same concern.) Further, there was trepidation that foundation managers would concentrate on maintaining and improving the business to the detriment of their charitable duties. Moreover, when a business is held in this fashion (by a tax-exempt foundation), it may operate in a way that unfairly competes with other similar businesses whose owners must pay taxes on the income they derive from the enterprise.

BUSINESS ENTERPRISES

The term *business enterprise* is broadly defined in the federal tax law to include the active conduct of a trade or business, including any activity that is regularly carried on for the production of income from the sale of goods or the performance of services, and that constitutes an unrelated trade or business (discussed later in this chapter). Where an activity carried on for profit is an unrelated business, no part of it may be excluded from classification as a business enterprise merely because it does not result in a profit.

Thus, just as is the case with the unrelated business rules, a threshold determination must be made as to whether the *business* involved is a *related* or *unrelated* one. For example, a private foundation proposed to build, maintain, and lease a public ice arena. This facility, which was planned to conform to National Hockey League and college rink specifications, was expected to include a pro shop, coffee shop, concession area, day care center, and cocktail lounge; other contemplated facilities were conference, gymnastics, and athletic medicine facilities. The foundation proposed to lease this arena at fair rental value rates. On the face of it, this undertaking might appear to be a commercial (unrelated) one. The IRS, however, concluded that the development, ownership, and leasing of the arena would promote the health and welfare of the community and lessen the burdens of local government. Thus, this bundle of activities was held to not constitute a business enterprise for purposes of the excess business holdings rules.

A bond or other evidence of indebtedness is not a holding in a business enterprise unless it is otherwise determined to be an equitable interest in the enterprise. Thus, an ostensible indebtedness will be treated as a business holding if it is essentially an equity holding in disguise. A leasehold interest in real property is not an interest in a business enterprise, even if the rent is based on profits, unless the leasehold interest is an interest in the income or profits of an unrelated trade or business.

The term *business enterprise* does not include a functionally related business (see p. 188), a program-related investment (see Chapter 7), or a trade or business that is a passive income business (see next section).

PASSIVE INCOME BUSINESSES

For purposes of the excess business holdings rules, exempted from the concept of the *business enterprise* is a trade or business of which at least 95% of the gross income is derived from passive sources. Thus, stock in a passive holding company is not considered a holding in a business enterprise, even if the company is controlled by the foundation. The foundation, however, is treated as owning its proportionate share of the interests in a business enterprise held by the company. Tax-exempt title-holding companies can be utilized to house passive business operations.

The notion of *passive source income* is derived from the unrelated business rules (see p. 190). Consequently, passive income includes items considered passive in nature for purposes of these rules, including:

- Dividends, interest, and annuities
- Royalties, including overriding royalties, whether measured by production or by gross or taxable income from the property

- Rental income from real property and from personal property leased with real property, if the rent attributable to the personal property is incidental (less than 50% of the total rent)

- Gains or losses from sales, exchanges, or other dispositions of property (other than stock in trade held for regular sale to customers)

- Income from the sale of goods, if the seller does not manufacture, produce, physically receive or deliver, negotiate sales of, or keep inventories in the goods.

The fact that the unrelated debt-financed income rules (discussed later in this chapter) may apply to an item of passive income does not alter the character of the income as passive for purposes of the excess business holdings rules.

INVESTMENT PARTNERSHIPS

The term *business enterprise* may not encompass certain partnerships that engage solely in investment activities, even though less than 95% of the partnership's income may be derived from passive sources (see previous section).

This aspect of the law began to develop when the IRS considered the formation and operation of an investment partnership by 15 private foundations, each of which was a disqualified person with respect to the others (see Chapter 2). The partnership agreement prohibited the admission of partners that are not private foundations; one of the foundations served as the managing general partner. An investment management company that provided services to the manager foundation provided investment management and administrative services to this investment partnership without charge. Each foundation's investment in and capital commitment to the investment partnership did not exceed 20% of the value of its investment portfolio.

The purpose of this investment partnership was to enable each of these private foundations to invest in equity interests in private businesses and private equity funds not otherwise available to them and to achieve greater diversification in investments. The investments generally were made in other (lower-tier) limited partnerships, to which this investment partnership will subscribe as a limited partner. The investment partnership's gross income from nonpassive sources (such as income from partnerships engaged in an active business) could, as noted, exceed 5% annually.

This partnership agreement prohibited the investment partnership from making any investments that would cause any of the participating foundations to be involved in jeopardy investments (see Chapter 7). The partnership was forbidden to directly engage in an operating business. The agreement prohibited the partnership from making any investment that would cause the combined interests of any partner/foundation and all disqualified persons with respect to that partner in any business enterprise to exceed the permitted business holdings (discussed later in this chapter) of the partner. The investment partnership could not purchase property from, sell property to, exchange property with, or lease property to or from a disqualified person with respect to any of the partners (see Chapter 6). The partnership could not receive credit from or extend credit to a disqualified person with respect to any of the partners (*id.*). The partnership was precluded from purchasing or selling investments in an attempt to manipulate the price of the investments to the advantage of a disqualified person (*id.*).

If this investment partnership were a business enterprise, the investment of each of the participating foundations would be an excess business holding, whenever the combined profit interests of each foundation and its disqualified persons was in excess of the 20% level. The IRS conceded that a "strict reading" of the law would limit the concept of the passive income business to organizations receiving at least 95% of their gross income from passive sources. Nonetheless, because this partnership's activities consisted of investing in private business, mostly as a limited partner in other limited partnerships, and because limited partnership interests "may represent passive investments," the IRS ruled that this investment partnership is not treated as a business enterprise for purposes of the excess business holdings rules.

In a buttressing of its position, the IRS reviewed the legislative history of these rules. The agency said that Congress "only sought to prevent private foundations from engaging in active businesses." The IRS observed that a contrary conclusion would prevent a participating foundation from indirectly (i.e., through the partnership) investing in limited partnership interests, even though it could invest in these interests directly. The IRS wrote that the "mere interposition" of this investment partnership "should not produce a different result."

The IRS continued in its rationalizing, noting that "this is a situation that calls for the application of the constructive ownership rule" (discussed later in this chapter). Under this rule, the investment partnership will not hold an impermissible interest in any business enterprise that would result in indirect excess holding for any of its foundation partners. The IRS concluded that, given that the partners could directly hold these interests in business enterprises, and given that the investment partnership is formed for "valid business reasons," the foundations should be allowed to form and hold interests in the partnership to achieve the same result indirectly.

This is a significant development for private foundations, providing them with an opportunity to invest in a more sophisticated manner and for greater returns. An irony is that the federal tax statutory law provides tax-exempt status for a similar type of entity that is an investment pool for schools, colleges, and universities. The private foundation community has been pushing for similar legislation for foundations, with no success. With this IRS policy in place, the need for and likelihood of such legislation is even further reduced.

PERCENTAGE LIMITATIONS

As noted, the excess business holdings rules generally limit to 20% the permitted ownership of a corporation's voting stock or other interest in a business enterprise that may be held by a private foundation and all disqualified persons combined. Thus, as a general rule, a foundation and its substantial contributors, managers, their family members, and related organizations cannot collectively own more than 20% of an active business enterprise.

Usually, ownership of a corporation is determined by means of voting stock. For these purposes, the percentage of voting stock held by a person in a corporation is normally determined by reference to the power of stockholders to vote for the election of directors, disregarding treasury stock and stock that is authorized but unissued.

Where all disqualified persons with respect to a private foundation together do not own more than 20% of the voting stock of an incorporated business enterprise, the foundation can own any amount of nonvoting stock. Equity interests that do not have voting power attributable to them are classified as nonvoting stock. Stock carrying contingent voting rights is treated as nonvoting stock, for this purpose, until the event triggering the right to vote occurs. (An illustration is preferred stock that can be voted only if dividends are not paid.)

If effective control of a business enterprise can be shown to the satisfaction of the IRS to be elsewhere (i.e., other than by a private foundation and its disqualified persons), a 35% limit may be substituted for the 20% limit. The term *effective control* means possession of the power, whether direct or indirect, and whether or not actually exercised, to direct or cause the direction of the management and policies of a business enterprise. Effective control can be achieved by means such as ownership of voting stock, use of voting trusts, and/or contractual arrangements. It is the reality of control that is decisive, rather than its form or the ways in which it may be exercisable. For this 35% rule to apply, a private foundation must demonstrate by affirmative proof that an unrelated party, or group of parties, does in fact exercise control over the business enterprise involved.

A private foundation must, however, directly or indirectly hold more than 2% of the voting stock or other value of a business enterprise before either of these limitations becomes applicable. The holdings of related foundations are aggregated for the purpose of computing this 2% amount. This aggregation rule exists, of course, to preclude the use of multiple foundations as a means of subverting the law by converting this de minimis rule into a method of evading the excess business holdings rules.

PERMITTED AND EXCESS HOLDINGS

The *permitted business holdings* of a private foundation are those that are within the 20% or 35% limitations.

General Rules

Excess business holdings, therefore, constitute the amount of stock or other interest in a business enterprise that a private foundation must dispose of, by transferring it to a person (other than a disqualified person), in order for the remaining holdings of the foundation in the enterprise to constitute permitted holdings. If a foundation, however, disposes of an interest in a business enterprise but imposes one or more material restrictions or conditions that prevent free use of or prevent disposition of the transferred shares, the foundation is treated as continuing to own the interest until the restrictions or conditions are eliminated.

When a purchase of stock or other interest in a business enterprise by a disqualified person creates an excess business holding by a private foundation, the foundation has 90 days—from the date it knows, or has reason to know, of the event that caused it to have the excess holdings—to dispose of the excess holdings. The penalty taxes imposed because of a foundation's excess business holding (discussed later in this chapter) are not imposed if the holdings are properly reduced within this 90-day period. The period can be extended to include any period during which a foundation is prevented by federal or state securities law from disposing of the excess holdings.

An interest purchased by a private foundation that causes the ownership of a business holding (combined with that of disqualified persons) to exceed the permissible limits must be disposed of immediately; the foundation in this circumstance becomes subject to the taxes. If the foundation did not have knowledge, or any reason to know, that its holdings had become excessive, the 90-day-period rule applies and the initial tax will not be assessed.

Whether a private foundation is treated as knowing or having reason to know of the acquisition of holdings by a disqualified person depends on the facts and circumstances of each case. Factors to be considered are the fact that the foundation did not learn of acquisitions made by disqualified persons through the use of procedures reasonably calculated to discover the holdings, the diversity of foundation holdings, and the existence of large numbers of disqualified persons who have little or no contact with the foundation and/or its managers.

Partnerships, Trusts, and Proprietorships

The excess business holdings rules often focus on holdings in the form of stock. These rules, as noted, however, also apply with respect to holdings in unincorporated business entities, such as partnerships, limited liability companies, joint ventures, and trusts. In the case of a general or limited partnership, or other joint venture, the terms *profits interest* and *capital interest* are substituted, for purposes of the foregoing rule, for *voting stock* and *nonvoting stock*, respectively. A private foundation's holdings as a limited partner are not equivalent to nonvoting stock. In the case of a sole proprietorship, a private foundation cannot have any holdings (because, by definition, the owner of such a proprietorship is a 100% owner). For any other unincorporated business or a trust, the term *beneficial interest* is used instead of *voting stock*; no amount of an equivalent to nonvoting stock is allowed.

The interest of a private foundation and its disqualified persons in a partnership is determined using the federal tax law's distributive share concepts. Absent a partnership agreement, a foundation's ownership in a partnership is measured by the portion of assets that the foundation is entitled to receive on withdrawal from or dissolution of the entity.

For example, a private foundation owning 45% of a partnership is considered to own 45% of the property owned by the partnership. Thus, if the partnership owned 50% of the stock of a corporation, the foundation is regarded as owning 22.5% of the corporation's stock. Therefore, in this example, the foundation would, absent applicability of the 35% limitation, have excess holdings of 2.5%. This would not normally be the case where a foundation holds an interest in a limited partnership, which does not accord the foundation the requisite power to direct or cause the direction of the management and policies of a business enterprise. A right on the part of the limited partner/foundation to veto the general partner's actions, however, may constitute sufficient control to cause the 20% (or 35%) limitation to be applicable.

A private foundation may not operate a business enterprise (other than an exempted one) as a sole proprietorship, in that such a business arrangement by definition entails a 100% ownership of the enterprise.

Constructive Ownership

In computing the holdings of a private foundation, or a disqualified person with respect to a foundation, in a business enterprise, any stock or other interest owned, directly or indirectly, by or for a corporation, partnership, estate, or trust is considered as being owned proportionately by or for its shareholders, partners, or beneficiaries. Exempted from this constructive ownership rule (subject to certain exceptions) are holdings of corporations that are engaged in an active trade or business. A passive parent of an affiliated group of active businesses is treated as an active business for these purposes.

An interest in a business enterprise over which a private foundation or a disqualified person has a power of appointment, exercisable in favor of the foundation or disqualified person, is disqualified person holding the power of appointment.

Stock held in a split-interest trust (see Chapter 9) is not considered constructively owned by a private foundation where the foundation's sole relationship with the trust is that it has an income or remainder interest in it.

Disposition Periods

If a private foundation obtains holdings in a business enterprise in a manner other than by purchase, and these holdings cause the foundation to have excess business holdings, the foundation has five years to reduce these holdings to permissible levels. The excess holdings (or an increase in excess holdings) resulting from this type of transaction are treated as being held by a disqualified person—rather than by the foundation—during the five-year period beginning on the date the foundation obtained the holdings.

Acquisitions by gift, devise, bequest, legacy, or intestate succession are the subjects of this five-year rule, as are certain increases in holdings in a business enterprise that are the result of a readjustment of the enterprise. In the case of an acquisition of holdings in a business enterprise by a private foundation pursuant to the terms of a will or trust, the five-year period does not commence until the date on which the distribution of the holdings from the estate or trust occurs.

This five-year rule does not apply to a transfer of holdings in a business enterprise by a private foundation to another foundation that is related to the transferor foundation. This rule also does not apply to an increase in the holdings of a foundation in a business enterprise that is part of a plan by which disqualified persons will purchase additional holdings in the same enterprise during the five-year period beginning on the date of the change. The purchase of holdings by an entity whose holdings are treated as constructively owned by a foundation, its disqualified persons, or both is treated as a purchase by a disqualified person if the foundation and/or its disqualified persons have effective control of the entity or otherwise can control the purchase.

If a private foundation and/or its disqualified persons hold an interest in specific property under the terms of a will or trust, and if the foundation and/or its disqualified persons agree to the substitution of holdings in a business enterprise for the property, the holdings are regarded as obtained by purchase by a disqualified person.

When a private foundation has a program-related investment (see Chapter 7) (and thus does not have an interest in a business enterprise by reason of that investment) and subsequently the investment fails to qualify as a program-related one (so that the holding becomes an interest in a business enterprise), for purposes of this five-year rule, the interest becomes one acquired other than by purchase as of the date of nonqualification as a program-related investment. A similar rule applies with respect to passive holdings and to other circumstances in which an interest not originally in an active business enterprise becomes such an interest.

The IRS has the authority to allow a private foundation an additional five-year period for the disposition of excess business holdings in cases of unusually large gifts or bequests of diverse business holdings or holdings with complex corporate structures if:

- The foundation establishes that diligent efforts to dispose of the holdings were made during the initial five-year period and disposition within that initial period was not possible (except at a price substantially below fair market value) by reason of the size and complexity or diversity of the holdings.

- Before the close of the initial five-year period, the foundation submits to the IRS a plan for disposition of all of the excess business holdings involved in the extension, submits the plan to the appropriate state attorney general or similar official, and submits to the IRS any response received by the foundation from a state official to the plan during the initial period.

- The IRS determines that the plan can reasonably be expected to be carried out before the close of the extension period.

Rulings from the IRS illustrate situations in which the IRS has granted extensions of this nature for private foundations that have made the requisite diligent effort. A plan developed by an independent financial consultant to assist a foundation in selling its holdings, in conjunction with a substantial contributor's family members who owned interests in the same business enterprise, was approved by the IRS. Likewise, the IRS granted the extension, where a foundation made "diligent and continuous" efforts to sell real estate but was impeded by the need for substantial capital improvements and conversions in order to secure a purchaser. Further, a foundation garnered this extension where disposition of the foundation's interest in a business during the initial five-year period was not feasible and an investment banker advised the foundation that the interest in the enterprise should be able to be sold for their true value over the coming three to four years. The IRS concluded, by contrast, that a foundation was not adequately diligent and thus denied a request for one of these extensions.

Some History

These rules have a complex past. They (like most of the private foundation rules) were initiated in 1969; interests held as of that year were termed *present holdings*. The excess business holdings rules discussed above did not apply to present holdings; rather, a 50% limitation applied or, if lower, the actual percentage of holdings. If a private foundation with present holdings reduced its percentage of holdings in a business enterprise, it generally could not thereafter increase the amount of holdings (the nicely termed *downward rachet rule*). If, however, the reduction caused the holdings to fall below the 20% (or, if applicable, the 35%) level, they could be increased to those levels.

Any excess ownership held at that time had to be divested by the foundation, with the period of disposition (or phase) being 10, 15, or 20 years, depending on the percentage of combined ownership. These rules, which played out in 1989, caused major dispositions of securities holdings by private foundations in the 1970s and 1980s, some in the form of public secondary offerings. On more than one occasion, a foundation's management was quite unhappy with a forced divestiture of stock.

FUNCTIONALLY RELATED BUSINESSES

The penalties for excess business holdings do not apply with respect to holdings in functionally related businesses. This type of business is not considered a *business enterprise*. A *functionally related business* is a business or activity:

- The conduct of which is substantially related (aside from the mere provision of funds for the tax-exempt purpose) to the exercise or performance by the private foundation of its charitable purpose(s)

- In which substantially all of the work is performed for the foundation without compensation (i.e., by volunteers)

- Carried on by the foundation primarily for the convenience of its employees, members, patients, visitors, or students (such as a small restaurant or gift shop operated for an exempt museum or hospital)

- That consists of the selling of merchandise, substantially all of which was contributed to the foundation

- Carried on within a larger aggregate of similar activities or within a larger complex of other endeavors that is related to the charitable purposes of the foundation (again, other than the need for funds)

As an example of the first of these types of functionally related businesses, the IRS concluded that a music publishing company that concentrated on classical music was related to the purposes of a private foundation that promoted music education and the choice of music as a career, and thus was a functionally related business. Likewise, the IRS ruled that a racetrack and campground constituted functionally related businesses, inasmuch as they were conducted in conjunction with a museum operated by a foundation. Similarly, a farm in a foreign country, previously operated as a for-profit business by the founder of a foundation, became operated by the foundation after his death as an exempt demonstration project and thus a functionally related business. Further, a grant by a foundation to a for-profit corporation for the purpose of funding a medical malpractice reinsurance program, to enable physicians in an area to continue to practice, constituted a qualifying distribution (see Chapter 4) because the reinsurance company was a functionally related business.

IMPOSITION OF EXCISE TAX PENALTIES

The penalties that can be imposed in this context principally are initial and additional taxes, levied on the private foundation involved.

Initial Tax

An initial excise tax (also known as a first-tier tax) is imposed on a private foundation in an instance of excess business holdings in a business enterprise for each tax year that ends during the taxable period. The amount of this tax is 10% of the total value of all of the foundation's excess business holdings in each of its business enterprises. This tax is determined using the greatest value of the foundation's excess holdings in an enterprise during the year. The valuation is determined in accordance with the estate tax rules.

The *taxable period* is the period beginning with the first day on which there are excess holdings and ending on the earliest of the following dates:

- The date on which the IRS mails a notice of deficiency with respect to the initial tax in respect of the excess holdings

- The date on which the excess holding is eliminated

- The date on which the initial tax in respect of the excess holdings is assessed

If the deficiency is self-admitted by the filing of Form 4720, the period ends when the return is filed.

Additional Tax

If the initial tax is imposed and the excess business holdings are not disposed of by the close of the taxable period, an additional tax (also known as a second-tier tax) is imposed on the private foundation. The amount of this tax is 200% of the value of the excess business holdings. The additional tax is imposed at the end of the taxable period.

CORRECTION

An excess business holding must be corrected (unless the foundation involved wants to watch the IRS confiscate its assets [discussed later in this chapter]). The *correction period* is the period beginning on the date on which the taxable event occurs and ending 90 days after the date of mailing of a notice of deficiency with respect to the additional tax imposed on the event. This period may be extended by any period in which a deficiency cannot be assessed and any other period that the IRS determines is reasonable and necessary to bring about correction of the taxable event. In this setting, a *taxable event* is an act or failure to act giving rise to liability for tax under the excess business holdings rules. This event occurs on the first day on which there are excess business holdings. *Correction* means complete elimination of the excess holdings. The correction period is suspended during any litigation.

TAX ABATEMENT

The IRS has the discretion to abate this initial tax when a private foundation establishes that the violation was due to reasonable cause and not to willful neglect, and timely corrects the violation. Where the act or failure to act that gave rise to the additional tax is corrected within the correction period, the tax will not be assessed, or if assessed will be abated, or if collected will be credited or refunded. The collection period is suspended during the course of any litigation.

A request for abatement is submitted on Form 4720. Details about any corrective action taken and the value of recovered property must be described. If the matter remains uncorrected, an explanation is to be attached. The information provided is the basis on which the IRS will decide as to whether to abate a tax.

THIRD-TIER TAX REGIME

As noted, the sanctions underlying the excess business holdings rules include a first-tier and a second-tier tax. The termination tax (see Chapter 3) serves as a third-tier tax. This is the ultimate sanction, with the federal government able to confiscate the value of all federal tax benefits the foundation and its substantial contributors ever received derived from tax exemption and charitable tax deductions, applicable where a foundation engaged in willful, flagrant, or repeated acts or failures to act that cause voluntary, conscious, and intentional transgressions of the excess business holdings rules.

UNRELATED BUSINESS LAW STATUTORY FRAMEWORK

For nearly 60 years, the federal tax law has categorized the activities of tax-exempt organizations as those that are related to the performance of exempt functions and those that are not. The revenue occasioned by the latter type of activities, *unrelated activities*, is subject to tax. Gross revenues gained from unrelated activities are potentially taxable; however, in computing unrelated business taxable income, the organization is entitled to deduct only expenses incurred that are directly related to the conduct of the unrelated business.

For organizations that are incorporated, the net revenue from unrelated activities is subject to the regular federal corporate income tax. The federal tax on individuals applies to the unrelated activities of organizations that are not corporations (usually, trusts). Unlike many of the private foundation rules, the law as to related and unrelated activities does not impose any taxes on the directors and officers of tax-exempt entities.

To decide whether any of its activities are taxable, an otherwise tax-exempt organization must first ascertain whether a particular activity is a business, then determine whether it is regularly carried on, then whether activities are related or unrelated, and then (if necessary) whether one or more exceptions are available. The judgments that go into assigning activities into these two categories are at the heart of one of the greatest controversies facing nonprofit organizations.

The objective of the unrelated business income tax is to prevent unfair competition between tax-exempt organizations and for-profit, commercial enterprises. The rules are intended to place the unrelated business activities of an exempt organization on the same tax basis as those of a nonexempt business with which it competes.

To be tax exempt, a nonprofit organization must be organized and operated *primarily* for exempt purposes (see Chapter 3). The federal tax law allows a tax-exempt organization to engage in a certain amount of income-producing activity that is unrelated to its exempt purposes. Where the organization derives net income from one or more unrelated business activities, known as *unrelated business taxable income*, a tax is imposed on that income. A nonprofit organization's tax exemption will be denied or revoked if an appropriate portion to its activities is not promoting one or more of its exempt purposes.

Business activities may preclude the initial qualification of an otherwise tax-exempt organization. If the organization is not being operated principally for exempt purposes, it will fail the *operational test* (see Chapter 3). If its articles of organization empower it to carry on substantial activities that are not in furtherance of its exempt purpose, it will not meet the *organizational test* (*id.*).

A nonprofit organization may still satisfy the operational test, even when it operates a business as a substantial part of its activities, as long as the business promotes the organization's exempt purpose. If the organization's primary purpose is carrying on a business for profit, it is denied exempt status, perhaps on the ground that it is a *feeder organization*.

Occasionally, the IRS will assume a different stance toward the tax consequences of one or more unrelated businesses when it comes to qualification for tax exemption. That is, the IRS may conclude that a business is unrelated to an organization's exempt purpose and thus is subject to the unrelated business income tax. Yet the IRS may also agree that the purpose of the unrelated business is such that the activity helps further the organization's exempt function (by generating funds for exempt purposes), even if the business activity is more than one-half of total operations. In this circumstance, then, the exempt organization can be in the anomalous position of having a considerable amount of taxable business activity and still be tax-exempt.

AFFECTED TAX-EXEMPT ORGANIZATIONS

Nearly all types of tax-exempt organizations are subject to the unrelated business rules. They include religious organizations (including churches), educational organizations (including universities, colleges, and schools), health care organizations (including hospitals), scientific organizations (including major research institutions), private foundations, and similar organizations. Beyond the realm of charitable entities, the rules are applicable to social welfare organizations (including advocacy groups), labor organizations (including unions), trade and professional associations, fraternal organizations, employee benefit funds, and veterans' organizations.

Special rules tax all income not related to exempt functions (including investment income) of social clubs, homeowners' associations, and political organizations.

Some exempt organizations are not generally subject to the unrelated income rules, simply because they are not allowed to engage in any active business endeavors. The best example of this is private foundations, where the operation of an active unrelated business (internally or externally) would likely trigger application of the excess business holdings restrictions. Generally, an exempt title-holding company cannot have unrelated business taxable income; an exception permits such income in an amount up to 10% of its gross income for the tax year, where the income is incidentally derived from the holding of real property.

Instrumentalities of the United States, like governmental agencies generally, are exempt from the unrelated business rules. These rules are, however, applicable to colleges and universities that are agencies or instrumentalities of a government, as well as to corporations owned by such institutions of higher education.

CONDUCT OF *BUSINESS*

For purposes of the federal tax rules, the term *trade or business* includes any activity that is carried on for the production of income from the sale of goods or the performance of services. Most activities that would constitute a trade or business under basic tax law principles are considered a trade or business for the purpose of the unrelated business rules. That definition is a statutory one; a court may ignore that definition and compose its own, such as by holding that the activity simply does not rise to the level of business functions.

This definition of the term *trade or business*—often referred to simply as *business*—embraces nearly every activity of a tax-exempt organization; only passive investment activities and the provision of administrative services among related organizations generally escape this classification. In this sense, a nonprofit organization is viewed as a bundle of activities, each of which is a business. (It must be emphasized that this term has nothing to do with whether a particular business is related or unrelated; there are related businesses and unrelated businesses.)

The IRS is empowered to examine each of a nonprofit organization's activities in search of unrelated business. Each activity can be examined as though it existed wholly independently of the others; an unrelated activity cannot, as a matter of law, be hidden from scrutiny by tucking it in among a host of related activities. As Congress chose to state the precept, an "activity does not lose identity as a trade or business merely because it is carried on within a larger aggregate of similar activities or within a larger complex of other endeavors which may, or may not, be related to the exempt purposes of the organization." This is known as the *fragmentation rule*, by which—as a matter of legal fiction—a nonprofit organization's disparate activities may be fragmented and each discrete fragment reviewed in isolation. For example, the activity of advertising in a nonprofit organization's exempt publication is severed from the publication activity and regarded as an unrelated activity, even though otherwise the publication activity is a related business.

The federal law also provides that, where an activity "carried on for profit constitutes an unrelated trade or business, no part of such trade or business shall be excluded from such classification merely because it does not result in profit." In other words, just because an activity results in a loss in a particular year, that is insufficient basis for failing to treat the activity as an unrelated one. Conversely, the mere fact that an activity generates a profit is not alone supposed to lead to the conclusion that the activity is unrelated (although on occasion that is the conclusion).

An activity that consistently results in annual losses likely will not be regarded as a *business*. If that is the only unrelated activity, then it cannot be an *unrelated business*. Some nonprofit organizations, however, have more than one unrelated business. They can offset the losses generated by one business against the gains enjoyed by another business in calculating unrelated business taxable income. But if the loss activity is not a business, its losses cannot be credited against unrelated gain.

It is common for a tax-exempt organization to provide management or other administrative services to another exempt organization. These services, where they are not inherently exempt functions, are known as *corporate services*. The general rule is that the provision of these types of services, even where the exempt organizations involved have the same exempt status, is a business. (Indeed, the providing of corporate services is generally considered by the IRS to be an unrelated business.) Nonetheless, where the relationship between the exempt organizations is that of parent and subsidiary, or is analogous to that of parent and subsidiary, the financial dealings will be regarded as a *matter of accounting*, which means they will be disregarded for federal income tax purposes.

Just as the element of *profits* is not built into the statutory definition of the term *trade or business*, so, too, is the factor of *unfair competition* missing from that definition. Yet unfair competition was the force that animated enactment of the unrelated business rules; the IRS and the courts sometimes take the matter of competition into consideration in assessing whether an activity is related or unrelated to exempt purposes.

Another term absent from the statutory definition of *business* is *commerciality*. Nothing in that definition authorizes the IRS and the courts to conclude that an activity is an unrelated one solely because it is conducted in a commercial manner, which basically means it is undertaken the way a comparable activity is carried on by for-profit businesses (see below). Yet, they engage in the practice anyway.

REGULARLY CARRIED ON BUSINESSES

To be considered an unrelated business, an activity must be *regularly carried on* by a nonprofit organization. That is, income from an activity is considered taxable only when (assuming the other criteria are satisfied) the activity is conducted more often than sporadically or infrequently. The factors that determine whether an activity is regularly carried on are the frequency and continuity of the activities, and the manner in which the activities are pursued.

These factors are to be evaluated in light of the purpose of the unrelated business rules, which is to place nonprofit organizations' business activities on the same tax law basis (what some are wont to call a *level playing field*) as those of their nonexempt competitors. Specific business activities of a tax-exempt organization will generally be deemed to be regularly carried on if they are, as noted, frequent and continuous, and pursued in a manner that is generally similar to comparable commercial activities of for-profit organizations.

Where a nonprofit organization duplicates income-producing activities performed by commercial organizations year-round, but conducts these activities for a period of only a few weeks a year, they do not constitute the regular carrying on of a business. Similarly, occasional or annual income-producing activities, such as fundraising events, do not amount to a business that is regularly carried on. The conduct of year-round business activities, such as the operation of a parking lot one day every week, however, constitutes the regular carrying on of a business. Where commercial entities normally undertake income-producing activities on a seasonal basis, the conduct of the activities by an exempt organization during a significant portion of the season is deemed the regular conduct of the activity. For this purpose, a season may be a portion of the year (such as the summer) or a holiday period.

Generally, the law, in ascertaining regularity, looks only at the time consumed in the actual conduct of the activity. The IRS, however, is of the view that time expended preparing for the event (*preparatory time*) should also be taken into account. This can convert what appears to be an exempted activity into a taxable business.

Outsourcing has become a popular management technique for nonprofit organizations. They often attempt to outsource unrelated activities (and try to bring the profits in as nontaxable income, usually royalties [discussed later in this chapter]). This arrangement entails a contract that sometimes casts the party with whom the nonprofit organization is contracting as the organization's *agent*. While this is meritorious from a management perspective (such as to ensure quality), it is a bad idea from the tax law viewpoint. Pursuant to the law of *principal* and *agent*, the activities of the agent are attributable to the principal. In this setting, the nonprofit organization is the principal. Attribution of the agent's activities to the exempt organization obliterates what would otherwise be the tax law outcome from the outsourcing, by treating the exempt organization as if it directly is conducting the outsourced activity.

RELATED OR UNRELATED?

The term *unrelated trade or business* is defined to mean "any trade or business the conduct of which [by a tax-exempt organization] is not substantially related (aside from the need of such organization for income or funds or the use it makes of the profits derived) to the exercise or performance by such organization of its charitable, educational, or other purpose or function constituting the basis for its exemption." The parenthetical clause means that an activity is not related, for these purposes, simply because the organization uses the net revenue from the activity in furtherance of exempt purposes.

The revenue from a regularly conducted trade or business is subject to tax, unless the activity is substantially related to the accomplishment of the organization's exempt purposes. The key to taxation or nontaxation in this area is the meaning of the words *substantially related*. Yet the law provides merely that, to be substantially related, the activity must have a *substantial causal relationship* to the accomplishment of an exempt purpose.

The fact that an asset is essential to the conduct of an organization's exempt activities does not shield from taxation the unrelated income produced by that asset. The income-producing activities must still meet the causal relationship test if the income is not to be subject to tax. This issue arises when a tax-exempt organization owns a facility or other assets that are put to a dual use. For example, the operation of an auditorium as a motion picture theater for public entertainment in the evenings is regarded as an unrelated activity even though the theater is used exclusively for exempt functions during the daytime hours. The fragmentation rule (discussed earlier in this chapter) allows this type of use of a single asset or facility to be split into two businesses.

Activities should not be conducted on a scale larger than is reasonably necessary for the performance of exempt functions. Activities in excess of what is needed for the achievement of exempt purposes may be seen as unrelated businesses.

There is a host of court opinions and IRS rulings providing illustrations of related and unrelated activities. Colleges and universities operate dormitories and bookstores as related businesses but can be taxed on travel tours and the conduct of sports camps. Hospitals may operate gift shops, snack bars, and parking lots as related businesses but may be taxable on sales of pharmaceuticals to the general public and on performance of routine laboratory tests for physicians. Museums may, without taxation, sell items reflective of their collections but are taxable on the sale of souvenirs and furniture. Trade associations may find themselves taxable on sales of items (such as uniforms, tools, and manuals) and particular services to members, for which dues and subscription revenue are nontaxable. Fundraising events may be characterized as unrelated activities, particularly where the activity is regularly carried on or compensation is paid.

UNRELATED BUSINESS TAXABLE INCOME

As noted above, to be subject to the unrelated business income tax, the revenue involved must be derived from an activity that satisfies (or, depending on one's point of view, fails) three tests. Thus, *unrelated business taxable income* is gross income derived by a tax-exempt organization from an unrelated trade or business that is regularly carried on by it, less any allowable deductions that are directly connected with the carrying of the trade or business. (This definition does not incorporate the application of certain *modifications* discussed later in this chapter).

Some tax-exempt organizations are members of partnerships. In computing its unrelated business taxable income, it must (subject to the modifications) include its share (whether or not distributed) of the partnership's gross income from the unrelated business and its share of the partnership deductions directly connected with the gross income. (This is an application of what the tax law terms the *look-through rule*.) A tax-exempt organization's share (whether or not distributed) of the gross income of a publicly traded partnership must be treated as gross income derived from an unrelated business, and its share of the partnership deductions is allowed in computing unrelated business taxable income (again, subject to the modifications).

EXCEPTED ACTIVITIES

The foregoing general rules notwithstanding, certain businesses conducted by tax-exempt organizations are exempted from unrelated business income taxation. One of the frequently used exemptions from this taxation is for a business in which substantially all the work is performed for the organization without compensation. Thus, if an exempt organization conducts an unrelated business using services provided substantially by volunteers, the net revenue from that business is spared taxation. This exemption protects from taxation many ongoing fundraising activities for charitable organizations. Caution must be exercised, however, because *compensation* is not confined to a salary, wage, or fee; the slightest amount of remuneration (such as gratuities) can nullify an individual's status as a *volunteer*.

Also exempted is a business carried on by the organization primarily for the convenience of its members, students, patients, officers, or employees. This exception is available, however, only to organizations that are charitable, educational, and the like, or are governmental colleges and universities.

Exemption is accorded a business that consists of the selling of merchandise, substantially all of which has been received by the exempt organization as contributions. This exemption shelters the revenue of exempt thrift stores from unrelated income taxation. Its use, though, is not confined to thrift shops. For example, it can protect auction revenue from taxation—even if auctions are regularly carried on. Likewise, this exemption applies in the case of used vehicle donation programs; the charity involved is not taxed as though it is in the used car business.

Unrelated trade or business does not include qualified public entertainment activities. A *public entertainment activity* is any entertainment or recreational activity traditionally conducted at fairs or expositions promoting agricultural and educational purposes. Typically, these activities attract the public to fairs or expositions or promote the breeding of animals or the development of products or equipment.

To be *qualified*, a public entertainment activity must be conducted (1) in conjunction with an international, national, regional, state, or local fair or exposition; (2) in accordance with the provisions of state law that permit the activity to be operated or conducted solely by a qualifying organization or by a governmental agency; or (3) in accordance with the provisions of state law that permit a qualifying organization to be granted a license to conduct no more than 20 days of the activity, on payment to the state of a lower percentage of the revenue from the licensed activity than the state requires from nonqualifying organizations.

To warrant application of the public entertainment activities exception, a *qualifying organization* must be a tax-exempt charitable, social welfare, or labor organization that regularly conducts, as one of its substantial exempt purposes, an agricultural or educational fair or exposition.

The term *unrelated trade or business* also does not include *qualified convention and trade show activities*. Activities of this nature, traditionally conducted at conventions, annual meetings, or trade shows, are designed to attract attention from persons in an industry. There is no requirement for these persons to be members of the sponsoring organization. The purposes of these shows are to display industry products; to stimulate interest in, and demand for, industry products or services; or to educate persons within the industry in the development of new products and services or new rules and regulations affecting industry practices.

To be *qualified*, a convention and trade show activity must be carried out by a qualifying organization in conjunction with an international, national, regional, state, or local convention, annual meeting, or show that the organization is conducting. One of the purposes of the organization in sponsoring the activity must be the promotion and stimulation of interest in, and demand for, the products and services of that industry in general, or the education of attendees regarding new developments or products and services related to the exempt activities of the organization. The show must be designed to achieve its purpose through the character of the exhibits and the extent of the industry products displayed. A *qualifying organization* is a charitable, social welfare, or labor organization or a trade association, which regularly conducts such a show as one of its substantial exempt purposes.

For a charitable, veterans', or other organization, as to which contributions are deductible, the term *unrelated business* does not include activities relating to a distribution of low-cost articles that is incidental to the solicitation of charitable contributions. A *low-cost article* is an item that has a maximum cost of $5 (indexed for inflation) to the organization that distributes the article (directly or indirectly). A *distribution* qualifies under this rule if it is not made at the request of the recipients, if it is made without their express consent, and if the articles that are distributed are accompanied by a request for a charitable contribution to the organization and a statement that the recipients may retain the article whether or not a contribution is made.

For a charitable, veterans', or other organization to which deductible contributions may be made, the term *business* does not include exchanging with another like organization the names and addresses of donors to or members of the organization, or the renting of these lists to another like organization.

Still other exceptions apply with respect to certain local organizations of employees, the conduct of certain games of chance, and the rental of poles by mutual or cooperative telephone or electric companies.

EXCEPTED INCOME

Certain types of passive and other income (principally research revenue) are exempt from the unrelated business income tax.

Because the unrelated income tax applies to businesses actively conducted by tax-exempt organizations, most types of passive income are exempt from taxation. This exemption generally embraces dividends, interest, securities loan payments, annuities, royalties, rent, capital gains, and gains on the lapse or termination of options written by exempt organizations. Income in the form of rent, royalties, and the like from an active business undertaking is taxable; that is, merely labeling an item of income as rent, royalties, and so forth does not make it tax free.

The following exemptions apply to the conduct of research: income derived from research (1) for the United States or any of its agencies or instrumentalities, or any state or political subdivision of a state; (2) performed for any person at a college, university, or hospital; and (3) performed for any person at an organization operated primarily for purposes of carrying on fundamental research, the results of which are freely available to the general public.

Some organizations do not engage in *research*; rather, they merely test products for public use just prior to marketing or undertake certification tasks. Other organizations, principally universities and scientific research institutions, are engaging in research, but their discoveries are licensed or otherwise transferred to for-profit organizations for exploitation in the public marketplace. This closeness between businesses and nonprofit organizations—known as *technology transfer*—can raise questions as to how much commercial activity is being sheltered from tax by the research exception.

For the most part, the tax law is clear regarding what constitutes *dividends*, *interest*, an *annuity*, *rent*, and *capital gain*. However, there can be considerable controversy concerning what constitutes a *royalty*. The term, not defined by statute or regulation, is being defined by the courts.

Generally, a *royalty* is a payment for the use of one or more valuable intangible property rights. In the tax-exempt organization setting, this is likely to mean payment for the use of an organization's name and logo. The core issue usually is the extent to which the exempt organization receiving the (ostensible) royalty can provide services in an attempt to increase the amount of royalty income paid to it. This issue was the subject of extensive litigation spanning many years, principally involving revenue from the rental of mailing lists and revenue derived from affinity card programs. The resulting rule is that these services are permissible as long as they are insubstantial. Beyond that, the IRS may contend that the exempt organization is in a *joint venture*, which is an active business undertaking that defeats the exclusion.

A specific deduction of $1,000 is available. This means that the first $1,000 of unrelated business income is spared taxation.

EXCEPTIONS TO EXCEPTIONS

There are two exceptions to the foregoing exceptions, one involving unrelated debt-financed income, the other concerning income from subsidiaries.

A tax-exempt organization may own *debt-financed property*; the use of the property may be unrelated to the organization's exempt purposes. In a situation where both facts are present, when the exempt organization computes its unrelated business taxable income, income from the debt-financed property must be included as gross income derived from an unrelated business. The income is subject to tax in the same proportion that the property is financed by debt. The debt involved must be what the federal tax law terms *acquisition indebtedness*. This body of law applies even where the income is paid to an exempt organization in one of the otherwise protected forms, such as interest or rent.

Some tax-exempt organizations elect to spin off their unrelated activities to taxable subsidiaries. The tax on the net income of the unrelated business is then not borne directly by the exempt organization. The managers of an exempt organization may be averse to reporting any unrelated business income, or the unrelated activity may be too large in relation to related activity.

If funds are transferred from a taxable subsidiary to an exempt parent, that income will be taxable as unrelated business income to the parent, if it is interest, rent, royalties, or capital gains. This is the outcome where the parent has, directly or indirectly, more than 50% control of the subsidiary. As an exception to an exception to an exception, if the subsidiary pays dividends to the tax-exempt parent, the dividends are not taxable to the parent because they are not deductible by the subsidiary.

FOUNDATIONS AND UNRELATED BUSINESS RULES

As noted, the principal reason that private foundations have minimal entanglement with the unrelated business rules is the limitation on ownership of business enterprises imposed by the excess business holding rules. A foundation generally cannot engage in unrelated business activity because that would be the conduct of one or more sole proprietorships (discussed earlier in this chapter). A foundation can, however, engage in activities that are not *business enterprises* (*id.*), such as an activity where at least 95% of the gross income of the business is derived from passive sources. Income from these sources generally is the same as the forms of income sheltered from taxation under the modification rules (*id.*), such as dividends, interest, royalties, annuities, most forms of rent, and capital gains. By definition, a functionally related business (*id.*) is not an unrelated business.

SUMMARY

This chapter provided a summary of the excess business holding rules, including a discussion of the concepts of business enterprises and passive businesses, the investment partnership rules, the applicable percentage limitations, permitted and excess holdings, and functionally related businesses. The chapter described the various tax penalties applicable in this context and the tax abatement rules, as well as the third-tier tax regime. The chapter concluded with an explanation of the unrelated business rules, including the concepts of related and unrelated businesses, the exceptions to the unrelated business rules, and an explanation as to how the unrelated business rules apply in the private foundation setting.

9

CHARITABLE GIVING

The purpose of this chapter is to summarize the federal tax law rules concerning deductible charitable giving, with emphasis on the application of these rules to private foundations. A seemingly simple subject, the law pertaining to the making of and deductibility of gifts to charitable organizations is complex. This is particularly the case with respect to planned giving. Specifically, this chapter will:

- Analyze the elements of a gift.

- Discuss the advantages of gifts of property.

- Summarize the rules concerning qualified appreciated stock.

- Summarize the percentage limitations on deductibility.

- Discuss the planned giving techniques.

- Address the charitable giving rules from the standpoint of private foundations.

BASIC CONCEPTS

The basic concept of the federal income tax deduction for a charitable contribution is this: Corporations and individuals who itemize their deductions can deduct on their annual tax return, within certain limits, an amount equivalent to the amount contributed (money) or to the value of a contribution (property) to a qualified donee. A *charitable contribution* for income tax purposes is a gift to or for the use of one or more qualified donees.

Deductions for charitable gifts are also allowed under the federal gift tax and estate tax laws. A charitable estate tax deduction is allowed for the value of all transfers from a decedent's estate to or for the use of charitable organizations. A charitable gift tax deduction is available for transfers by contribution to or for the use of charitable organizations. The extent of these charitable deductions is not dependent on whether the charitable donee is a public charity or a private foundation (see Chapter 1); percentage limitations do not apply to these deductions.

Donors and the charitable organizations they support commonly expect gifts to be in the form of outright transfers of money or property. For both parties (donor and donee), a gift is usually a unilateral transaction, in a financial sense: the donor parts with the contributed item; the charity acquires it.

The advantages to the donor, from the making of a charitable gift, generally are the resulting charitable deduction and the gratification derived from the giving. Planned giving (discussed later in this chapter) provides additional financial and tax advantages to the donor. Overall, these are the economic advantages that can result from a charitable gift:

- A federal, state, and/or local tax deduction
- Avoidance of capital gains taxation
- Creation of or an increase in cash flow
- Improved tax treatment of income
- Free professional tax and investment management services
- Opportunity to transfer property between the generations of a family
- Receipt of benefits from the charitable donee

A contribution to a private foundation can provide these advantages—and more. This is because a contributor to a foundation usually is a founder of the foundation, and likely also is a trustee and officer of it. Thus, the contributor, in the case of a foundation gift, usually retains control over the money and/or property that is the subject of the gift. This is not to countenance or advocate wrongdoing; it is merely a statement of fact that gives rise to unique circumstances not normally found in the charitable giving setting. Indeed, in this context, the contributor (and/or one or more family members) may also be an employee of the donee foundation.

DEFINING *CHARITABLE GIFT*

A fundamental requirement of the charitable contribution deduction law is that the cash or property transferred to a charitable organization must be transferred in the form of a *gift*. Just because money is paid or property is transferred to a charity does not necessarily mean that the payment or transfer is a gift. When a tax-exempt university's tuition, an exempt hospital's health care fee, or an exempt association's dues are paid, there is no gift and thus no charitable deduction for the payment.

Basically, a gift has two elements: it involves a transfer that is *voluntary* and is motivated by something other than *consideration* (something being received in return for a payment). Where payments are made to receive something in exchange (education, health care, etc.), the transaction is a purchase. The law places more emphasis on what is received by the payor than on the payment or transfer. The income tax regulations state that a transfer is not a contribution when made "with a reasonable expectation of financial return commensurate with the amount of the transfer." A single transaction, however, can be partially a gift and partially a purchase (see below); when a charity is the payee, only the gift portion is deductible.

The U.S. Supreme Court, in a famous pronouncement, observed that a gift is a transfer motivated by "detached or disinterested generosity." The Court also characterized a gift as a transfer stimulated "out of affection, respect, admiration, charity, or like impulses." Thus, the focus in this area for the most part has been an objective analysis, comparing what the "donee" parted with and what (if anything) the "donor" received net in exchange.

Another factor, that of *donative intent*, is sometimes taken into consideration. A set of tax regulations states that, for any part of a payment made in the context of a charity auction to be deductible as a charitable gift, the patron must have donative intent. More broadly, a congressional committee report contains this statement: "The term 'contribution or gift' is not defined by statute, but generally is interpreted to mean a voluntary transfer of money or other property without receipt of adequate consideration and with donative intent. If a taxpayer receives or expects to receive a quid pro quo in exchange for a transfer to charity, the taxpayer may be able to deduct the excess of the amount transferred over the fair market value of any benefit received in return provided the excess payment is made with the intention of making a gift."

A federal court of appeals described the matter as to what is a gift this way: It is a "particularly confused issue of federal taxation." The statutory law on the subject, said this court, is "cryptic," and "neither Congress nor the courts have offered any very satisfactory definitions" of the terms *gift* and *contribution* (which are, for these purposes, basically synonymous).

QUALIFIED DONEES

Qualified donees are charitable organizations (including educational, religious, and scientific entities), certain fraternal organizations, certain cemetery companies, and most veterans' organizations. Contributions to both private foundations and public charities (see Chapter 1) are deductible, but the law favors gifts to public charities.

Federal, state, and local governmental bodies are charitable donees. State or local law, however, may preclude a governmental entity from accepting charitable gifts. In most jurisdictions, a charitable organization can be established to solicit deductible contributions for and make grants to governmental bodies. This is a common technique for public schools, colleges, universities, and hospitals.

An otherwise nonqualifying organization may be allowed to receive a deductible charitable gift, where the gift property is used for charitable purposes or received by an agent for a charitable organization. An example of the former is a gift to a trade association that is earmarked for a charitable fund within the association. Examples of an agent for a charity is a title-holding company that holds a property for charitable purposes and a for-profit company that acquires and disposes of vehicles as part of a charity's used vehicle donation program.

GIFTS OF PROPERTY

Aside from the eligibility of the gift recipient, the other basic element in determining whether a charitable contribution is deductible is the nature of the property given. Essentially, the distinctions are between outright giving and planned giving, and between gifts of cash and gifts of property. In many instances, the tax law differentiates between personal property and real property, and tangible property and intangible property (securities).

The federal income tax treatment of gifts of property is dependent on whether the property is capital gain property. The tax law makes a distinction between *long-term capital gain* and *short-term capital gain*. Property that is not capital gain property is *ordinary income property*. These three terms are based on the tax classification of the type of revenue that would be generated on sale of the property. Short-term capital gain property is generally treated the same as ordinary income property. Therefore, the actual distinction is between capital gain property (really long-term capital gain property) and ordinary income property.

Capital gain property is a capital asset that has appreciated in value and, if sold, would give rise to long-term capital gain. To result in long-term capital gain, property must be held for at least 12 months. Most forms of capital gain property are securities and real estate.

The charitable contribution deduction for capital gain property is often equal to its fair market value or at least is computed using that value. Thus, a critical determination in ascertaining the extent of a charitable deduction can be the value of the property. In general, the fair market value of an item of property is the price at which the property would change hands between a willing buyer and a willing seller, neither being under any compulsion to buy or sell and both having reasonable knowledge of relevant facts. The IRS amplified this rule, holding that the "most probative evidence of fair market value is the price at which similar quantities of . . . [the property] are sold in arms'-length transactions." The IRS also determined that the fair market value of gift property is determined by reference to the "most active and comparable marketplace at the time of the donor's contribution." (The fair market value of an item of property is frequently the subject of litigation.)

Inasmuch as the charitable deduction for a gift of property is often based on the fair market value of the property, a donor can be economically benefited where the property has increased in value since the date on which the donor acquired the property. Property in this condition has *appreciated* in value; it is known as *appreciated property*. This gain is the amount that would have been recognized for tax purposes had the donor sold the property; it is sometimes referred to as the *appreciation element*.

Gifts of ordinary income property generally produce a deduction equivalent to the donor's cost basis in the property. The law provides exceptions to this basis-only rule; an example is a gift by a corporation out of its inventory (discussed later in this chapter). A charitable deduction based on the full fair market value of an item of appreciated property (with no recognition of the built-in capital gain) is a critical feature of the federal tax law incentives for charitable giving. This incentive is limited in the case of contributions of appreciated property to private foundations (discussed later in this chapter).

LIMITATIONS ON DEDUCTIBILITY

The extent of charitable contributions that can be deducted for a particular tax year is limited to a certain amount, which for individuals is a function of the donor's *contribution base*—essentially, an amount equal to the individual's adjusted gross income. This level of allowable annual deductibility is determined by five percentage limitations. They are dependent on several factors, principally the nature of the charitable recipient and the nature of the property contributed. The examples used below assume an individual donor with an annual contribution base of $100,000.

The first three limitations apply to gifts to public charities and to private operating foundations.

First, there is a percentage limitation of 50% of the donor's contribution base for gifts of cash and ordinary income property. A donor with a $100,000 contribution base may, in a year, make deductible gifts of these items up to a total of $50,000. If an individual makes contributions that exceed the 50% limitation, the excess generally may be carried forward and deducted in one to five subsequent years. Thus, if this donor gave $60,000 to public charities in year 1 and made no other charitable gifts in that year, he or she would be entitled to a deduction of $50,000 in year 1 and the remaining $10,000 would be available for deductibility in year 2.

The second percentage limitation is 30% of the donor's contribution base for gifts of capital gain property. A donor thus may, in a year, contribute up to $30,000 of qualifying stocks, bonds, real estate, and like property, and receive a charitable deduction for that amount. Any excess (more than 30%) of the amount of these gifts is subject to the carryforward rule. If a donor gave $50,000 in capital gain property in year 1 and made no other charitable gifts that year, he or she would be entitled to a charitable contribution deduction of $30,000 in year 1 and the $20,000 would be available in year 2.

A donor who makes gifts of cash and capital gain property to public charities (and/or private operating foundations) in any one year generally is limited by a blend of these percentage limitations. For example, if the donor in year 1 gives $50,000 in cash and $30,000 in appreciated capital gain property to a public charity, his or her charitable deduction in year 1 is $30,000 of capital gain property and $20,000 of the cash (to keep the deduction within the overall 50% ceiling); the other $30,000 of cash would be carried forward to year 2 (or to years 2 through 5, depending on the donor's circumstances).

The third percentage limitation allows a donor of capital gain property to use the 50% limitation, instead of the 30% limitation, where the amount of the contribution is reduced by all of the unrealized appreciation in the value of the property. This election is usually made by donors who want a larger deduction in the year of the gift for an item of property that has not appreciated in value to a great extent. Once made, this election is irrevocable.

The fourth and fifth percentage limitations apply to gifts to private foundations and certain other charitable donees (other than public charities and private operating foundations). These other donees are generally veterans' and fraternal organizations.

Under the fourth percentage limitation, contributions of cash and ordinary income property to private foundations and other entities may not exceed 30% of the individual donor's contribution base. The carryover rules apply to this type of gift. If the donor gives $50,000 in cash to one or more private foundations in year 1, his or her charitable deduction for that year (assuming no other charitable gifts) is $30,000, with the balance of $20,000 carried forward into subsequent years (up to 5).

The carryover rules blend with the first three percentage limitations. For example, if in year 1 a donor gave $65,000 to charity, of which $25,000 went to a public charity and $40,000 to a private foundation, his or her charitable deduction for that year would be $50,000: $30,000 for the gift to the private foundation and $20,000 for the gift to the public charity. The remaining $10,000 of the gift to the foundation and the remaining $5,000 of the gift to the public charity would be carried forward into year 2.

The fifth percentage limitation is 20% of the contribution base for gifts of capital gain property to private foundations and other charitable donees. There is a carryforward for any excess deduction amount. For example, if a donor gives appreciated securities, having a value of $30,000, to a private foundation in year 1, his or her charitable deduction for year 1 (assuming no other charitable gifts) is $20,000; the remaining $10,000 may be carried forward.

Deductible charitable contributions by corporations in any tax year may not exceed 10% of pretax net income. Excess amounts may be carried forward and deducted in subsequent years (up to 5). For gifts by corporations, the federal tax laws do not differentiate between gifts to public charities and gifts to private foundations. As an illustration, a corporation that grosses $1 million in a year and incurs $900,000 in expenses in that year (not including charitable gifts) may generally contribute to charity and deduct in that year an amount up to $10,000 (10% of $100,000); in computing its taxes, this corporation would report taxable income of $90,000. If the corporation contributed $20,000 in that year, the numbers would remain the same, except that the corporation would have a $10,000 charitable contribution carryforward.

A corporation on the accrual method of accounting can elect to treat a contribution as having been made in a tax year if it is actually donated during the first $2\frac{1}{2}$ months of the following year. Corporate gifts of property are generally subject to the deduction reduction rules, discussed next.

A business organization that is a *flow-through entity* generates a different tax result when it comes to charitable deductions. (These organizations are partnerships, other joint ventures, small business [S] corporations, and limited liability companies.) Entities of this nature, even though they may make charitable gifts, do not claim charitable contribution deductions. Instead, the deduction is passed through to the partners, members, or other owners on an allocable basis and they claim their share of the deduction on their tax return.

Thus, aside from these percentage limitations, the ability in instances of gifts of property to base a charitable deduction on the full fair market value of the property often turns on this public charity/private foundation dichotomy. As a general rule, the only time the deduction can be based on the property's fair value (and enable the contributor to avoid recognition of the appreciation element [capital gain]) is when the charitable donee is a public charity or a private operating foundation. By contrast, where a contribution is made to a charitable organization that is a private foundation, a deduction reduction rule usually applies, unless the contributed property is qualified appreciated stock (discussed later in this chapter).

DEDUCTION REDUCTION RULES

A donor (individual or corporation) who makes a gift of *ordinary income property* to a charitable organization (public or private) must confine the charitable deduction to an amount equal to the donor's cost basis in the property. The deduction is not based on the fair market value of the property; it must be reduced by the amount that would have been gain (ordinary income) if the property had been sold. As an example, if a donor gave to a charity an item of ordinary income property having a value of $1,000, for which he or she paid $600, the resulting charitable deduction would be $600.

Any donor who makes a gift of *capital gain property* to a public charity generally can compute the charitable deduction using the property's fair market value at the time of the gift, regardless of the basis amount and with no taxation of the appreciation (the capital gain inherent in the property). Suppose, however, a donor makes a gift of capital gain tangible personal property (such as a work of art) to a public charity and the use of the gift property by the donee is unrelated to its tax-exempt purposes (see Chapter 3). The donor must reduce the deduction by an amount equal to all of the long-term capital gain that would have been recognized had the donor sold the property at its fair market value as of the date of the contribution.

Generally, a donor who makes a gift of capital gain property to a private foundation must reduce the amount of the otherwise allowable deduction by all of the appreciation element (built-in capital gain) in the gift property. An individual, however, is allowed full fair market value for a contribution to a private foundation of certain publicly traded stock (known as *qualified appreciated stock*).

QUALIFIED APPRECIATED STOCK

A significant exception to the deduction reduction rule that is unique to private foundations is that it does not apply where the contribution is of qualified appreciated stock. That is, where this exception is applicable, the charitable contribution deduction for a contribution of stock to a foundation is based on the fair market value of the stock at the time of the gift.

The term *qualified appreciated stock* means any stock:

- For which, as of the date of contribution, market quotations are readily available on an established securities market
- That is capital gain property

Market quotations are readily available on an established securities market, according to the tax regulations, if:

- The security is listed on the New York Stock Exchange, the American Stock Exchange, or any city or regional exchange where quotations are published on a daily basis.
- The security is regularly traded in the national or a regional over-the-counter market, for which published quotations are available.

- The security is a share of an open-ended investment company (i.e., a mutual fund) for which quotations are published on a daily basis in a newspaper of general circulation throughout the United States.

Securities are not considered publicly traded if (1) the securities are subject to restrictions that materially affect the value of the securities to the donor or prevent the securities from being freely traded or (2) if the amount claimed or reported as a deduction with respect to the contribution of the securities is different from the amount listed in the market quotations that are readily available on an established securities market.

The IRS, applying the first of these two rules, held that stock that cannot be sold or exchanged by reason of the federal securities law rules confining sales of control stock to small portions (Securities and Exchange Commission Rule 144) cannot qualify as qualified appreciated stock. Moreover, the IRS ruled that stock traded by means of the Over-the-Counter Bulletin Board Service is not qualified appreciated stock because market quotations are not readily available, in that they can be obtained only by consulting a broker, subscribing to a service, or obtaining a copy of the one newspaper that lists the stock.

By contrast, in one of the most enlightened and well-reasoned rulings ever issued by the IRS in the tax-exempt organization context, the IRS held (in 2007) that stock to be contributed to a private foundation was qualified appreciated stock, because the market quotations for the stock were readily available due to accessibility of the information on Internet sites. Having determined, by reviewing daily trade data for the stock on Internet financial sites for a one-year period, that the stock was *regularly traded*, the IRS contemplated the phrase *published quotations are available*. The agency concluded that the trades in the stock were posted on Internet sites immediately following the transaction (so that *quotations are available*) and that "virtually anyone in the world with access to the Internet" can "view current and historical market quotations" for this stock (so that the quotations were *published*). The IRS smartly observed that the tax regulations were written (in 1988) "before access to the Internet was universal and before availability of financial information on the Internet was as extensive as now."

One court case addressed the concept of qualified appreciated stock. The court held that stock contributed to a private foundation did not give rise to a charitable contribution deduction based on its fair market value because the stock did not constitute qualified appreciated stock. The stock involved was that of a bank holding company. The shares were not listed on the New York Stock Exchange, the American Stock Exchange, or any city or regional stock exchange; the shares were not regularly traded in the national or any regional over-the-counter market for which published quotations were available. The shares were not those of a mutual fund. A brokerage firm occasionally provided a suggested share price based on the net asset value of the bank. The procedure for someone wishing to purchase or sell shares of this corporation was to contact an officer of the bank or a local stock brokerage firm specializing in the shares. An attempt would be made to match a potential seller with a potential buyer; the shares were not sold frequently. The court held that the stock did not constitute qualified appreciated stock because the market quotations requirement was not satisfied.

Further, qualified appreciated stock does not include any stock contributed to a private foundation to the extent that the amount of stock contributed (including prior gifts of stock by the donor) exceeds 10% (in value) of all of the outstanding stock of the corporation. In making this calculation, an individual must take into account all contributions made by any member of his or her family. The fact that a foundation disposed of qualified appreciated stock is irrelevant in making this computation.

In applying this limitation with respect to future contributions of qualified appreciated stock, the values of prior contributions of the same stock are based on the value of the stock at the time of their contribution. That is, for this purpose, the prior contributions of stock are not revalued each time there is another contribution of the same stock.

TWICE-BASIS DEDUCTIONS

As a general rule, when a corporation makes a charitable gift of property from its inventory, the resulting charitable deduction cannot exceed an amount equal to the donor's cost basis in the donated property. In most instances, this basis amount is rather small, being equal to the cost of producing the property. Under certain circumstances, however, corporate donors can receive a greater charitable deduction for gifts out of their inventory. Where the tests are satisfied, the deduction can be equal to cost basis plus one-half of the appreciated value of the property. The charitable deduction may not, in any event, exceed an amount equal to twice the property's cost basis.

Five requirements have to be met for this twice-basis charitable deduction to be available:

1. The donated property must be used by the charitable donee for a related use.

2. The donated property must be used solely for the care of the ill, the needy, or infants.

3. The property may not be transferred by the donee in exchange for money, other property, or services.

4. The donor must receive a written statement from the donee representing that the use and disposition of the donated property will be in conformance with these rules.

5. Where the donated property is subject to regulation under the Federal Food, Drug, and Cosmetic Act, the property must fully satisfy the act's requirements on the date of transfer and for the previous 180 days.

For these rules to apply, the donee must be a public charity; that is, it cannot be a private foundation or a private operating foundation (see Chapter 1).

Similarly computed charitable deductions are available for contributions of scientific property used for research and contributions of computer technology and equipment for educational purposes.

PARTIAL-INTEREST GIFTS

Most charitable gifts are of all ownership of a property: the donor parts with all right, title, and interest in the property. A gift of a *partial interest*, however, is also possible—a contribution of less than a donor's entire interest in the property.

As a general rule, charitable deductions for gifts of partial interests in property, including the right to use property, are not available. The exceptions, which are many, are:

- Gifts made in trust form (using a *split-interest trust*)

- Gifts of an outright remainder interest in a personal residence or farm

- Gifts of an undivided portion of the donor's entire interest in an item of property

- Gifts of a lease on, option to purchase, or easement with respect to real property granted in perpetuity to a public charity exclusively for conservation purposes

- A remainder interest in real property granted to a public charity exclusively for conservation purposes

Contributions of income interests in property in trust are basically confined to the use of charitable lead trusts. Aside from a charitable gift annuity and gifts of remainder interests, there is no charitable deduction for a contribution of a remainder interest in property unless it is in trust and is one of three types: a charitable remainder annuity trust, a charitable remainder unitrust, or a pooled income fund (discussed later in this chapter).

Defective charitable split-interest trusts may be reformed to preserve the charitable deduction where certain requirements are satisfied.

GIFTS OF OR USING INSURANCE

Another type of charitable giving involves life insurance. To secure an income tax charitable deduction, the gift must include all rights of owner-ship in a life insurance policy. Thus, an individual can donate a fully paid-up life insurance policy to a charitable organization and deduct (for income tax purposes) its value. Or an individual can acquire a life insurance policy, give it to a charity, pay the premiums, and receive a charitable deduction for each premium payment made.

For the donation of an insurance policy to be valid, the charitable organization must be able to demonstrate that it has an insurable interest in the life of the donor of the policy (unless state statutory law eliminates the requirement). From an income tax deduction standpoint, it is not enough for a donor to simply name a charitable organization as the or a beneficiary of a life insurance policy. There is no income tax charitable contribution deduction for this philanthropic act. Although the life insurance proceeds become part of the donor's estate, however, there will be an offsetting estate tax charitable deduction.

There is a use of life insurance in the charitable giving context that essentially has been outlawed and thus is to be avoided. This use is embodied in the charitable split-interest insurance plan.

PLANNED GIVING

Planned giving is the most sophisticated form of charitable giving. For the most part, planned gifts are partial-interest gifts. In a broader sense, planned giving encompasses contributions made via decedents' estates and by use of life insurance. Planned gifts are common in the private foundation con-text, particularly those made by means of charitable remainder trusts and charitable lead trusts (discussed later in this chapter).

Introduction

There are two basic types of planned gifts. One type is a legacy: under a will, a gift comes out of an estate (as a bequest or a devise). The other type is a gift made during a donor's lifetime, using a trust or other agreement.

These gifts once were termed *deferred gifts* because the actual receipt of the contribution amount by the charity is deferred until the happening of some event (usually the death of the donor or subsequent death of the donor's spouse). This term, however, has fallen out of favor. Some donors (to the chagrin of the gift-seeking charities) gained the impression that it was their tax benefits that were being deferred.

A planned gift usually is a contribution of a donor's interest in money or an item of property, rather than an outright gift of the money or property in its entirety. (The word *usually* is used because gifts involving life insurance do not neatly fit this definition and because an outright gift of property, in some instances, is treated as a planned gift.) Technically, this type of gift is a conveyance of a partial interest in property; planned giving is (usually) partial-interest giving.

An item of property conceptually has within it two interests: an income interest and a remainder interest.

The *income interest* within an item of property is a function of the income generated by the property. A person may be entitled to all of the income from a property or to some portion of the income—for example, income equal to 6% of the fair market value of the property, even though the property is producing income at the rate of 9%. This person is said to have the (or an) income interest in the property. Two or more persons (such as spouses or siblings) may have income interests in the same property; these interests may be held concurrently or consecutively.

The *remainder interest* within an item of property is equal to the projected value of the property, or the property produced by reinvestments, at some future date. Put another way, the remainder interest in property is an amount equal to the present value of the property (or its offspring) when it is to be received at a subsequent point in time.

These interests are measured by the value of the property, the age of the donor(s), and the period of time that the income interest(s) will exist. The actual computation is made by means of actuarial tables, usually those promulgated by the Department of the Treasury.

An income interest or a remainder interest in property may be contributed to charity, but a deduction is almost never available for a charitable gift of an income interest in property. (This is more of an estate-planning technique.) By contrast, the charitable contribution of a remainder interest in an item of property will—assuming all of the technical requirements are satisfied—give rise to a (frequently sizable) charitable deduction.

When a gift of a remainder interest in property is made to a charity, the charity will not acquire that interest until the income interest(s) in the property have expired. The donor receives the charitable contribution deduction for the tax year in which the recipient charity's remainder interest in the property is established. On the occasion of a gift of an income interest in property to a charity, the charity acquires that interest immediately and retains it until such time as the remainder interest commences.

Basically, under the federal tax law, a planned gift must be made by means of a trust if a charitable contribution deduction is to be available. The trust used to facilitate a planned gift is known as a *split-interest trust* because it is the mechanism for satisfying the requirements involving the income and remainder interests. In other words, this type of trust is the medium for—in use of a legal fiction—splitting the property into its two component categories of interests. Split-interest trusts are charitable remainder trusts, pooled income funds, and charitable lead trusts.

There are some exceptions to the general requirements as to the use of a split-interest trust in the planned giving context. The principal exception is the charitable gift annuity, which entails a contract rather than a trust. Individuals may give a remainder interest in their personal residence or farm to charity and receive a charitable deduction without utilizing a trust. Other exceptions are listed in the preceding discussion of partial-interest gifts.

A donor, although desirous of financially supporting a charity, may be unwilling or unable to fully part with property because of a present or perceived need for the income that the property generates and/or because of the capital gains taxes that would be experienced if the property were sold. The planned gift is likely to be the solution in this type of situation: The donor may satisfy his or her charitable desires and yet continue to receive income from the property (or property that results from reinvestment). The donor also receives a charitable deduction for the gift of the remainder interest, which will reduce or eliminate the tax on the income from the gift property. There is no tax imposed on the capital gain inherent in the property. If the gift property is not throwing off sufficient income, the trustee of the split-interest trust may dispose of the property and reinvest the proceeds in more productive property. The donor may then receive more income from the property in the trust than was received prior to the making of the gift.

The various planned-giving vehicles are explored next.

Charitable Remainder Trusts

The most widespread form of planned giving involves a split-interest trust know as the *charitable remainder trust*. The term is nearly self-explanatory: The entity is a trust by which a remainder interest destined for charity has been created. Each charitable remainder trust is designed specifically for the particular circumstances of the donor(s), with the remainder interest in the gift property designated for one or more charities. (Occasionally, because of miscommunication with the donor[s], lack of skill in use of a word processor, or incompetence, a remainder trust will be drafted that is the wrong type ([discussed later in this chapter].) The IRS generously characterizes these trusts as the product of *scrivener's error*, and will recognize the qualification of the corrected trust, which must be undertaken by court-supervised reformation.

A qualified charitable remainder trust must provide for a specified distribution of income, at least annually, to or for the use of one or more beneficiaries (at least one of which is not a charity). This flow of income must be for life or for a term of no more than 20 years, with an irrevocable remainder interest to be held for the benefit of the charity or paid over to it. The beneficiaries are the holders of the income interests and the charity has the remainder interest.

How the income interests in a charitable remainder trust are ascertained depends on whether the trust is a *charitable remainder annuity trust* (income payments are in the form of a fixed amount, an annuity) or a *charitable remainder unitrust* (income payments are in the form of an amount equal to a percentage of the fair market value of the assets in the trust, determined annually). (Recently promulgated tax regulations have changed the concept of *trust income*, doing away with the traditional precepts of income and principal, with as yet unknown consequences for some charitable remainder unitrusts.)

There are four types of charitable remainder unitrusts. The one described in the preceding paragraph is known as the *standard charitable remainder unitrust* or the *fixed percentage charitable remainder unitrust*. There are two types of unitrusts that are known as *income exception charitable remainder unitrusts*. One of these types enables income to be paid to the income interest beneficiary once there is any income generated in the trust; this is the *net income charitable remainder unitrust*. The other type of income-exception unitrust is akin to the previous one, but can make catch-up payments for prior years' deficiencies once income begins to flow; this is the *net income make-up charitable remainder unitrust*. The fourth type of unitrust is allowed to convert (flip) once from one of the income exception methods to the fixed-percentage method for purposes of calculating the unitrust amount; this is the *flip charitable remainder unitrust*.

The income payout of both of these types of trusts is subject to a 5% minimum. That is, the annuity must be an amount equal to at least 5% of the value of the property initially placed in the trust. Likewise, the unitrust amount must be an amount equal to a least 5% of the value of the trust property, determined annually. These percentages may not be greater than 50%. Also, the value of the remainder interest in the property must be at least 10% of the value of the property contributed to the trust.

Nearly any kind of property can be contributed to a charitable remainder trust. Typical gift properties are cash, securities, and/or real estate. Yet a charitable remainder trust can accommodate gifts of artworks, collections, and just about any other forms of property. One of the considerations must be the ability of the property (or successor property, if sold) to generate sufficient income to satisfy the payout requirement with respect to the income interest beneficiary or beneficiaries.

All categories of charitable organizations—public charities and private foundations—are eligible to be remainder interest beneficiaries of as many charitable remainder trusts as they can muster. The amount of the charitable deduction will vary for different types of charitable organizations, however, because of the percentage limitations.

Often, a bank or other financial institution serves as the trustee of a charitable remainder trust. The financial institution should have the capacity to administer the trust, make appropriate investments, and timely adhere to all income distribution and reporting requirements. It is not unusual,

however, for the charitable organization that is the remainder interest beneficiary to act as trustee. If the donor or a related person is named the trustee,
the *grantor trust* rules may apply: The gain from the trust's sale of appreciated
property is taxed to the donor.

Conventionally, once the income interest expires, the assets in a charitable remainder trust are distributed to the charitable organization (or
organizations) that is the remainder interest beneficiary. If the assets (or
a portion of them) are retained in the trust, the trust will be classified as a
private foundation, unless it can qualify as a public charity (most likely, a
supporting organization) (see Chapter 1).

There have been some abuses in this area. One problem has been the
use of short-term (such as a term of two years) charitable remainder trusts
to manipulate the use of assets and payout arrangements for the tax benefit
of the donors. Certain of these abuses were stymied by legislation creating
some of the previously discussed percentage rules. The tax regulations were
revised in an attempt to prevent transactions by which a charitable remainder trust is used to convert appreciated property into money while avoiding
tax on the gain from the sale of the assets. (Some of these arrangements
were so audacious that the vehicles garnered the informal name *chutzpah
trust.*)

Inasmuch as charitable remainder trusts are split-interest trusts, they
are subject to at least some of the prohibitions that are imposed on private
foundations, most notably the rules concerning taxable expenditures and
self-dealing (see Chapters 5 and 6). For example, the IRS has an informal
procedure for the premature termination of a charitable remainder trust,
where the termination does not give rise to self-dealing because the procedure devised for allocation of the trust's assets to beneficiaries is reasonable.

A qualified charitable remainder trust generally is exempt from federal
income taxation. For many years, however, the law was that, in any year in
which a remainder trust had unrelated business taxable income (see Chapter 8), the trust lost its tax-exempt status. Beginning in 2007, that rule no
longer applies. Now, when one of these trusts has unrelated business taxable
income, it must pay an excise tax of 100% on that income, but otherwise it
retains its tax exemption.

Pooled Income Funds

Another planned giving technique involves gifts to charity via a *pooled income
fund*. Like a charitable remainder trust, a pooled income fund is a form of
split-interest trust.

A donor to a qualified pooled income fund receives a charitable deduction for giving the remainder interest in the donated property to charity.
The gift creates income interests in one or more noncharitable beneficiaries;
the remainder interest in the gift property is designated for the charity that
maintains the fund.

The pooled income fund's basic instrument (a trust agreement or a declaration of trust) is written to facilitate gifts from an unlimited number of donors, so the essential terms of the transactions must be established in advance for all participants. The terms of the transfer cannot be tailored to fit any one donor's particular circumstances (as is done with the charitable remainder trust). The pooled income fund constitutes, literally, a pool of gifts.

Each donor to a pooled income fund contributes an irrevocable remainder interest in the gift property to (or for the use of) an eligible charitable organization. Each donor creates an income interest for the life of one or more beneficiaries, who must be living at the time of the transfer. The properties transferred by the donors must be commingled in the fund (thereby creating the necessary pool of gifts).

Each income interest beneficiary must receive income at least once each year. The pool amount is determined by the rate of return earned by the fund for the year. Beneficiaries receive their proportionate share of the fund's income. The dollar amount of the income share is based on the number of units owned by the beneficiary; each unit must be based on the fair market value of the assets when transferred. Thus, a pooled income fund is essentially an investment vehicle whose funding is motivated by charitable intents.

A pooled income fund must be maintained by one or more charitable organizations. Usually, there is only one charity per fund. The charity must exercise control over the fund; it does not have to be the trustee of the fund (although it can be), but it must have the power to remove and replace the trustee. A donor or an income beneficiary of the fund may not be a trustee. A donor may be a trustee or officer of the charitable organization that maintains the fund, however, as long as he or she does not have the general responsibilities with respect to the fund that are ordinarily exercised by a trustee.

Unlike other forms of planned giving, a pooled income fund is restricted to only certain categories of charitable organizations. Most types of public charities can maintain a pooled income fund; private foundations and some other charities cannot.

Charitable Lead Trusts

Most forms of planned giving have a common element: The donor transfers to a charitable organization the remainder interest in an item of property, and one or more noncharitable beneficiaries retain the income interest. A reverse sequence may occur, however—and that is the essence of the *charitable lead trust.*

The property transferred to a charitable lead trust is apportioned into an income interest and a remainder interest. Like the charitable remainder trust and the pooled income fund, this is a split-interest trust. An income interest in property is contributed to a charitable organization, either for a term of years or for the life of one individual (or the lives of more than one individual). The remainder interest in the property is reserved to return, at the expiration of the income interest (the *lead period*), to the donor or pass to some other noncharitable beneficiary or beneficiaries. Often, the property passes from one generation (the donor's) to another.

The tax regulations limit the types of individuals whose lives can be used as *measuring lives* for determining the period of time the charity will receive the income flow from a charitable lead trust. The only individuals whose lives can be used as measuring ones are those of the donor, the donor's spouse, and/or a lineal ancestor of all the remaining beneficiaries. This regulation project is designed to eliminate the practice of using the lives of seriously ill individuals to move assets and income away from charitable beneficiaries prematurely and, instead to private beneficiaries. These trusts are sometimes referred to as *vulture trusts* or *ghoul trusts*.

The charitable lead trust can be used to accelerate into one year a series of charitable contributions that would otherwise be made annually. There can be a corresponding single-year deduction for the "bunched" amount of charitable gifts.

In some circumstances, a charitable deduction is available for the transfer of an income interest in property to a charitable organization. There are stringent limitations, however, on the deductible amount of charitable contributions of these income interests.

Charitable Gift Annuities

Still another form of planned giving is the *charitable gift annuity*. It is not based on use of a split-interest trust. Instead, the annuity is arranged in an agreement between the donor and the charitable donee. The donor agrees to make a gift and the donee agrees, in return, to provide the donor (and/or someone else) with an annuity.

With one payment, the donor is engaging in two transactions: the purchase of an annuity and the making of a charitable gift. The contribution gives rise to the charitable deduction. One sum is transferred; the money in excess of the amount necessary to purchase the annuity is the charitable gift portion. Because of the dual nature of the transaction, the charitable gift annuity transfer constitutes a *bargain sale*.

The annuity resulting from the creation of a charitable gift annuity arrangement (like an annuity generally) is a fixed amount paid at regular intervals. The exact amount paid depends on the age of the beneficiary, which is determined at the time the contribution is made. Frequently, the annuity payment period begins with the creation of the annuity payment obligation. The initiation of the payment period can be postponed to a future date; this type of arrangement is termed the *deferred payment charitable gift annuity*.

A portion of the annuity paid is tax free because it is a return of capital. Where appreciated securities (or other capital gain property) are given, there will be capital gain on the appreciation that is attributable to the value of the annuity. If the donor is the annuitant, the capital gain can be reported ratably over the individual's life expectancy. The tax savings occasioned by the charitable contribution deduction may, however, shelter the capital gain (resulting from the creation of a charitable gift annuity) from taxation.

Inasmuch as the arrangement is by contract between the donor and donee, all of the assets of the charitable organization are subject to liability for the ongoing payment of the annuities. (With most planned giving techniques, the resources for payment of the income are confined to those in a split-interest trust.) That is why some states impose a requirement that charities must establish a reserve for the payment of gift annuities—and why many charitable organizations are reluctant to embark on a gift annuity program. Charities that are reluctant to commit to the ongoing payment of annuities can eliminate the risk by reinsuring them.

SUMMARY

This chapter provided a summary of the federal tax charitable giving rules, including definition of the term *gift*, identification of the nonprofit organizations that are eligible to receive a deductible charitable contribution, special rules as to gifts of property, rules concerning qualified appreciated stock, and the limitations on deductibility of charitable contributions. Federal tax law in this context is additionally complicated because of the deduction reduction rules and the twice-basis deduction rules. The chapter also summarized the rules as to planned giving, including underlying principles and the use of charitable remainder trusts, pooled income funds, charitable lead trusts, and charitable gift annuities. The nonlawyer may be surprised to find that something as seemingly simple as giving to charity can spawn these exceedingly complex bodies of law.

10

REPORTING AND DISCLOSURE REQUIREMENTS

The purpose of this chapter is to summarize the various federal and state reporting requirements imposed on private foundations. It is amply clear that, tax-exempt status notwithstanding, these organizations are required to engage in a considerable amount of reporting. This aspect of nonprofit law is compounded when the various disclosure requirements are taken into account. The prevailing view is that the operations of nonprofit organizations, as a price of tax-exempt status, must be *transparent*. Specifically, this chapter will:

- Review the basics of the federal tax law reporting requirements.
- Review the elements of the private foundation annual information return.
- Summarize the unrelated business income tax return.
- Summarize the state law filing requirements.
- Describe the federal tax law disclosure requirements.

FEDERAL TAX LAW REPORTING BASICS

Nearly every organization that is exempt from federal income taxation must file an annual information return with the IRS. This return generally calls for the provision of much information, some of it financial and some in prose form. This document, being an *information return*, rather than a *tax return*, is available for public inspection (discussed later in this chapter).

Various Forms

For most tax-exempt organizations, this information return that must be filed annually is Form 990. Private foundations, however, file an information return that is uniquely styled for them—Form 990-PF. Small organizations (other than private foundations), that is, entities that have gross receipts that are less than $100,000 and total assets that are less than $250,000 in value at the end of the reporting year, file Form 990-EZ. Other forms in the 990 series are Form 990-N, 990-T, and 990-W (discussed later in this chapter).

Filing Exceptions

The requirement for the filing of an annual information return does not apply to:

- Churches (including interchurch organizations of local units of a church)
- Integrated auxiliaries of churches
- Conventions or associations of churches
- Financing, fund management, or retirement insurance program management organizations functioning on behalf of the foregoing organizations
- Certain other entities affiliated with a church or convention or association of churches
- Most religious orders (to the exclusive extent of their religious activities)
- State and local institutions
- Certain schools and mission societies
- Governmental units
- Affiliates of governmental units (which can include nonprofit, tax-exempt organizations)
- Organizations (other than private foundations) that have gross receipts that normally are not in excess of $25,000 annually
- Foreign organizations (other than private foundations) that normally do not receive more than $25,000 in gross receipts annually from

sources within the United States and that do not have any significant activity (including lobbying or political activity) in the United States

Filing Due Dates

The annual information return is due on or before the 15th day of the 5th month following the close of the organization's tax year. Thus, the return for a calendar year organization should be filed by May 15 of each year. One or more extensions may be obtained. These returns are filed with the IRS service center in Ogden, Utah.

The filing date for an annual information return may fall due while the organization's application for recognition of tax-exempt status (see Chapter 3) is pending with the IRS. In that instance, the organization should nonetheless file the information return (rather than a tax return) and indicate on it that the application is pending.

Penalties

Failure to timely file the annual information return, without reasonable cause or an exception, can generally give rise to a $20-per-day penalty. The organization must pay for each day the failure continues, up to a maximum of $10,000. For larger organizations (those with annual gross receipts in excess of $1 million), the per-day penalty is $100 and the maximum penalty is $50,000.

An additional penalty can be imposed, at the same rate and up to the same maximum, on the individual(s) responsible for the failure to file, absent reasonable cause. Other fines and even imprisonment can be imposed for willfully failing to file returns or for filing fraudulent returns and statements with the IRS.

FORM 990-PF

As noted, Form 990-PF is the annual information return that must be filed by all private foundations (tax exempt and taxable). This return is also filed by nonexempt charitable trusts. There are no exceptions to these filing requirements.

Introduction of Return

At the outset of the Form 990-PF, the filing private foundation indicates whether the return is the initial one, the final one, or an amended one, and whether there is a name and/or address change. Other information required in the opening portion of the return includes the foundation's name, mailing address, telephone number, employer identification number, accounting method, and asset value as of year-end. The foundation must indicate whether its application for recognition of exemption (see Chapter 3) is pending, whether it is a foreign organization, and whether its foundation status was terminated or if it is in a termination period (*id.*).

Part I

Part I of the Form 990-PF is an analysis of the foundation's revenue and expenses. The filing foundation must attach a schedule of the contributions it received during the reporting year. Most of the other revenue concerns investment income, primarily interest, dividends, and rent, as well as capital gain.

The expenses to be reported primarily are outlays for compensation (including compensation paid to trustees, directors, and officers), employee benefits (including pension contributions), professional fees (including legal and accounting), occupancy, travel (such as for meetings and conferences), and printing. Most other expenses (if any) need to be reported on a schedule.

Revenue and expenses are netted. The foundation also is required to report its net investment income and adjusted net income.

Part II

Part II of the Form 990-PF is a balance sheet. Thus, the foundation reports its assets and liabilities in this part of the return. The asset list includes cash, accounts receivable (including receivables from trustees, directors, officers, and other disqualified persons), securities (stocks and bonds), and real estate. Liabilities include accounts payable, loans from disqualified persons, and mortgages and other notes payable.

The filing foundation computes its total net assets or fund balances (for the beginning and end of the year), and total liabilities and net assets/fund balances. Part III of the return is an analysis of changes in net assets or fund balances.

Part IV

Part IV of the Form 990-PF is a determination of capital gains and losses for purposes of the tax on investment income (see Chapter 3). This reporting includes a list and description of the types of capital gain property sold, an indication as to how the property was acquired (purchase or contribution), the date of acquisition, the date of sale, the gross sales price, the basis in the property, the expenses of sale, and the capital gain or loss.

Part V

Part V of the Form 990-PF is used to report the foundation's qualification for the reduced tax on net investment income (see Chapter 3). Here the foundation reports its qualifying distributions for the five-year base period and other information, to determine if it is eligible for the 1% tax on net investment income (rather than the general 2% tax).

Part VI

Part VI of the Form 990-PF is the portion of the return used to calculate the excise tax based on net investment income (see Chapter 3). This part is also used to reflect any credits and prior payments made in connection with this tax, as well as any penalty for underpayment of the tax.

Part VII-A

Part VII-A of the Form 990-PF is used to provide answers to some pointed questions posed by the IRS as to activities during the tax year, including:

- Whether the foundation attempted to influence legislation or participate or intervene in a political campaign (see Chapters 3 and 5).

- Whether the foundation engaged in any activities not previously reported to the IRS.

- Whether the organization made any changes to its governing instruments not previously reported to the IRS.

- Whether the foundation had unrelated business income of $1,000 or more (see Chapter 8) and, if so, whether it filed a Form 990-T (discussed later in this chapter).

- Whether there was a liquidation, termination, dissolution, or substantial contraction.

- Whether the organizational test for private foundations was satisfied (see Chapter 3).

- The states to which the foundation reports or with which it is registered.

- Whether the foundation is claiming status as a private operating foundation (see Chapter 1).

- Whether any persons became substantial contributors (see Chapter 2) (if so, a schedule is required).

- Whether the foundation directly or indirectly owned a controlled entity.

- Whether the foundation acquired a direct or indirect interest in certain insurance contracts.

- Whether the foundation complied with the public inspection requirements for its annual information returns and its application for recognition of exemption (discussed later in this chapter).

Part VII-B

Part VII-B of the Form 990-PF is used to provide answers to more pointed questions posed by the IRS as to activities during the tax year, as to which the filing of a Form 4720 may be required, including:

- Whether the foundation engaged in any self-dealing transactions (see Chapter 6).

- Whether the foundation complied with the mandatory payout rule (see Chapter 4).

- Whether the foundation had any business holdings (see Chapter 8).

- Whether the foundation made any investment that would jeopardize its charitable purpose (see Chapter 7).

- Whether the foundation made any taxable expenditures (see Chapter 5).

- Whether the foundation received any funds, directly or indirectly, to pay premiums on a personal benefit contract (see Chapter 3).

- Whether the foundation was a party to a prohibited tax shelter transaction (*id.*).

Part VIII

In Part VIII of the Form 990-PF, the foundation is required to report:

- All trustees, directors, officers, and foundation managers, and their compensation.

- Compensation of five highest-paid employees (if not in prior list).

- Compensation of five highest-paid independent contractors for professional services.

Part IX-A

In Part IX-A of the Form 990-PF, the foundation summarizes its four largest direct charitable activities, including relevant statistical information such as the number of organizations and other beneficiaries served, conferences convened, and research papers produced, and the expenses associated with each of these activities.

Part IX-B

In Part IX-B of the Form 990-PF, the foundation describes the two largest program-related investments (see Chapter 7) that it made (if any), along with any other program-related investments.

Part X

Part X of the Form 990-PF is used by the foundation to compute its minimum investment return (see Chapter 4). Thus, the foundation reports the fair market value of its assets not used, or held for use, directly in carrying out its charitable purposes, minus any applicable acquisition indebtedness. It then calculates the amount of cash deemed held for charitable activities (generally, 1.5% of assets value) and subtracts that amount from the assets value amount, to arrive at the net value of its noncharitable-use assets. The foundation's minimum investment return is 5% of that net value amount.

Part XI

Part XI of the Form 990-PF is used by the foundation to compute its distributable amount (*id.*). Thus, the foundation subtracts the amounts of its excise tax on net investment income and any income taxes from its minimum investment return. To the resulting amount the foundation adds any recoveries of amounts previously treated as qualifying distributions, then subtracts certain deductible amounts to arrive at the distributable amount.

Part XII

Part XII of the Form 990-PF is used by the foundation to report its qualifying distributions (*id.*). The foundation reports the amounts (1) paid to accomplish charitable purposes (including administrative expenses and program-related investments), (2) paid to acquire assets used (or held for use) directly in carrying out charitable purposes, and (3) set aside for specific charitable projects (pursuant to either the suitability test or the cash distribution test), the total of which is the foundation's qualifying distributions.

Part XIII

Part XIII of the Form 990-PF is used by the foundation to report amounts of undistributed income for the prior year (if any), any excess distributions carryover to the reporting year, any excess distributions carryover to the succeeding year, and related items.

Part XIV

Part XIV of the Form 990-PF is used by the foundation to report (if it can) why it qualifies as a private operating foundation for the reporting year.

Part XV

Part XV of the Form 990-PF is used by the foundation (if it has at least $5,000 in assets during the year) to report certain supplementary information:

- A list of any of the foundation's managers who have contributed more than 2% of the total contributions received by the foundation before the close of any tax year, if they have contributed more than $5,000 (see Chapter 2).

- A list of any of the foundation's managers who own at least 10% of the stock of a corporation (or an equally large portion of the ownership of another type of business entity) of which the foundation has at least a 10% interest.

- Whether the foundation only makes grants to preselected charitable organizations and does not accept unsolicited requests for funds.

- Certain information if the foundation makes grants to individuals or to organizations under other conditions.

- Information about grants paid during the year or approved for future payment (such as the name and address of the recipient, the public charity status (see Chapter 1) of the recipient (if applicable), the purpose of the grant, and the amount of the grant).

Part XVI

Part XVI of the Form 990-PF is used to provide an analysis of the foundation's income-producing activities. The foundation reports, in Part XVI-A, the gross amount of its program service revenue, investment income (such as interest, dividends, and rent), gain from the sale of assets, revenue from special events, and any other forms of revenue. Then the foundation reports whether these income items are forms of unrelated business income, forms of unrelated income that are not taxable due to an exclusion, or forms of related income (see Chapter 8). If the income is related business income, the foundation explains, in Part XVI-B, how the underlying activities pertain to the accomplishment of the foundation's charitable purposes.

Part XVII

In Part XVII of the Form 990-PF, the foundation provides information regarding transfers to, and transactions and relationships with, noncharitable tax-exempt organizations. These transfers include transfers from the reporting foundation of cash or other assets, sales of assets, purchases of assets, rental of assets, loans or loan guarantees, reimbursement arrangements, and performance of services. The foundation reports as to whether it is directly or indirectly affiliated with or related to one or more of these exempt organizations.

FORM 990-T

Revenue and expenses associated with unrelated business activity by a tax-exempt organization (see Chapter 8) are annually reported to the IRS on

Form 990-T. This is a *tax return*, not an information return. Thus, an exempt organization, including a private foundation, with unrelated business taxable income must file the Form 990-T in addition to its Form 990, 990-PF, or 990-EZ. The Form 990-T is the return on which the source or sources of unrelated business income is reported, along with directly related deductions and the unrelated business income tax (if any) is computed. These reporting obligations are less where the unrelated business gross income is no more than $10,000.

Separate schedules pertain to rental income, unrelated debt-financed income, investment income that must be treated as unrelated business income, income (other than dividends) from controlled organizations, and advertising and other exploited exempt activity income.

FORM 990

Form 990 is an annual information return filed by most tax-exempt organizations (but not by private foundations). Foundation managers should nonetheless be familiar with this return because it is the return filed by the foundation's public charity grant recipients. Also, the IRS has recently significantly redesigned the Form 990, with implications for private foundations, such as in the realm of governance (see Chapter 12).

FORM 990-N

As noted, certain small organizations are not required to file a Form 990 (see above). Beginning in 2008, however, these organizations are required to electronically file with the IRS a short form, largely for the purpose of letting the IRS know that they exist (also known as the *e-postcard*). This short form is Form 990-N. Private foundations do not file these forms because all foundations are required to file Form 990-PF.

STATE LAW REQUIREMENTS

The states impose filing requirements on nonprofit entities. Usually, these requirements are the most defined for corporations, although there often is somewhat similar law for trusts.

If the entity is a corporation, its articles of incorporation (and perhaps its bylaws) must be filed with the state. There may be an annual reporting requirement, such as an annual report required of corporations. If the organization is doing business in more than one state, each state involved will have a filing requirement. A charitable organization may be required to adhere to the filing requirements of one or more state charitable solicitation acts (statutes regulating the fundraising process). There may be filing rules under local ordinances.

Some states and local governments accept a copy of the federal annual information return in place of all or part of their financial report forms. This may be the case if the filing is pursuant to a charitable solicitation law or in connection with an annual report for a state in which the organization is doing business.

State or local filing rules may require the organization to attach to the annual information return one or more elements of information, including additional financial statements (such as a complete analysis of functional expenses or a statement of changes in net assets), notes to financial statements, additional financial schedules, a report on the financial statements by an independent accountant, and/or answers to additional questions.

FEDERAL TAX LAW DISCLOSURE REQUIREMENTS

Various forms of disclosure requirements are imposed on private foundations.

Applications for Recognition of Exemption

To be tax-exempt, private foundations (and nearly all other types of charitable organizations) are required to file an application for recognition of exemption with the IRS (as discussed in Chapter 3). In either case, once the application is filed and the IRS has acted on the matter, the application becomes a public document, subject to disclosure by the exempt organization. A question on the annual information return inquires as to whether the organization has complied with this disclosure requirement.

Tax-exempt organizations that have a determination letter from the IRS recognizing their tax-exempt status are required to provide a copy of their application for recognition of exemption to requesting members of the public. This must be done, without charge, at the organization's principal, regional, and district offices during regular business hours. Generally, the copy must be provided to a requestor on the business day the request is made. In the case of an in-person request, where unusual circumstances exist so that fulfillment of the request on the same day places an unreasonable burden on the exempt organization, the copy must be provided on the next business day following the day on which the unusual circumstances cease to exist or the fifth business day after the date of the request, whichever occurs first. A tax-exempt organization that receives a written request for a copy of the application must mail the copy within 30 days from the date it receives the request.

A tax-exempt organization is not required to comply with requests for copies of its application for recognition of exemption if the organization has made the document widely available. The application is made *widely available* by posting the document on a web site that the organization establishes and maintains. It can also satisfy the exception if the document is posted as part of a database of similar documents of other exempt organizations on a web site established and maintained by another entity.

If the IRS determines that a tax-exempt organization is the subject of a harassment campaign and that compliance with the requests that are part of the campaign would not be in the public interest, the organization is not required to fulfill a request for a copy that it reasonably believes is part of the campaign.

If a tax-exempt organization denies an individual's request for a copy of an application for recognition of exemption, and the individual wishes to alert the IRS to the possible need for enforcement action, he or she may send a statement to the appropriate IRS district office, describing the reason why the individual believes the denial was in violation of these requirements. There is no private right of action in this setting.

There is a penalty for failure to comply with this disclosure requirement, amounting to $20 per day.

Annual Information Returns

Private foundations (and just about every other type of tax-exempt organization) are required to file annual information returns with the IRS. These returns are public documents that are subject to disclosure by the exempt organization. A question on the annual information return inquires as to whether the organization has complied with this disclosure requirement.

Tax-exempt organizations are required to provide copies of their annual information returns to members of the requesting public. This requirement pertains to the most recent three annual information returns. The same rules, as summarized with respect to the disclosure and dissemination of applications for recognition of exemption, apply with respect to annual information returns. This includes the exception for returns that are posted on the Internet and the harassment campaign exception.

There is a penalty for failure to comply with this disclosure requirement, amounting to $20 per day ($10,000 per return).

Unrelated Business Income Tax Returns

The public inspection and disclosure requirements applicable to annual information returns are applicable to the unrelated business income tax returns filed by charitable organizations, including private foundations.

Gift Substantiation Requirements

The federal tax law contains charitable gift substantiation rules. Pursuant to this body of law, a donor who makes a separate charitable contribution of $250 or more (in amount or value) in a year, for which a charitable contribution deduction is claimed, must obtain written substantiation from the donee charitable organization.

More specifically, the rule is that the charitable deduction is not available for a separate charitable contribution of $250 or more unless the donor has obtained written substantiation from the charitable donee of the contribution in the form of a contemporaneous written acknowledgment. Thus, donors cannot rely solely on a canceled check or similar documentation as substantiation for a gift of at least $250. Such documentation suffices as substantiation for smaller gifts.

An *acknowledgment* meets this requirement if it includes the following information: (1) the amount of money and a description (but not value) of any property other than money that was contributed; (2) whether the donee organization provided any goods or services in consideration, in whole or in part, for any money or property contributed; and (3) a description and good faith estimate of the value of any goods or services involved or, if the goods or services consist solely of intangible religious benefits, a statement to that effect. The phrase *intangible religious benefit* means an intangible benefit provided by a religious organization and that generally is not sold in a commercial transaction outside the donative context. An acknowledgment is considered to be *contemporaneous* if the contributor obtains the acknowledgment on or before the earlier of (1) the date on which the donor filed a tax return for the tax year in which the contribution was made or (2) the due date (including extensions) for filing the return.

There are other defined terms. The phrase *goods or services* means money, property, services, benefits, and privileges. Certain goods or services, however, are disregarded for these purposes: those that have insubstantial value and certain annual membership benefits offered to an individual in exchange for a payment of $75 or less per year. A charitable organization provides goods or services *in consideration* for a donor's transfer if, at the time the donor makes the payment to the charity, the donor receives or expects to receive goods or services in exchange for the payment. Goods or services a charitable organization provides in consideration for a payment by a donor include goods or services provided in a year other than the year in which the payment was made. A *good faith estimate* means a charitable organization's estimate of the fair market value of any goods or services, without regard to the manner in which the organization in fact made the estimate.

As noted, this substantiation rule applies in connection with separate payments. *Separate* payments are generally treated as separate contributions and are not aggregated for the purpose of applying the $250 threshold. In cases of contributions paid by withholding from wages, the deduction from each paycheck is treated as a separate payment. The IRS has the authority to issue antiabuse rules in this area (addressing practices such as the writing of multiple checks to the same charity on the same date) but has not done so.

The written acknowledgment of a separate gift is not required to take any particular form. Thus, these acknowledgments may be made by letter, postcard, email, or computer-generated form. A donee charitable organization may prepare a separate acknowledgment for each contribution or may provide donors with periodic (such as annual) acknowledgments that set forth the required information for each contribution of $250 or more made by the donor during the period.

A court made the administration of this area of the law considerably more difficult. This is because it held that these rules apply with respect to verbal (unwritten) *expectations* or *understandings* a donor may have of the charitable recipient when making a contribution. This court thus equated, for these purposes, expectations with goods or services. How representatives of charitable organizations are supposed to divine their donors' inner thoughts when giving is not clear.

It is the responsibility of a donor to obtain the written substantiation and maintain it in his or her records. (Again, the allowability of the charitable contribution deduction is dependent on compliance with these rules.) A charitable organization that knowingly provides a false written substantiation to a donor may be subject to a penalty for aiding and abetting an understatement of tax liability.

These substantiation rules do not apply to transfers of property to charitable remainder trusts or to charitable lead trusts. The requirements are, however, applicable to transfers to pooled income funds (see Chapter 9). In the case of these funds, the contemporaneous written acknowledgment must state that the contribution was transferred to the charitable organization's pooled income fund and indicate whether any goods or services (in addition to the income interest) were provided in exchange for the transfer. The contemporaneous written acknowledgment, however, need not include a good faith estimate of the income interest.

Quid Pro Quo Contributions

Among the practices that entail payments that are partially gifts and partially payments for goods or services are special event programs, whereby the patron receives something of value (such as a ticket to a theater performance or a dinner, the opportunity to play in a sports tournament, and auctions), yet makes a payment in excess of that value amount. In these circumstances, the amount paid that is in excess of the value received by the patron is a charitable gift.

In an analogous area, the IRS held that payments by corporate sponsors of college and university bowl games are not charitable gifts to the bowl game associations, but must be treated by the associations as forms of unrelated business income because the corporate sponsors received a valuable package of advertising services. This controversial ruling led to IRS and congressional hearings, proposed regulations, and finally legislation.

This statutory law shields *qualified sponsorship payments* from taxation. A payment of this nature is one made by a person engaged in a trade or business, from which the person did not receive a substantial return benefit other than the use or acknowledgment of the name or logo (or product lines) of the person's trade or business in connection with the organization's activities. This use or acknowledgment does not include advertising of the person's products or services. *Advertising* entails qualitative or comparative language, price information or other indications of savings or value, or an endorsement or other inducement to purchase, sell, or use the products or services.

The federal tax law imposes certain disclosure requirements on charitable organizations that receive quid pro quo contributions. A question on the annual information return inquires as to whether the organization has complied with these disclosure requirements.

A *quid pro quo contribution* is a payment made partly as a contribution and partly in consideration for goods or services provided to the payor by the donee organization. The term does not include a payment made to an organization, operated exclusively for religious purposes, in return for which the donor receives solely an intangible religious benefit that generally is not sold in a commercial transaction outside the donative context.

Specifically, if a charitable organization (other than a state, possession of the United States, a political subdivision of a state or possession, the United States, and the District of Columbia) receives a quid pro quo contribution in excess of $75, the organization must, in connection with the solicitation or receipt of the contribution, provide a written statement that (1) informs the donor that the amount of the contribution that is deductible for federal income tax purposes is limited to the excess of the amount of any money and the value of any property other than money contributed by the donor over the value of the goods or services provided by the organization, and (2) provides the donor with a good faith estimate of the value of the goods or services.

In other words, this law is designed to cause a donor or patron to know that the only amount deductible in these circumstances as a charitable gift (if any) is the amount paid to the charity in excess of any benefits provided by the charity. A charitable organization may use any reasonable methodology in making this good faith estimate as long as it applies the methodology in good faith. A good faith estimate of the value of goods or services that are not generally available in a commercial transaction may be determined by reference to the fair market value of similar or comparable goods or services. Goods or services may be similar or comparable even though they do not have the unique qualities of the goods or services that are being valued. Where the goods or services are available on a commercial basis, the commercial value is used.

For purposes of the $75 threshold, separate payments made at different times of the year with respect to fundraising events generally will not be aggregated. The IRS has the authority to promulgate antiabuse rules in this area (addressing practices such as the writing of multiple checks to the same charity on the same date) but has not done so.

These rules do not apply where only *de minimis*, token goods or services (such as key chains and bumper stickers) are provided to the donor. In defining these terms, prior IRS announcements are followed. Nor do these rules apply to transactions that lack a donative element (such as the charging of tuition by a school, the charging of health care fees by a hospital, or the sale of items by a museum).

The law in this area is meager on the matter of *celebrity presence*. If a celebrity is present at an event and does nothing, or does something that is different from that for which he or she is celebrated, the value of the celebrity presence is zero. (An example of the latter is a tour of a museum conducted by an artist whose works are on display; the artist is renowned for the artwork, not for being a tour guide.) Presumably, if the celebrity performs as such, the charitable organization must utilize the commercial value of the performance.

No part of a payment can be considered a contribution unless the payor intended to make a payment in an amount that is in excess of the fair market value of the goods or services received. This requirement of *donative intent* has particular application in the instance of auctions conducted by charitable organizations. The procedure preferred by the law is that a charity holding an auction will publish a catalog that meets the requirements for a written disclosure statement, including the charity's good faith estimate of the value of items that will be available for bidding.

A penalty is imposed on charitable organizations that do not satisfy these disclosure requirements. For failure to make the required disclosure in connection with a quid pro quo contribution of more than $75, there is a penalty of $10 per contribution, not to exceed $5,000 per fundraising event or mailing. An organization may be able to avoid this penalty if it can show that the failure to comply was due to reasonable cause.

In general, a person can rely on a contemporaneous written acknowledgment provided in the gift substantiation context (discussed earlier in this chapter) or a written disclosure statement provided in the quid pro quo transaction setting. An individual may not, however, treat an estimate of the value of goods or services as their fair market value if he or she knows, or has reason to know, that the treatment is unreasonable.

Disclosure of Gifts of Property

A donor to a charitable organization is required to disclose to the IRS, by means of the appropriate federal income tax return, certain information in the case of a claimed deduction for noncash contributions in excess of $500. This filing requirement is applicable in the case of contributions by individuals, partnerships, personal service corporations, closely held corporations, and other corporations. C corporations (that are not personal service corporations or closely held corporations) are required to make this disclosure only if the amount claimed as a charitable deduction is more than $5,000.

This disclosure is made by means of IRS Form 8283. The form consists of Sections A and B. A donor may need to complete one of these sections or the other, or both, depending on the type of property contributed and the amount claimed as a charitable deduction. This form is filed with the donor's tax return for the year of the gift.

The donor includes in Section A only references to items (or groups of similar items [discussed later in this chapter]) for which the donor claimed a deduction of $5,000 or less per item (or group of similar items). The following information is required in Part I: the name and address of the donee organization, a description of the donated property in sufficient detail, the date of the contribution, the date the donated property was acquired by the donor, how the property was acquired by the donor, the donor's cost or adjusted basis in the property, the fair market value of the property, and the method used to determine this fair market value.

Also, the donor is required to list the following publicly traded securities even if the claimed deduction is more than $5,000: securities listed on an exchange in which quotations are published daily, securities regularly traded in national or regional over-the-counter markets for which published quotations are available, and securities that are shares of a mutual fund for which quotations are published on a daily basis in a newspaper of general circulation throughout the United States.

The donor must respond to questions in Part II about any partial-interest gifts (see Chapter 9) and/or any conditions placed on contributed property. If this part applies to more than one item of property, a separate statement must be attached to the return, providing the required information for each property.

The donor references in Section B (appraisal summary [discussed later in this chapter]) only items (or groups of similar items) for which the donor claimed a deduction of more than $5,000 per item (or group). (This rule does not apply with respect to publicly traded securities that are reportable in Section A.) Generally, the donor must have a written appraisal from a qualified appraiser (see below) that supports the information provided in Section B, Part I. If the total deduction for art is $20,000 or more, the donor must attach a complete copy of the signed appraisal; a photograph of the artwork must be provided to the IRS on request.

A separate qualified appraisal and a separate Form 8283 are required for each item of property, except for an item that is part of a group of similar items. If the donor gave similar items to more than one charitable donee for which the donor claimed a total deduction of more than $5,000, the donor must attach a separate form for each donee.

The donor should complete Part II of Section B for each item included in Part I of the section that has an appraised value of $500 or less. Because the donor does not have to show the value of these items in Part I of the donee's copy of the Form 8283, these items should be identified for the donee in Part II. Then, the donee does not have to file with the IRS if the property is sold within two years of the gift.

If the donor was required to obtain an appraisal, the appraiser must complete Part III of Section B to be qualified (discussed later in this chapter). The charitable organization that received the property is required to complete Part IV of the section. The donor must provide a copy of Section B of Form 8283 to the donee.

Dispositions of Contributed Property

Charitable organizations that dispose of certain charitable deduction property (see below) within two years of the gift must disclose the transaction to the IRS. This is accomplished by filing Form 8282. The charitable donee is required to file the form within 125 days after the date of disposition of the property.

This form does not have to be filed if, at the time the original donee signed the appraisal summary, the donor signed a statement on Form 8283 (see above) that the appraised value of the specific item was not more than $500. If the Form 8283 references more than one similar item, this rule applies only to those items that are clearly identified as having a value of $500 or less. Also, the charitable donee is not required to file this form if an item is consumed or distributed, without consideration, in fulfillment of its exempt purpose or function.

If the gift property is transferred by the donee charitable organization (the *original donee*) to another charitable organization (the *successor donee*) within the two-year period, the original donee must provide the successor donee with the name, address, and tax identification number of the organization; a copy of the appraisal summary; and a copy of the Form 8282 involved, within 15 days of filing by the original donee.

The first two of these items must be furnished to the successor donee within 15 days after the latest of the date the original donee transferred the property, the original donee signed the appraisal summary, or the original donee received a copy of the appraisal summary from the preceding donee if the charity is also a successor donee.

A successor donee must provide the original donee with the successor organization's name, address, and tax identification number within 15 days after the later of the date the property was transferred by the original organization or the date the successor organization received a copy of the appraisal summary.

A charitable organization must provide a copy of the completed Form 8282 to the original donor of the property.

A charitable organization may be subject to a penalty if it fails to timely file Form 8282, fails to include all of the information required to be shown on the form, or fails to include correct information on the form. Generally, this penalty is $50.

Appraisal Requirements

There are disclosure requirements in connection with the substantiation of deductions claimed by an individual, a closely held corporation, a personal service corporation, a partnership, or an S corporation for charitable contributions of certain property.

Property to which these rules apply is termed *charitable deduction property*. If the contributed property is a partial interest in an item of property (see Chapter 9), the appraisal must be of the partial interest. These requirements apply to contributions of property (other than money and publicly traded securities) if the aggregate claimed or reported value of the property—and all similar items of property for which deductions for charitable contributions are claimed or reported by the same donor for the same tax year whether donated to the same charitable donee—is in excess of $5,000.

The phrase *similar items of property* means property of the same generic category or type, such as stamp collections, coin collections, lithographs, paintings, photographs, books, non–publicly traded securities, parcels of land, buildings, clothing, jewelry, furniture, electronic equipment, household appliances, toys, everyday kitchenware, china, crystal, or silver.

For this type of gift, the donor must obtain a qualified appraisal and attach an appraisal summary to the federal income tax return on which the deduction is claimed. In the case of non-publicly traded stock, however, the claimed value of which does not exceed $10,000 but is greater than $5,000, the donor is not required to obtain a qualified appraisal but must attach a partially completed appraisal summary form to the federal income tax or information return on which the deduction is claimed.

A *qualified appraisal* is an appraisal document that relates to an appraisal that is made not earlier than 60 days prior to the date of contribution of the appraisal property; is prepared, signed, and dated by a qualified appraiser (or appraisers); contains the requisite information; and does not involve a prohibited type of appraisal fee.

The qualified appraisal must include a description of the property in sufficient detail for a person who is not generally familiar with the type of property to ascertain that the property that was appraised is the property contributed; the physical condition of the property (in the instance of tangible property); the date of contribution of the property; the terms of any agreement between the parties relating to any subsequent disposition of the property, including restrictions on the charitable organization's use of the gift property; the name, address, and tax identification number of the appraiser; the qualifications of the qualified appraiser (or appraisers); a statement that the appraisal was prepared for income tax purposes; the date or dates on which the property was appraised; the appraised fair market value of the property on the date of contribution; the method of valuation used to determine the fair market value of the property; and the specific basis for the valuation.

The qualified appraisal must be received by the donor before the due date (including extensions) of the return on which the deduction for the contributed property is first claimed or, in the case of a deduction first claimed on an amended return, the date on which the amended return is filed.

A separate qualified appraisal is required for each item of property that is not included in a group of similar items of property. One qualified appraisal is required for a group of similar items of property contributed in the same tax year, as long as the appraisal includes all of the required information for each item. The appraiser may select any items the aggregate value of which is appraised at $100 or less, for which a group description (rather than a specific description of each item) is adequate.

The tax regulations provide that the appraisal must be retained by the donor "for so long as it may be relevant in the administration of any internal revenue laws."

The *appraisal summary* must be made using Section B of Form 8283, signed and dated on behalf of the charitable donee and by the qualified appraiser (or appraisers), and attached to the donor's federal income tax return on which a deduction with respect to the appraised property is first claimed or reported. The signature by the representative of the charitable donee does not represent concurrence by the donee in the appraised value of the contributed property.

The appraisal summary must include the name and taxpayer identification number of the donor (such as the Social Security number of an individual); a description of the donated property in requisite detail; a brief summary of the condition of the property at the time of the gift (in the case of tangible property); the manner and date of acquisition of the property by the donor; the cost basis of the property; the name, address, and taxpayer identification number of the charitable donee; the date the donee received the property; a statement explaining whether the charitable contribution was made by means of a bargain sale and amount of any consideration received from the donee for the contribution; the name, address, and taxpayer identification number of the qualified appraiser (or appraisers); the appraised fair market value of the property on the date of contribution; and a declaration by the appraiser (discussed later in this chapter).

The rules pertaining to separate appraisals also apply with respect to appraisal summaries. A donor who contributed similar items of property to more than one charitable donee must, however, attach a separate appraisal summary for each donee.

Every donor who presents an appraisal summary to a charitable organization for signature must furnish a copy of the appraisal summary to the charitable organization. If the donor is a partnership or an S corporation, the donor must provide a copy of the appraisal summary to every partner or shareholder who receives an allocation of a deduction for a charitable contribution of property described in the appraisal summary. The partner or shareholder must attach the appraisal summary to the partner's or shareholder's federal income tax return. If a donor (or partner or shareholder of a donor) fails to attach the appraisal summary to the return, the charitable deduction will not be disallowed if the donor (or partner or shareholder of a donor) submits an appraisal summary within 90 days of being requested to do so by the IRS, as long as the failure to attach the appraisal summary was a good faith omission and certain other requirements are met (including timely completion of the appraisal).

An appraisal summary on Section B of Form 8283 must be filed by contributors where the total value of all noncash contributions exceeds $500 and is less than $5,000. This portion of the form must also be used to report contributions of publicly traded securities, even where the value of them is in excess of $5,000.

The term *qualified appraiser* means an individual who includes on the appraisal summary a declaration that:

- He or she holds himself or herself out to the public as an appraiser to perform appraisals on a regular basis.

- Because of the appraiser's qualifications as described in the appraisal, he or she is qualified to make appraisals of the type of property being valued.

- The appraiser is not one of the persons excluded by these rules from being a qualified appraiser.

- The appraiser understands that an intentionally false or fraudulent overstatement of the value of the property described in the qualified appraisal or appraisal summary may subject the appraiser to a civil penalty for aiding and abetting an understatement of tax liability, and consequently the appraiser may have appraisals disregarded.

Notwithstanding these requirements, an individual is not a qualified appraiser if the donor had knowledge of facts that would cause a reasonable person to expect the appraiser to falsely overstate the value of the donated property. Also, the donor, donee, or certain other related persons cannot be a qualified appraiser of the property involved in the gift transaction.

More than one appraiser may appraise the donated property, as long as each appraiser complies with these requirements, including signing the qualified appraisal and appraisal summary. If more than one appraiser appraises the property, the donor does not have to use each appraiser's appraisal for purposes of substantiating the charitable deduction.

Generally, no part of the fee arrangement for a qualified appraisal can be based on a percentage of the appraised value of the property. If a fee arrangement is based, in whole or in part, on the amount of the appraised value of the property that is allowed as a charitable deduction, after an IRS examination or otherwise, it is treated as a fee based on a percentage of the appraised value of the property. (This rule does not apply in certain circumstances to appraisal fees paid to a generally recognized association that regulates appraisers.)

In any situation involving a gift of property, the charitable organization that is the recipient of the gift must value the property for its own record-keeping, reporting, and (if applicable) financial statement purposes. The charitable donee, however, is not required to share that valuation amount with the donor.

These rules are subject to the *doctrine of substantial compliance*. Pursuant to this doctrine, where the rules involved are procedural or directory in nature, strict adherence to them is not required; substantial compliance is sufficient. It has been held that in this context, the requirement that certain documentation be attached to the donor's federal income tax return is directory rather than mandatory.

A separate set of rules applies appraisal requirements to regular corporations (that is, corporations other than those referenced above; termed *C corporations*). These rules, in general, require these corporations to obtain a qualified independent appraisal to validly claim a charitable contribution deduction for gifts of most items of property, other than money, having a value in excess of $5,000.

There are special rules concerning contributions of inventory. C corporations are required to include summary information in their annual federal income tax return, such as a description of the inventory contributed and the valuation method used. This information is to be embodied in a *partially completed appraisal summary*.

These substantiation requirements must be complied with if the charitable contribution deduction is to be allowed.

FILING REQUIREMENTS AND TAX-EXEMPT STATUS

If a tax-exempt organization that is required to file a notice (Form 990-N) with the IRS in lieu of an annual information return fails to provide the notice for three consecutive years, the organization's exempt status is revoked by operation of law. This revocation rule also applies with respect to annual information returns or a combination of annual information returns and notices.

As noted, these notice rules do not apply to private foundations. Foundations, however, should check on the status of prospective grantees, to avert the possibility of making a grant to an organization that has lost its tax-exempt status (without the exercise of expenditure responsibility [see Chapter 5]).

ELECTRONIC FILING

Private foundations, irrespective of asset size, must file their annual information returns electronically, if during the year involved they filed at least 250 returns with the IRS (such as Forms W-2 and 1099).

SUMMARY

This chapter provided a summary of the federal tax law reporting requirements imposed on tax-exempt organizations, with emphasis on the annual information return that private foundations are mandated to file. State law reporting requirements were described. The chapter described the many federal tax law disclosure requirements imposed on private foundations (and tax-exempt charitable organizations generally). The chapter concluded with reference to the filing rules in relation to tax-exempt status and the electronic filing rules.

11

ALTERNATIVES TO PRIVATE FOUNDATIONS

The purpose of this chapter is to analyze charitable entities that prospective contributors, tax-exempt organizations, and others may want to consider as alternatives to the private foundation. Essentially, there are three options: a type of public charity other than a supporting organization, a supporting organization, and a donor-advised fund. Several variables animate the decision as to which vehicle to utilize. Specifically, this chapter will:

- Inventory the factors to consider when contemplating the formation of a charitable entity.
- Explain the advantages of public charity status.
- Explore more law concerning supporting organizations.
- Describe the creative uses of supporting organizations.
- Summarize the law concerning donor-advised funds.
- Provide a comparative analysis as to private foundations and their alternatives.

FACTORS TO CONSIDER

There are ten factors to consider when contemplating the establishment of a private foundation or some other charitable entity:

1. The form of the entity (see Chapter 3). The elements to take into account in this regard include the attendant federal and state reporting

243

requirements (see Chapter 10), limitations as to personal liability (see Chapter 12), and the need for a governing board.

2. Whether those who are creating the entity want to have ongoing control over it. This frequently is the pivotal factor.

3. Tax-exempt status for the entity, including whether application for recognition of exemption (see Chapter 3) is required.

4. Whether contributions to the entity will be deductible as charitable gifts and, if so, to what extent (see Chapter 9).

5. The nature of the programs of the organization.

6. The extent of the law regulating the programs and other operations of the organization (see, e.g., Chapters 3 through 8).

7. Whether the organization wants to engage in fundraising.

8. Whether the organization wants to receive grants from private foundations.

9. Whether the organization is going to have employees, which may include the founder(s) and/or their family members.

10. Whether the organization is being established by one or more individuals, by a tax-exempt organization, or by a for-profit corporation.

PRIVATE FOUNDATIONS

How does the standard private foundation stack up against the foregoing checklist? Here are the answers:

1. The form of the entity is discussed elsewhere (see Chapters 3 and 12). The choice essentially is a nonprofit corporation or trust. If concerns about personal liability are paramount, the corporate form will be selected. Where privacy is of primary concern or the entity is being created by will, the trust form will be used. Concerns about annual reporting to the IRS are a negative factor because the Form 990-EZ is complex; this is somewhat of a neutral factor now that the redesigned Form 990 is much more expansive and encompassing. A private foundation must have a governing board.

2. If control is a factor (and, as noted, it usually is), the private foundation is certain to be the first choice. The creators of a foundation can, and almost always do, maintain control over it. As discussed throughout, this is often the principal element that causes the selection of the private foundation as the preferred entity.

3. An application for recognition of tax exemption (Form 1023) must be filed, and be successful, for a private foundation to be tax exempt.

4. The charitable contribution deduction, obviously, is often a major factor in this mix. Contributions to a private foundation are deductible, although the federal charitable giving rules are, in places, tilted against foundations, such as the more restrictive percentage limitations on the deductibility of gifts by individuals and the rules concerning deductible gifts of property. If a gift of a large amount of money is involved, the percentage limitations may discourage selection of the private foundation (with that negativity perhaps tempered by the deduction carryforward rules). If a gift of appreciated property is being contemplated, and the property is not qualified appreciated stock, use of a standard private foundation will likely not be appealing because the charitable deduction will be confined to the donor's cost basis in the property. Often, this factor and the control factor are the major competing ones.

5. If the plan is for the charitable organization to have one or more active programs, the private foundation may not be the best choice, although the private operating foundation should be considered. Certainly, for example, if a school or hospital is under consideration, the private foundation is not the choice; it may be the choice, however, if a museum is being contemplated. Foundations are ideal where the charitable activity is grant-making.

6. If the putative founders of a charitable entity are fearful of government regulation and penalties, the private foundation will probably end up at the bottom of the list (see Chapters 4 through 8).

7. If the plan includes fundraising of any consequence, the private foundation will not be the choice, simply because active and ongoing fundraising would cause the entity to be a publicly supported charity (or perhaps another form of public charity).

8. The private foundation is not the answer if the charitable entity-in-waiting expects to receive grants from foundations. A private foundation generally cannot obtain a payout credit for the making of a grant to another private foundation (see Chapter 4).

9. The private foundation is the ideal charitable vehicle where the founders and/or their family members are to be its employees. A creator of a foundation can be a board member, an officer, and an employee of the organization. It is essential, however, to avoid self-dealing and private inurement problems, that compensation be reasonable.

10. If one or more individuals are establishing the charitable organization, the private foundation certainly is a legitimate candidate. If a for-profit

company is forming a charitable entity, the choice is almost certain to be the foundation, funded solely by the company. If the charitable organization is being established by a public charity, the organization would almost never be a private foundation. If another type of tax-exempt organization is forming a charitable entity, it may or may not be a foundation, depending on the type of exempt organization.

PUBLIC CHARITIES IN GENERAL

A public charity is an obvious alternative to a private foundation (see Chapter 1). Yet the choice here is far more theoretical than real. If, for example, the entity under consideration is to be a church, school, college, university, hospital, medical research organization, large fundraising charity, or supporting organization, the appropriate public charity form would be selected; a private foundation would not be (or should not be) contemplated. (Supporting organizations are discussed more fully on p. 248.)

The Checklist

Here is how public charities in general (other than supporting organizations) fare in relation to the preceding ten-factor checklist:

1. The typical public charity is likely to be formed as a nonprofit corporation. These organizations almost always have federal and state reporting requirements (as to the former, it is usually the Form 990). It is possible that the charitable organization to be established will be a church or some other religious organization that is not required to file an annual information return but that choice of tax-exempt organization is unlikely. Public charities always have governing boards.

2. Those who create a public charity can—as a matter of pure law—control it. In our society, however, this type of control is not well regarded. There is a pervasive view (based on good governance principles, not law) that the members of boards of public charities (or at least a majority of them) should be *independent* or somehow be representative of the public or the community. The IRS and the courts are quick to find unwarranted private benefit in control situations involving public charities; this endangers tax-exempt status.

3. To be tax-exempt, most public charities are required to file an application for recognition of exemption with, and receive a favorable determination from, the IRS.

4. Contributions to public charities are deductible, almost always to the fullest extent permitted by law.

5. Public charities conduct a variety of programs. It is rare for a public charity (again, other than a supporting organization) to be merely a grant-making entity. A public charity can operate an unrelated business, whereas a private foundation is likely to be precluded from doing so (see Chapter 8).

6. Public charities are subject to the federal tax and other law regulating their operations but not to the extent that private foundations are regulated.

7. If a charitable organization wants to engage in fundraising to any appreciable extent, it will be a public charity. For example, churches, schools, hospitals, and research organizations solicit contributions and grants. Many fundraising entities are donative publicly supported charitable organizations.

8. Public charities generally can receive grants from private foundations. Foundations generally receive a payout credit for making grants to public charities; indeed, this is the most common form of foundation grant-making.

9. Public charities obviously can have employees, which may include their founder(s) and/or their family members. It is essential, however, to avoid excess benefit transaction and private inurement problems, that compensation be reasonable.

10. Individuals and tax-exempt organizations can establish public charities. So, too, can for-profit companies, although that is infrequent.

Public Charities as Successors

More likely, a public charity, while not the choice when a private foundation is clearly more appropriate, will be a successor to a foundation. A charitable organization can terminate its private foundation status (see Chapter 3) and morph into a public charity. The obvious candidate for this successor status is the supporting organizations, but private foundations have evolved into schools, research entities, publicly supported charities, and the like.

The opportunities in this regard are nearly boundless and definitely not static. As an illustration, consider a private foundation that for years has been making scholarship grants to gifted children. The foundation may decide to become a school (a form of public charity) for gifted children, thereby more directly educating these children. Or it may utilize a portion of its resources to form the school, then convert the balance of itself to a supporting organization (public charity) with respect to the school (two public charities for the price of one private foundation).

Tax-exempt organization parents usually spawn public charities, not private foundations. An exempt business association may want a related charitable organization to be a fundraising arm, a research or publishing vehicle, an endowment, or a training entity; this related organization will be a public charity, not a private foundation. Exempt social welfare organizations are fond of having related charitable or educational entities; these are rarely private foundations. A labor union's apprentice training facility is likely to be housed in a public charity, not a private foundation. In other instances, however, a private foundation will be a necessary choice for an exempt social club, veterans' organization, or fraternal group.

No law confines an individual or organization to the formation of only one organization, however. There are individuals who have formed and control a private foundation and a private operating foundation, or a private foundation and a form of public charity. Limited only by money, time, and energy, an individual or group of individuals can establish as many charities as they wish, some public, some private. Mixing and matching of this nature is nearly limitless.

SUPPORTING ORGANIZATIONS

The supporting organization (discussed in Chapter 1) is, on the face of these matters, the most likely alternative to the private foundation. This is because a typical supporting organization looks and operates much like a private foundation. That is, a supporting organization (1) is a tax-exempt charitable organization, (2) that often is funded only with investment income, (3) and that often makes grants to other charitable organizations rather than maintain its own programs. A major difference between the two is that the supporting organization's support and benefit is frequently targeted to one entity. Also, quite frequently, the beneficiary entity with respect to a supporting organization controls the supporting organization. The supporting organization, then, can often be viewed as a foundation that is dedicated to one entity (the supported organization).

Recent years, however, have not been kind to supporting organizations, in terms of law development. Abuses (or the potential for abuses) have caused Congress to crack down hard on supporting organizations, enacting legislation (some of it misguided) that has substantially increased the regulation of these organizations and, in too many instances, is crippling their use. Even more burdensome and harmful regulation is in the works, in the form of Treasury Department and IRS regulations and rules. As a consequence, supporting organizations are not the attractive alternative to private foundations they once were.

Before summarizing this new law, it is critical to reiterate the major distinctions between the private foundation and the supporting organization. One major factor is *control*. As discussed, the founders of a private foundation can control it. As also discussed, the founders of a supporting organization cannot (if they are disqualified persons) control it. An individual or family contemplating the establishment of a charitable organization is likely to select the foundation alternative solely because of this control factor. A compelling, countervailing factor, however, is the charitable contribution deduction. An individual with highly appreciated real estate, for example, to contribute to a charity being formed is almost certainly going to be torn between the much larger charitable deduction available if the donee is a supporting organization (public charity) and the ability to control the charity if the donee is a private foundation. On occasion, the deduction factor will trump the control factor. (Again, an individual can form and fund two charitable entities, one public, one private.)

Recent Law

As discussed (see Chapter 1), supporting organizations are public charities because they generally are sufficiently related to one or more charitable organizations that are *institutions* or are *publicly supported organizations* so that the requisite degree of public control and involvement is considered present. These entities are operated exclusively for the benefit of, to perform the functions of, or to carry out the purposes of one or more eligible supported organizations. Supporting organizations are of four types: parent and subsidiary (Type I), common control (Type II), functionally integrated (Type III), and nonfunctionally integrated. A supporting organization may not be controlled, directly or indirectly, by one or more disqualified persons (other than foundation managers or eligible supported organizations).

Congress, in 2006, passed new law, much of it rather intricate, in connection with supporting organizations. Some of this law involved application of some of the private foundation rules to supporting organizations. Other law brought in specific application of the intermediate sanctions rules. The most stringent provisions of new law are directed at Type III supporting organizations, particularly those that are not functionally integrated with a supported organization.

A grant-making private foundation (as contrasted with a private operating foundation) may not treat as a qualifying distribution (see Chapter 4) an amount paid to a Type III supporting organization that is not a functionally integrated Type III supporting organization (discussed later in this chapter) or to any other type of supporting organization if a disqualified person with respect to the foundation directly or indirectly controls the supporting organization or a supported organization of the supporting organization. An amount that does not count as a qualifying distribution under this rule is regarded as a taxable expenditure (see Chapter 5).

An organization is not considered to be operated, supervised, or controlled by a qualified supported organization (the general criterion for a Type I organization) or operated in connection with a supported organization (the general criterion for Type IIIs) if the organization accepts a contribution from a person (other than a qualified supported organization) who, directly or indirectly, controls, either alone or with family members and/or certain controlled entities, the governing board of a supported organization. A supporting organization is considered to not be operated in connection with a supported organization unless the supporting organization is only operated in connection with one or more supported organizations that are organized in the United States.

The private foundation excess business holdings rules (see Chapter 8) are applicable to Type III supporting organizations, other than functionally integrated Type III supporting organizations. Until more specific guidance is issued, a *functionally integrated Type III supporting organization* is a Type III supporting organization that is not required by the tax regulations to make payments to supported organizations. Solely for purposes of certain due diligence requirements (discussed later in this chapter), an entity is a functionally integrated Type III supporting organization if it is engaged in activities for or on behalf of a supported organization that are activities to perform the functions of, or to carry out the purposes of, a supported organization and, but for the involvement of the supporting organization, would normally be engaged in by the supported organization (the *but for* test).

These excess business holdings rules also apply to a Type II supporting organization if the organization accepts a contribution from a person (other than a public charity that is not a supporting organization) who controls, either alone or with family members and/or certain controlled entities, the governing body of a supported organization of the supporting organization. Nonetheless, the IRS has the authority to not impose the excess business holdings rules on a supporting organization if the organization establishes that the holdings are consistent with the organization's tax-exempt status.

A supporting organization is required to file annual information returns with the IRS, irrespective of the amount of the organization's gross receipts. (Generally, small organizations, other than private foundations, do not have to file these returns.) A supporting organization must report its type on its annual information returns. The supported organization(s) must be identified on the returns. A Type III supporting organization must apprise each organization that it supports of information regarding the supporting organization in order to help ensure the responsiveness by the supporting organization to the needs or demands of the supported organization(s). A Type III supporting organization that is organized as a trust must establish to the satisfaction of the IRS that it has a sufficiently close and continuous relationship with the supported organization so that the trust is responsive to the needs or demands of the supported organization.

An excise tax is imposed on disqualified persons if they engage in one or more excess benefit transactions with public charities and/or social welfare organizations. (This rule is part of the *intermediate sanctions* regime, which is somewhat akin to the private foundation self-dealing rules [see Chapter 6].) A grant, loan, compensation, or other similar payment (such as an expense reimbursement) by any type of supporting organization to a substantial contributor (see Chapter 2) or a person related to a substantial contributor, as well as a loan provided by a supporting organization to certain disqualified persons with respect to the supporting organization, is automatically an excess benefit transaction. Thus, the entire amount paid to the substantial contributor, disqualified persons, and related parties is an excess benefit.

To demonstrate the complexity of this new body of law (as if the foregoing is not sufficient), one of the ways that a charitable organization can qualify as a Type III supporting organization is to satisfy a *responsiveness test* and an *integral part test* (see Chapter 1). Before these law changes, there were two ways in which the responsiveness test could be met. One way to meet this test was to be a charitable trust, with the supported organization(s) specified in the trust instrument and the supported organization(s) accorded the power to enforce the trust and compel and accounting. That approach to satisfaction of the test was eliminated by statute. Consequently, trusts previously classified as Type III supporting organizations may be classified as private foundations. (A trust can continue to qualify as a supporting organization if it meets the other was to satisfy the responsiveness test and thus remain a Type III entity, or if it meets the requirements of a Type I or II supporting organization.) The IRS provided some transitional relief in this regard by stating that charitable trusts that became private foundations by reason of this law change could file the standard annual information return (Form 990) for tax years beginning before January 1, 2008, and begin filing the private foundation annual information return (Form 990-PF) (see Chapter 10) for subsequent years.

A supporting organization must annually demonstrate that one or more of its disqualified persons (other than its managers and supported organization[s]) do not, directly or indirectly, control it. This is done by means of a certification on its annual information return.

Another law change enacted in 2006 provided certain individuals the opportunity to distribute, from their individual retirement arrangements, funds to public charities without the amounts includible in the gross income of the contributors. (This income exclusion rule was in effect for only two years and has expired; the rule may be resuscitated.) Under this law, however, distributions to any type of supporting organization did not qualify for the exclusion.

The Department of the Treasury, at the direction of Congress, is undertaking a study on the organization and operation of supporting organizations, considering whether (1) the deductions allowed for income, estate, or gift taxes for charitable contributions to supporting organizations are appropriate in consideration of the use of contributed assets or the use of the assets of these organizations for the benefit of the person making the charitable contribution, and (2) these issues are also issues with respect to other forms of charitable organizations or charitable contributions.

Private Foundations' Due Diligence Requirements

The IRS, at the end of 2006, issued guidance regarding certain elements of the law, enacted earlier that year, that affect supporting organizations, donor-advised funds, and private foundations that make grants to supporting organizations.

Grants to Supporting Organizations   The federal tax law imposes, as noted, certain burdens where a private foundation makes a grant to (1) a Type III supporting organization that is not functionally integrated with one or more supported organizations or (2) any other type of supporting organization if one or more disqualified persons with respect to the private foundation directly or indirectly controls the supporting organization or one of its supported organizations. In one of these instances, the grant fails to constitute a qualifying distribution (see Chapter 4) and is a taxable expenditure unless the private foundation exercises expenditure responsibility with respect to the grant (see Chapter 5). Similar rules apply (with treatment of the payment as a taxable distribution) in connection with distributions from donor-advised funds (discussed later in this chapter).

Pursuant to this guidance, a grantor, acting in good faith, may, in determining whether the grantee is a public charity, rely on information from the IRS Business Master File or the grantee's current IRS determination letter recognizing the grantee's tax exemption and indicating the grantee's public charity status. In addition, a grantor, acting in good faith, may rely on a written representation from a grantee and certain specified documents (see bullet points below) in determining the grantee's supporting organization type. In any event, the grantor must verify that the grantee is listed in the IRS's Publication 78 or obtain a copy of the grantee's determination letter.

To establish that a grantee is a Type I or II supporting organization, a grantor, acting in good faith, may rely on a written representation signed by a trustee, director, or officer of the grantee that the grantee is a Type I or II supporting organization, provided that:

- The representation describes how the grantee's trustees, directors, and/or officers are selected, and references any provision in the governing documents that establish a Type I or II relationship between the grantee and its supported organization(s).

- The grantor collects and reviews copies of the governing documents of the grantee and, if relevant, of the supported organization(s).

To establish that a grantee is a functionally integrated Type III supporting organization, a grantor, acting in good faith, may rely on a written representation signed by a trustee, director, or officer of the grantee that the grantee is a functionally integrated Type III supporting organization, provided that:

- The grantee's representation identifies the one or more supported organizations with which the grantee is functionally integrated.

- The grantor collects and reviews copies of governing documents of the grantee (and, if relevant, of the supported organization[s]) and any other documents that set forth the relationship of the grantee to its supported organization(s), if the relationship is not reflected in the governing documents.

- The grantor reviews a written representation signed by a trustee, director, or officer of each of the supported organizations with which the grantee represents that it is functionally integrated, describing the activities of the grantee and confirming that, but for the involvement of the grantee engaging in activities to perform the functions of, or to carry out the purposes of, the supported organization, the supported organization would normally be engaged in those activities itself (discussed later in this chapter).

As an alternative to the foregoing, a grantor may rely on a reasoned written opinion of counsel of either the grantor or the grantee concluding that the grantee is a Type I, Type II, or Type III functionally integrated supporting organization.

A private foundation considering a grant to a Type I, Type II, or Type III functionally integrated supporting organization may need to obtain a list of the grantee's supported organizations from the grantee to determine whether any of the supported organizations is controlled (discussed later in this chapter) by disqualified persons with respect to the foundation. Likewise, a sponsoring organization considering a grant from a donor-advised fund to one of these types of supporting organizations may need to obtain such a list to determine whether any of the supported organizations is controlled by the fund's donor or donor advisor (and any related parties).

Standards for Determining Control   Until regulations are issued, in determining whether a disqualified person with respect to a private foundation controls a supporting organization or one of its supported organizations, the standards as to control established in the mandatory payout regulations (see Chapter 4) apply. Under these standards, an organization is controlled by one or more disqualified persons with respect to a foundation if any of these persons may, by aggregating their votes or positions of authority, require the supporting or supported organization to make an expenditure or prevent the supporting or supported organization from making an expenditure, regardless of the method by which the control is exercised or exercisable.

Similarly, a supported organization is controlled by one or more donors or donor advisors (and any related parties) of a donor-advised fund if any of these persons may, by aggregating their votes or positions of authority, require a supported organization to make an expenditure or prevent a supported organization from making an expenditure, irrespective of the method by which the control is exercised or exercisable.

Because of this guidance, coupled with the statutory law changes that preceded it, one might wonder whether private foundation grants to supporting organizations are doomed. Foundations are unlikely to take the time and make the effort to go through the collection and review processes, and secure the requisite written representations to determine a supporting organization's type. These developments may give rise to a general antipathy on the part of private foundations toward grants to all supporting organizations.

The Checklist

Here is how supporting organizations fare in relation to the ten-factor checklist:

1. Supporting organizations are almost always nonprofit corporations or trusts. As discussed, however, there are some disadvantages to use of trusts in this context. These organizations have the usual state law reporting requirements; they have to file annual information returns irrespective of size or revenue. Supporting organizations always have governing boards.

2. Supporting organizations cannot be controlled by their founders (substantial contributors) and other disqualified persons. As has been noted, this is the biggest deterrent to the use of supporting organizations in this context.

3. To be tax-exempt, every supporting organization, unless it is very small, must file an application for recognition of exemption with, and receive a favorable determination from, the IRS.

4. Contributions to supporting organizations are deductible, almost always to the fullest extent permitted by law. This frequently is the principal reason why a supporting organization is selected instead of a private foundation. The prospective donor wants to make a gift of appreciated property and obtain a full fair market value charitable deduction in circumstances where the deduction would be confined to the donor's cost basis if the gift were made to a private foundation. When forced to choose, some donors (but not the majority of them) will take the higher deduction over control.

5. Supporting organizations conduct a variety of programs. Often, they are fundraising vehicles and/or holders of an endowment for the parent entity. As such, they can be grant-makers to their parent organizations. They can, however, operate charitable programs, particularly when the parent organization does not, for whatever reason, want to directly conduct a program. A supporting organization can operate an unrelated business, whereas a private foundation is likely to be precluded from doing so (see Chapter 8).

6. As just noted, a principal function of a supporting organization is to be a fundraising entity. There is a problem in this regard, however, as is reflected in the next factor.

7. Most supporting organizations can receive grants from private foundations. Because of the pall cast on foundation granting to some supporting organizations, however, private foundations often are reluctant to engage in the due diligence process that is required before they make these grants. A few private foundations (and their number may be growing) have adopted a policy of simply not making grants to any supporting organizations. This can be a major frustration for supporting organizations that have fundraising as their primary purpose. This unfortunate outcome is traceable to one of the most misguided of law changes made in 2006.

8. Supporting organizations obviously can have employees. Before the 2006 law changes, a founder of a supporting organization could, as is the case with private foundations, be an employee of the organization. But now the payment of compensation (even if it is reasonable) by any type of supporting organization to a substantial contributor or a person related to a substantial contributor is automatically an excess benefit transaction, triggering tax penalties (discussed earlier in this chapter). This is another example of the overkill wrought in 2006. The rules here are tougher than is the case for private foundations (where reasonable compensation to disqualified persons is permitted).

9. If one or more individuals are establishing the charitable organization, the supporting organization certainly is a legitimate candidate. It is, as noted, the most likely alternative to the private foundation. A public charity (other than most supporting organizations) can (indeed, often does) establish a supporting organization, as can tax-exempt social welfare organizations, labor organizations, and associations. (Other exempt organizations, such as social clubs and fraternal groups, can establish related charities but these affiliated entities cannot formally qualify as supporting organizations.) A for-profit company is not likely to form a supporting organization (although it can make deductible charitable contributions to supporting organizations).

CREATIVE USES OF SUPPORTING ORGANIZATIONS

Despite the heavy damage inflicted on supporting organizations by the 2006 law additions, they still can be used, mostly by public charities, to creative advantage. Here are some examples:

- A common reason for establishment of a supporting organization by a public charity is to form a related fundraising entity (despite the previously discussed drawbacks). It is common for charitable organizations to place the fundraising function in a separate organization. Some boards like fundraising; some don't. (Because of the 2006 law changes, some of these related fundraising entities are being structured as publicly supported charities [discussed later in this chapter].)

- Another frequent reason that a public charity will form a supporting organization is to place its endowment in a separate entity. Some charities are more comfortable having their endowment in a separate vehicle, usually a nonprofit corporation.

- Some public charities have property that they want held in a separate organization, perhaps for liability reasons. A supporting organization is a good candidate in this regard (as is a single-member limited liability company or a tax-exempt title-holding company). Just holding the property can be the requisite support or benefit.

- Some public charities prefer to operate one or more programs in a separate vehicle. Again, the supporting organization can serve this purpose. Just operating the program can be the requisite support or benefit.

- A supporting organization can serve as a type of *holding company* (despite the commercial-sounding nature of that term). Usually, a supporting organization is at the bottom of an organizational chart, providing its support or benefit *up* to the parent. But a supporting organization can also be at the top of the organizational arrangement, as a coordinating entity with respect to a cluster of public charities *below* it. Structures of this nature are, for example, common in the tax-exempt health care field.

- Private foundations sometimes convert to public charities (see Chapters 1 and 3). The supporting organization is the most likely entity of choice in this regard.

Being brewed in the halls of the IRS are regulations, prompted by Congress, that will force payout requirements (akin to those now imposed on private foundations [see Chapter 4]) on most, if not all, supporting organizations. The impact of a payout rule on supporting organizations, other than those used for fundraising, is not clear at this time.

The foregoing six reasons are the principal ones for establishment, by a public charity, of a supporting organization. Here are two additional, albeit perhaps esoteric, reasons why a public charity might use a supporting organization:

1. Assume that the public charity involved is a publicly supported charity (see Chapter 1). Also assume that a prospective donor wants to make a charitable contribution to this organization; the proposed gift, however, is so large that it would severely adversely affect the charity's public support ratio. The unusual grant exception is not available. You are the lawyer for this public charity. What would you advise? Would you advise the charity to decline the gift? If so, you are likely to suddenly have a *former* client. The better advice would be to quickly form a Type I supporting organization and cause the gift to be made to it. (The donor's charitable deduction would be the same.) Once the gift is safely in the supporting organization, the parent can begin thinking of ways to bring portions of it up to it incrementally.

2. A public charity may be contemplating entry into a joint venture. Its lawyer, however, is fretful that participation in this venture by the charity may endanger its tax-exempt status, by reason of the private benefit doctrine (see Chapter 3). The solution: create a supporting organization and cause it to join the venture. If something goes amiss, it is the supporting organization's exemption that gets zapped, not the parent's.

IRS SHELL GAME

The IRS, in the aftermath of the 2006 law revisions and additions, offered the charitable community a remarkable opportunity, in the form of a public charity status shuffle as a stratagem for evading the new tax law restrictions. (This is the kind of thing lawyers are supposed to conjure up, not government agencies.) The IRS, in late 2006, announced a process by which tax-exempt charitable organizations may jettison their public charity status, as supporting organizations, so as to avoid the tax law problems engendered by the new rules. This IRS move was prompted principally by the law concerning distributions from individual retirement plans and the inability of private foundations to make qualifying distributions to certain supporting organizations.

This IRS announcement stated that "organizations currently classified as supporting organizations . . . may wish to seek reclassification" so as to be another type of public charity. A charitable organization seeking to change its public charity classification "for reasons related to changes made" in 2006 is required to submit a written request for reclassification, with the request expressly requesting reclassification and including one of two IRS forms that reflect the nature of the organization's revenue.

This IRS announcement is both extraordinary and extremely unsettling. It is extraordinary because the IRS openly acknowledges, and offers an end run around, two of the most egregious law changes devised by Congress in 2006. It is extremely unsettling because it brazenly offers charities an escape from reach of the new law by merely altering (if they can) the basis for their public charity status. This moving of the shells does not contribute to good tax policy. If an organization is of such a contaminated nature as to be tainted under either or both of these rules, what business is it of the IRS to suggest that a change in public charity status is a fix?

[The Internal Revenue Code sections for public charities are 509(a)(1) for the institutions, 509(a)(1) or 509(a)(2) for the publicly supported charities, and 509(a)(3) for supporting organizations. The inherently evil nature of the public charity does not somehow just magically disappear because the IRS rejiggles it to be a (1) or a (2) instead of a (3).]

For example, a supporting organization could launch a fundraising campaign and become a publicly supported charity. Or a supporting organization may otherwise qualify as a public charity. It could nonetheless persist with the same board, officers, programs, location, and the like. Yet this transformed entity would no longer be subject to these two troublesome rules.

By the way, the IRS missed one. A small charitable organization, now a supporting organization, that converts to another type of public charity, can avoid filing annual information returns. Because of a 2006 law change, all supporting organizations are required to file these returns.

The core problem, of course, is with the ill-conceived statutory law; the solution to this dilemma is to repeal these unnecessary harsh (and, as the IRS would have it, pointless) provisions. In the meantime, the IRS's efforts to exhort form-over-substance tax planning are way out of line. The invitation from the IRS to do the public charity status shuffle was an affront to everyone involved in creating this legislation.

DONOR-ADVISED FUNDS IN GENERAL

One of the most controversial entities in the realm of charitable organizations is the *donor-advised fund*. These funds are created and maintained within public charities, such as community foundations, colleges and universities, churches, and charitable gift funds. Indeed, these funds were invented by community foundations, which have existed for nearly 100 years. Today, there are billions of dollars in money and other assets reposing in donor-advised funds.

While this giving vehicle has been a part of the U.S. charitable giving scene for nearly a century, only recently has it become the subject of considerable scrutiny, criticism, and law. Several federal tax law issues are triggered by these funds, all resting on the fundamental fact that the donor-advised fund is an alternative to the private foundation. Some choose to state the matter somewhat differently, regarding these funds as a means of sidestepping or inappropriately avoiding the private foundation rules.

A donor-advised fund is not a separate legal entity. Rather, as noted, it is a fund within an organization that is classified as a public charity. This type of fund is often referred to as an *account* or sometimes as a *subaccount* of the host organization. These accounts usually are named, reflecting an individual, family, corporation, private foundation, or cause. A donor-advised fund can appear to be a legal entity—seemingly a charitable organization with many of the attributes of a private foundation.

The donor-advised fund should be contrasted with the donor-directed fund. In the case of a *donor-directed fund*, the donor or a designee of the donor has the *right* to direct the investment of the fund's assets and/or to direct grants from the fund for charitable purposes. By contrast, with the donor-advised fund, the donor or a designee of the donor has the mere *ability* to make *recommendations* (proffer advice) as to investment policy and/or the making of grants.

An unfortunate court opinion concerning these types of funds concluded that an organization that operated a fund could not be tax-exempt as a charitable entity, although the case was more about fraud and private benefit (see Chapter 3). Because of the fund's promotional materials, which emphasized donor self-interest rather than philanthropic intent, the court observed that the organization "served significant non-exempt purposes that focused primarily on providing personal, rather than public, benefits." It wrote that the organization's operations were "characterized at the least by willful neglect, and, more than likely, an active willingness to participate in a scheme designed to produce impermissible tax benefits." These materials and operations suggested, the court wrote, that the "donors in question did not truly relinquish ownership and control over the donated funds and property" but rather treated the organization as a "conduit for accomplishing the twin tax avoidance goals of building up their assets tax-free and then siphoning off the accumulated wealth to pay for personal expenditures." This case was an aberration, not in the donor-advised or even donor-directed fund mainstream; it essentially was a private benefit doctrine case adorned with usually ugly facts. Still, this development was not advantageous to the donor-advised fund cause.

In recent years, commercial investment companies have created donor-advised funds charitable entities. That is what triggered the furor. As long as use of these funds was confined to community foundations, there was no controversy. The attention accorded these funds, including criticism, then new law (again, in 2006) (discussed later in this chapter), started when other types of public charities began generating gifts by means of donor-advised funds.

GIFTS REVISTED

One of the fundamental issues raised by donor-advised funds is whether the transfers to them constitute gifts. That is, the question arises as to whether the transfer to such a fund is incomplete, in that the ostensible donor, by reserving an ability to advise, has in fact retained some form of right that precludes the transfer from being a completed gift.

There must be a gift before there can be a charitable gift. Integral to the concept of the charitable contribution deduction is the basic requirement that the payment of money or transfer of property to a charitable organization be in the form of a transaction that qualifies as a gift. The tax regulations contain this definition: A *contribution* is a "voluntary transfer of money or property that is made with no expectation of procuring financial benefit commensurate with the amount of the transfer." (This subject is explored more fully in Chapter 9.) Any condition (discussed later in this chapter) by which the donor retains dominion and control over the transferred money or property makes the gift incomplete. An incomplete gift cannot be the basis of a charitable contribution deduction.

This use of charitable gift funds implicates the law concerning conditional gifts. A *conditional gift* is a gift that is made subject to the occurrence of an event following the transaction (a *condition subsequent*). A gift can be made to a charitable organization containing binding covenants on the charitable donee.

Conditions subsequent that are not negligible can defeat the federal income tax charitable contribution deduction. In one case, donors transferred real property to a charitable trust but retained control over its future occupancy and sale; the entire charitable deductions were disallowed because of these retained rights (although they were incapable of valuation). The charitable deduction for a gift of a rare book collection to a charity was disallowed because the donor retained an unlimited right of access to the collection and the right to deny access to it to others. An illustration of an incidental condition subsequent was a gift of materials to a library, where the materials could not be copied or removed from the library without the donor's consent.

More to the point, the IRS ruled (before the statutory law came into being [discussed later in this chapter]) that a donor was entitled to a charitable contribution deduction for a gift of money or other property to a charitable organization, where the donor, or the donor's investment manager, retained the power, under certain conditions, to manage the gift property in a designated account.

Most public charities that utilize charitable gift funds have a standard agreement that makes it clear to the prospective donor that the gift property will belong exclusively to the charity and that the donor's ability to make recommendations regarding the subsequent use of the gift property is not a legal right.

DONOR-ADVISED FUNDS' STATUTORY CRITERIA

Legislation enacted in 2006 introduced a statutory definition of the term *donor-advised fund*. Essentially, it is a fund (or account) that is (1) separately identified by reference to contributions of one or more donors, (2) that is owned and controlled by a sponsoring organization, and (3) as to which a donor or a donor advisor has, or reasonably expects to have, advisory privileges with respect to the distribution or investment of amounts held in the fund by reason of the donor's status as a donor. A *sponsoring organization* is a public charity that maintains one or more donor-advised funds.

A donor-advised fund does not include funds that make distributions only to a single identified organization or governmental entity, or certain funds where a donor or donor advisor provides advice as to which individuals receive grants for travel, study, or similar purposes. The IRS has the authority to exempt a fund from treatment as a donor-advised fund under certain circumstances. Exercising this authority, the IRS announced that employer-sponsored disaster relief assistance funds do not constitute donor-advised funds.

A distribution from a donor-advised fund is taxable if it is to an individual or any other person for a noncharitable purpose, unless expenditure responsibility (see Chapter 5) is exercised with respect to the distribution. A tax, in the amount of 20% of the amount involved, is imposed on the sponsoring organization for making a taxable distribution. Another tax, of 5%, is imposed on the agreement of a fund manager to the making of a taxable distribution, where the manager knew that the distribution was a taxable one. The tax on fund management is subject to a joint and several liability requirement. This tax does not apply to a distribution from a donor-advised fund to most public charities (but not including a nonfunctionally integrated Type III supporting organization), the fund's sponsoring organization, or another donor-advised fund.

If a donor, donor advisor, or a person related to a donor or donor advisor with respect to a donor-advised fund provides advice as to a distribution that results in any of these persons receiving, directly or indirectly, a benefit that is more than incidental, an excise tax equal to 125% of the amount of the benefit is imposed on the person who advised as to the distribution and on the recipient of the benefit. Also, if a manager of the sponsoring organization agreed to the making of the distribution, knowing that the distribution would confer more than an incidental benefit on a donor, donor advisor, or related person, the manager is subject to an excise tax equal to 10% of the amount of the benefit. These taxes are also subject to a joint and several liability requirement.

A grant, loan, compensation, or other similar payment (such as reimbursement of expenses) from a donor-advised fund to a person that, with respect to the fund, is a donor, donor advisor, or related person automatically is treated as an excess benefit transaction for intermediate sanctions law purposes. This means that the entire amount paid to any of these persons is an excess benefit. Donors and donor advisors with respect to a donor-advised fund, and related persons, are disqualified persons for intermediate sanctions law purposes with respect to transactions with the donor-advised fund (although not necessarily with respect to transactions with the sponsoring organization).

The private foundation excess business holdings rules (see Chapter 8) apply to donor-advised funds. For this purpose, the term *disqualified person* means, with respect to a donor-advised fund, a donor, donor advisor, member of the family of either, or a 35% controlled entity of any such person (see Chapter 2).

A donor must obtain, with respect to each charitable contribution to a sponsoring organization to be maintained in a donor-advised fund, a contemporaneous written acknowledgment from the sponsoring organization that the organization has exclusive legal control over the funds or other assets contributed.

A sponsoring organization is required to disclose on its annual information return the number of donor-advised funds it owns, the aggregate value of assets held in the funds at the end of the organization's tax year involved, and the aggregate contributions to and grants made from these funds during the year. When seeking recognition of tax-exempt status, a sponsoring organization must disclose whether it intends to maintain donor-advised funds. As to this latter rule, the organization must provide information regarding its planned operation of these funds, including a description of procedures it intends to use to:

- Communicate to donors and donor advisors that assets held in the funds are the property of the sponsoring organization.

- Ensure that distributions from donor-advised funds do not result in more than incidental benefit to any person.

The Department of the Treasury was directed by Congress to undertake a study on the organization and operation of donor-advised funds, to consider whether:

- The deductions allowed for income, estate, or gift taxes for charitable contributions to sponsoring organizations are appropriate in consideration of the use of contributed assets or the use of the assets of these organizations for the benefit of the person making the charitable contribution.

- Donor-advised funds should be required to distribute for charitable purposes a specified amount in order to ensure that the sponsoring organization with respect to the funds is operating in a manner consistent with its tax-exempt or public charity status.

- The retention by donors to donor-advised funds of "rights or privileges" with respect to amounts transferred to these organizations (including advisory rights or privileges with respect to the making of grants or the investment of assets) is consistent with the treatment of these transfers as completed gifts.

- These issues are also issues with respect to other forms of charitable organizations or charitable contributions.

MORE ABOUT DONOR-ADVISED FUNDS

Additional considerations pertain to the creation, maintenance, and funding of donor-advised funds.

Deductibility of Contributions

Contributions to a sponsoring organization for maintenance in a donor-advised fund are not deductible for income tax purposes if the sponsoring organization is a fraternal society, a cemetery company, or a veterans' organization. Contributions to a sponsoring organization for such maintenance are not eligible for an estate or gift tax charitable deduction if the sponsoring organization is a fraternal society or a veterans' organization. Contributions to a sponsoring organization for such maintenance are not eligible for a charitable deduction for income, estate, or gift tax purposes if the sponsoring organization is a nonfunctionally integrated Type III supporting organization.

Public Support Considerations

Community foundations, charitable gift funds, and other charitable entities that sponsor donor-advised funds to a significant extent are classified as donative publicly supported charities (see Chapter 1). This is because the contributions to these organizations, although placed in these funds, are treated (in accordance with the various limitations) as public support for the sponsoring organizations. The IRS frets, from time to time, over the propriety of treating these organizations as publicly supported entities, on the theory that these charities may not be properly financially *supported* in a technical sense.

When a grant is made from a donor-advised fund to a charity—which may be termed the *ultimate beneficiary*—the grant amount can be regarded (in whole or in part) as public support for this ultimate beneficiary. In this setting, the same funds can end up being forms of public support twice—when contributed to the sponsoring organization and then when granted by the sponsoring organization (from the fund) to the ultimate beneficiary. Purists can find this double treatment troublesome. The IRS is not concerned about treatment of the grants as public support for the ultimate charitable recipient. What gives the agency pause is the classification of the gifts as public support for the *intermediate* entity (the sponsoring organization).

In some of its writings, the IRS posits the notion that gifts to sponsoring organizations, by means of a donor-advised fund, are *earmarked* gifts. From there, the IRS makes a distinction between a contribution *to* a charitable organization and one *for the use of* a charitable organization. The idea is that only contributions to a charitable organization can be treated as public support, as the charity is free to use the gifts in its charitable program. Then, the IRS asserts that an earmarked gift and a gift for the use of a charity are similar, in that "both have qualities of property held in trust." Following this logic, the IRS considers the intermediary entity (the sponsoring organization) the functional equivalent of a trustee for the ultimate charity, leading to the conclusion that the contributions are public support only for that charity and not the sponsoring organization.

While credit should be given for creativity, this line of analysis is fundamentally flawed. First, a contribution to a donor-advised fund is not an earmarked gift under the federal tax law; the gift reposes in an account that is owned by the sponsoring organization, which is legally free to do whatever it wants with the gift. Second, it is common for donors to make restricted gifts, where the restriction is a programmatic one (such as for research or scholarships); there is no authority that these restrictions conjure up a trust relationship. Third, the statutory definition of the word *support* does not embody this dubious dichotomy in this context between gifts to and for the use of charity.

To date, rulings issued by the IRS have not adhered to this approach. That is, these rulings (there are two of them) state that contributions to a donor-advised fund are forms of public support to the sponsoring organization. The IRS can always change its mind on this point but, for now, it appears that charities with donor-advised funds can report gifts to the funds as public support for these charities.

The Checklist

Here is how donor-advised funds fare in relation to the ten-factor checklist:

1. Here is where many of the advantages of the donor-advised fund come to the fore. These funds are not separate legal entities; they are accounts

within public charities. Thus, there are no federal or state reporting requirements for these funds; that function is taken care of by the sponsoring organization. There is no need for a governing board; the governing board of the fund is the governing board of the sponsoring organization. Simplicity of operation is among the donor-advised funds' greatest attributes.

2. The donor-advised fund is of no utility to a donor who wants to control the charitable donee. The fund must be owned by the sponsoring organization. The fund may not confer unwarranted private benefit on the donor, donor advisor, or related persons.

3. There is no need for the filing of an application for recognition of exempt status for a donor-advised fund. The fund takes on the tax-exempt (and public charity) status of its sponsoring organization. This is often seen as an advantage to the use of a donor-advised fund.

4. Contributions to a donor-advised fund are deductible, almost always to the fullest extent permitted by law. This is because the gift is to the sponsoring organization, which is a public charity. A difficulty here, however, is that nearly all donor-advised funds accept gifts only of money or liquid securities. A prospective donor of real estate or other property must look to the other options.

5. Program activity can be seen as a negative factor for donor-advised funds, inasmuch as active program undertakings are not the stuff of these funds. Like typical private foundations, a donor-advised fund is simply a grant-making vehicle. For some, however, this is a positive factor.

6. Donor-advised funds are now subject to some government regulation, but it is not onerous. It essentially comes down to avoiding private benefit and a slight increase in reporting (the burden of the sponsoring organization, not the donor). A donor-advised fund itself, however, does not have to comply with most of the laws applicable to public charities (see Chapter 3)—that is the responsibility of the sponsoring organization.

7. The donor-advised fund will not engage in fundraising. The founder of the fund, however, is free to attempt to get others to contribute to the fund.

8. A private foundation is not likely to make a grant to a donor-advised fund—but it can. This occurs most frequently where a foundation needs to quickly transfer a substantial amount of funds to meet its payout requirement (see Chapter 4). Rather than select a number of grantees in a rush, the foundation can make the grant to a donor-advised fund, thus becoming a *donor* with *advisory privileges*, and have

the funds transferred to various charitable organizations later pursuant to its advice.

9. Donor-advised funds do not have employees. Most sponsoring organizations, even before the law changes, did not allow grants from these funds to individuals. With the new law, however, the rules are clear: a distribution to an individual from a donor-advised fund is either a taxable distribution or an automatic excess benefit transaction. An individual establishing a charity with a purpose being the creation of an employer for himself, herself, and/or one or more family members must look to the private foundation or public charity (other than a supporting organization) alternatives.

10. If one or more individuals are establishing the charitable organization, the donor-advised fund certainly is a legitimate candidate–if grant-making is to be the sole purpose of the charity. (Here, not only is it less expensive to set up a donor-advised fund in comparison to a private foundation but the amount(s) contributed can be much less.) A for-profit company could establish a donor-advised fund, but that rarely happens. A public charity has no need for a donor-advised fund. A private foundation is not likely to create a donor-advised fund but may make a grant to one.

QUICK COMPARATIVE ANALYSIS

Chances are high that, when one or more individuals or a for-profit company decide to form a charitable organization, the entity of choice will be the private foundation. The reason: the ability to control the entity. Employment of founders and family members may be a factor in selecting the foundation option. Where, however, individuals are involved and a large charitable deduction based on fair market value is looming, the preferred approach is likely to be the supporting organization. Control of the organization is forfeited but the donors can still serve on the governing board (in the minority) and have influence over the policies and direction of the organization. If the founder is a public charity, the supporting organization will probably be the entity of choice, unless fundraising is a primary purpose, in which case the publicly supported charity will likely be the form selected.

Where individuals, companies, and perhaps private foundations want only a simple, grantmaking vehicle, the donor-advised fund may be the answer. This is particularly the case for individuals. All they have to do is create the fund (which is only slightly more complicated than opening a bank account), put the donor's name on it, make one or more charitable gifts, and periodically tender advice. The charity receiving funding from the donor-advised fund will receive a check, with the name of the fund on the check. It will be the same as a check from a private foundation. In the right set of circumstances (including an absence of concern about control), the donor-advised fund is, from the donor's standpoint, the most preferable of the alternatives to a private foundation: it is easy to establish, others do the work to maintain it, and the outside world sees the donor as a philanthropist.

SUMMARY

This chapter provided an inventory of the factors to consider when contemplating the establishment of a tax-exempt charitable entity. The advantages and disadvantages of public charity and private foundation status were discussed. More law concerning, and creative uses of, supporting organizations was explained. The law pertaining to donor-advised funds was summarized. The chapter concluded with a comparative analysis of private foundations and their alternatives.

12

GOVERNANCE PRINCIPLES AND TRUSTEE LIABILITY

The purpose of this chapter is to summarize the law and practices—some of them just emerging—concerning governance principles pertaining to private foundations and the matter of potential board member liability. Scandals embroiling for-profit corporations and accounting firms—involving fraud, tax avoidance, conflicts of interests, and questionable accounting practices—led to enactment of the Sarbanes-Oxley Act in 2002. The principles embodied in that legislation are quickly being imported into the nonprofit sector, largely by means of the voluntary adoption by charitable organizations of a variety of policies and procedures. Specifically, this chapter will:

- Summarize the basics of governance principles.
- Inventory evolving governance precepts.
- Identify the various policies a foundation may consider adopting.
- Summarize board member responsibilities and duties.
- List protections against director and officer liability.
- Address (revisit) the use of management companies.
- Reference the watchdog agencies' guidelines.

BASICS OF GOVERNANCE PRINCIPLES

Traditionally, the law as to governance of a nonprofit organization—corporation or otherwise—has been largely confined to state rules. These principles, however, are now quickly becoming part of the federal tax law

268

and/or organizations' practices. Although new federal law on the subject, in the form of legislation and regulations is not imminent, IRS forms and instructions are playing a major role in reshaping the charitable governance scene.

The essence of the emerging governance principles is that a charitable organization (and perhaps other types of tax-exempt entities) must be *managed* by its board of directors or board of trustees. It is becoming unacceptable for a board to meet infrequently and be merely the recipient of reports from an organization's officers and staff. The developing law is requiring the board of the nonprofit organization to become directly involved, be knowledgeable about the organization's programs and finances, understand the climate in which the entity operates, avoid conflicts of interest, place the objectives of the organization above personal desires—and *govern*.

These emerging principles are also forcing structural changes in the operations of nonprofit organizations. No longer are the operative documents only articles of organization and bylaws. The law is beginning to demand organizational and management policies and procedures, conflicts of interest policies, codes of ethics for senior officers, investment policies, and written program objectives and performance measures. Independent audit committees are becoming common. Lawyers, accountants, and other consultants must be hired directly by the board, not the executive staff. Compensation arrangements for top positions have to be approved at the board level. Independent auditors may have to be rotated periodically, such as every five years. Corporate executives may have to certify financial statements and perhaps annual information returns.

Even the appropriate size of the governing body is being debated. According to the law in most states, a nonprofit corporation must have at least three directors (or trustees). A few states require only one director. The appropriate number of directors for a charitable organization is a matter of some controversy. Although "one size certainly does not fit all," there is an emerging consensus among students of nonprofit governance that a charity's board should number in the range of 5 to 15.

EMERGING CONCEPTS

The basics as to governance principles are beginning to yield specific requirements. Board members do not, individually, have unilateral authority to make decisions about the organization's governance. Rather, the board has collective responsibilities. In 2007, Congress passed legislation that amended the congressional charter of the American National Red Cross to modernize its structure and otherwise strengthen its governance. Changes included a substantial reduction in the size of the organization's board, delegation to management of the day-to-day operations of the organization, elimination of distinctions as to how board members are elected, and transition of some board members into an advisory council.

The essence of the legislation is unique to the National Red Cross entity. Certainly some items in the following list do not apply to private foundations. Yet it outlines the collective responsibilities for nonprofit boards in general:

- Review and approve the organization's mission statement.

- Approve and oversee the organization's strategic plan and maintain strategic oversight of operational matters.

- Select, evaluate, and determine the level of compensation of the organization's chief executive officer.

- Evaluate the performance and establish the compensation of the senior leadership team and provide for management succession.

- Oversee the financial reporting and audit process, internal controls, and legal compliance.

- Ensure that the chapters of the organization are geographically and regionally diverse.

- Hold management accountable for performance.

- Provide oversight of the financial stability of the organization.

- Ensure the inclusiveness and diversity of the organization.

- Provide oversight of the protection of the brand of the organization (a responsibility rarely found in a list of this nature).

- Assist with fundraising on behalf of the organization.

NONPROFIT GOVERNANCE PRINCIPLES

Governance issues are dominating the nonprofit law scene. Much of this focus is on the duties and responsibilities of members of nonprofit boards, and the policies and practices they are expected to develop, implement, and maintain. Some of what is emerging is not directly applicable to private foundations, although much of it is. Three important recent developments illustrate these points: the principles of nonprofit governance promulgated by the Panel on the Nonprofit Sector established under the auspices of Independent Sector, a draft of a code of nonprofit ethics issued by the IRS, and the redesign by the IRS of the annual information return filed by most tax-exempt organizations (Form 990).

The Panel on the Nonprofit Sector, convened by Independent Sector, issued, on October 18, 2007, its principles for good governance for public and private charitable organizations. The principles are predicated on the need for a "careful balance between the two essential forms of regulation—that is, between prudent legal mandates to ensure that organizations do not abuse the privilege of their exempt status, and, for all other aspects of sound operations, well-informed self-governance and mutual awareness among nonprofit organizations." These principles, organized under four categories, are as follows (slightly edited for brevity):

Legal Compliance and Public Disclosure

- An organization must comply with applicable federal, state, and local law. If the organization conducts programs outside the United States, it must abide by applicable international laws and conventions that are legally binding on the United States.

- An organization should have a formally adopted, written code of ethics with which all of its directors, staff, and volunteers are familiar and to which they adhere.

- An organization should implement policies and procedures to ensure that all conflicts of interest, or appearance of them, within the organization and its board are appropriately managed though disclosure, recusal, or other means.

- An organization should implement policies and procedures that enable individuals to come forward with information on illegal practices or violations of organizational policies. This whistleblower policy should specify that the organization will not retaliate against, and will protect the confidentiality of, individuals who make good faith reports.

- An organization should implement policies and procedures to preserve the organization's important documents and business records.

- An organization's board should ensure that the organization has adequate plans to protect its assets—its property, financial and human resources, programmatic content and material, and its integrity and reputation—against damage or loss. The board should regularly review the organization's need for general liability and directors' and officers' liability insurance, as well as take other actions to mitigate risk.

- An organization should make information about its operations, including its governance, finances, programs, and other activities, widely available to the public. Charitable organizations should also consider making information available on the methods they use to evaluate the outcomes of their work and sharing the results of the evaluations.

Effective Governance

- An organization must have a governing body that is responsible for approving the organization's mission and strategic direction, annual budget and key financial transactions, compensation practices, and fiscal and governance policies.

- The board of an organization should meet regularly to conduct its business and fulfill its duties.

- The board of an organization should establish its size and structure, and periodically review these. The board should have enough members to allow for full deliberation and diversity of thinking on organizational matters. Except for very small organizations, this generally means there should be at least five members.

- The board of an organization should include members with the diverse background (including ethnic, racial, and gender perspectives), experience, and organizational and financial skills necessary to advance the organization's mission.

- A substantial majority of the board (usually at least two-thirds) of a public charity should be independent. Independent members should not be compensated by the organization, have their compensation determined by individuals who are compensated by the organization, receive material financial benefits from the organization except as a member of a charitable class served by the organization, or be related to or reside with any person described above.

- The board should hire, oversee, and annually evaluate the performance of the chief executive of the organization, and should conduct such an evaluation prior to any change in that individual's compensation, unless a multi-year contract is in force or the change consists solely of routine adjustments for inflation or cost of living.

- The board of an organization that has paid staff should ensure that separate individuals hold the positions of chief staff officer, board chair, and board treasurer. Organizations without paid staff should ensure that the position of board chair and treasurer are separately held.

- The board should establish an effective, systematic process for educating and communicating with board members to ensure that they are aware of their legal and ethical responsibilities, are knowledgeable about the programs and other activities of the organization, and can effectively carry out their oversight functions.

- Board members should evaluate their performance as a group and as individuals no less than every three years, and should have clear procedures for removing board members who are unable to fulfill their responsibilities.

- The board should establish clear policies and procedures setting the length of terms and the number of consecutive terms a board member may serve.

- The board should review the organization's governing instruments at least every five years.

- The board should regularly review the organization's mission and goals, and evaluate at least every five years the organization's goals, programs, and other activities to be sure they advance its mission and make prudent use of its resources.

- Board members are generally expected to serve without compensation, other than reimbursement for expenses incurred to fulfill their board duties. An organization that provides compensation to its board members should use appropriate comparability data to determine the amount to be paid, document the decision and provide full disclosure to anyone, on request, of the amount and rationale for the compensation.

Strong Financial Oversight

- An organization must keep complete, current, and accurate financial records. Its board should review timely reports of the organization's financial activities and have a qualified, independent financial expert audit or review these statements annually in a manner appropriate to the organization's size and scale of operations.

- The board of an organization must institute policies and procedures to ensure that the organization (and, if applicable, its subsidiaries) manages and invests its funds responsibly, in accordance with requirements of law. The full board should approve the organization's annual budget and monitor performance against the budget.

- An organization should not provide loans (or the equivalent, such as loan guarantees, purchasing or transferring ownership of a residence or office, or relieving a debt or lease obligations) to its directors or officers.

- An organization should spend a significant portion of its annual budget on programs that pursue its mission. The budget should provide sufficient resources for effective administration of the organization and, if it solicits contributions, for appropriate fundraising activities.

- An organization should establish clear, written policies for paying or reimbursing expenses incurred by anyone conducting business or traveling on behalf of the organization, including the types of expenses that can be paid or reimbursed and the documentation required. These policies should require that travel on behalf of the organization is to be undertaken in a cost-effective manner.

- An organization should neither pay for nor reimburse travel expenditures for spouses, dependents, or others who are accompanying someone conducting business for the organization unless they are also conducting the business.

Responsible Fundraising

- Solicitation materials and other communications addressed to prospective donors and the public must clearly identify the organization, and be accurate and truthful.

- Contributions must be used for purposes consistent with the donor's intent, whether as described in the solicitation materials or as directed by the donor.

- An organization must provide donors with acknowledgments of charitable contributions, in accordance with federal tax law requirements, including information to facilitate the donor's compliance with tax law requirements.

- An organization should adopt clear policies to determine whether acceptance of a gift would compromise its ethics, financial circumstances, program focus, or other interests.

- An organization should provide appropriate training and supervision of the people soliciting funds on its behalf to ensure that they understand their responsibilities and applicable law, and do not employ techniques that are coercive, intimidating, or intended to harass potential donors.

- An organization should not compensate internal or external fundraisers on the basis of a commission or percentage of the amount raised.

- An organization should respect the privacy of individual donors and, except where disclosure is required by law, should not sell or otherwise make available the names and contact information of its donors without providing them an opportunity to at least annually opt out of use of their names.

IRS DRAFT OF GOOD GOVERNANCE PRINCIPLES

In 2007, The IRS unveiled a draft of the agency's "Good Governance Practices" for charitable organizations. About one year later, the agency jettisoned this draft (discussed later in this chapter). Nonetheless, it is significant that the IRS issued this document; some of the practices are applicable to private foundations.

The IRS is of the view that a governing board of a charitable organization should be composed of persons who are informed and active in overseeing the organization's operations and finances. If a governing board tolerates a climate of secrecy or neglect, charitable assets are more likely to be used to advance an impermissible private interest. Successful governing boards include individuals who are not only knowledgeable and passionate about the organization's programs but also have expertise in critical areas involving accounting, finance, compensation, and ethics.

Organizations with very small or very large governing boards may be problematic: Small boards generally do not represent a public interest; large boards may be less attentive to oversight duties. If an organization's governing board is very large, it may want to establish an executive committee with delegated responsibilities or establish advisory committees.

The IRS suggested that charitable organizations review and consider the following to help ensure that directors understand their roles and responsibilities, and actively promote good governance practices. While adopting a particular practice is not a requirement for tax exemption, the agency believes that an organization that adopts some or all of these practices is more likely to be successful in pursuing its exempt purposes and earning public support.

The proposed principles, essentially reproduced verbatim, are as follows:

Mission Statement   A clearly articulated mission statement that is adopted by an organization's board of directors will explain and popularize the charity's purpose, and serve as a guide to the organization's work. A well-written mission statement shows why the charity exists, what it hopes to accomplish, and what activities it will undertake, where, and for whom.

Code of Ethics   The public expects a charity to abide by ethical standards that promote the public good. The board of directors bears the ultimate responsibility for setting ethical standards and ensuring that they permeate the organization and inform its practices. To that end, the board should consider adopting and regularly evaluating a code of ethics that describes behavior it wants to encourage and behavior it wants to discourage. The code of ethics should be a principal means of communicating to all personnel a strong culture of legal compliance and ethical integrity.

Whistleblower Policy   The board of directors should adopt an effective policy for handling employee complaints and establish procedures for employees to report in confidence suspected financial impropriety or misuse of the charity's resources.

Due Diligence   The directors of a charity must exercise due diligence consistent with a duty of care that requires a director to act in good faith, with the care an ordinarily prudent person in a like position would exercise under similar circumstances, and in a manner the director reasonably believes to be in the charity's best interests. Directors should see to it that policies and procedures are in place to help them meet their duty of care, such as by (1) being familiar with the charity's activities and knowing whether the activities promote the charity's mission and achieve its goals, (2) being fully informed about the charity's financial status, and (3) having full and accurate information to make informed decisions.

Duty of Loyalty   The directors of a charity owe it a duty of loyalty. This duty requires a director to act in the interest of the charity rather than in the personal interest of the director or some other person or organization. In particular, the duty of loyalty requires a director to avoid conflicts of interest that are detrimental to the charity. To that end, the board of directors should adopt and regularly evaluate an effective conflict-of-interest policy that (1) requires directors and staff to act solely in the interests of the charity without regard for personal interests; (2) includes written procedures for determining whether a relationship, financial interest, or business affiliation results in a conflict of interest; and (3) prescribes a certain course of action in the event a conflict of interest is identified. Directors and staff should be required to disclose annually in writing any known financial interest that the individual, or a member of the individual's family, has in any business entity that transacts business with the charity.

Transparency   By making full and accurate information about its mission, activities, and finances publicly available, a charity demonstrates transparency. The board of directors should adopt and monitor procedures to ensure that the charity's Form 990, annual reports, and financial statements are complete and accurate, are posted on the organization's public web site, and are made available to the public on request.

Fundraising Policy   Charitable fundraising is an important source of financial support for many charities. Success at fundraising requires care and honesty. The board of directors should adopt and monitor policies to ensure that fundraising solicitations meet federal and state law requirements and solicitation materials are accurate, truthful, and candid. Charities should keep their fundraising costs reasonable. In selecting paid fundraisers, a charity should use those that are registered with the state and that can provide good references. Performance of professional fundraisers should be continuously monitored.

Financial Audits   Directors must be good stewards of a charity's financial resources. A charity should operate in accordance with an annual budget approved by the board of directors. The board should ensure that financial resources are used to further charitable purposes by regularly receiving and reading up-to-date financial statements, including Form 990, auditor's letters, and finance and audit committee reports. If the charity has substantial assets or annual revenue, the board of directors should ensure that an independent auditor conduct an annual audit. The board can establish an independent audit committee to select and oversee the independent auditor. The auditing firm should be changed periodically (e.g., every five years) to ensure a fresh look at the financial statements. For a charity with lesser assets or annual revenue, the board should ensure that an independent certified public accountant conduct an annual audit. Substitute practices for very small organizations would include volunteers who would review financial information and practices. Trading volunteers between similarly situated organizations who would perform these tasks would also help maintain financial integrity without being too costly.

Compensation Practices   A successful charity pays no more than reasonable compensation for services rendered. Charities should generally not compensate persons for service on the board of directors, except to reimburse direct expenses of such service. Director compensation should be allowed only when determined to be appropriate by a committee composed of persons who are not compensated by the charity and have no financial interest in the determination. Charities may pay reasonable compensation for services provided by officers and staff.

Document Retention Policy   An effective charity will adopt a written policy establishing standards for document integrity, retention, and destruction. The document retention policy should include guidelines for handling electronic files. The policy should cover backup procedures, archiving of documents, and regular check-ups of the reliability of the system.

REDESIGNED ANNUAL INFORMATION RETURN

In 2007, the IRS substantially revised the general annual information return (Form 990) that is filed by most tax-exempt organizations. This return is not the annual return filed by private foundations (see Chapter 10). Nonetheless, this newly redesigned return includes a series of questions that directly reflect the agency's views as to governance principles applicable to nonprofit organizations. Indeed, this return is intended to influence and modify nonprofit organizations' behavior, in essence by forcing their governing boards to adopt certain policies and procedures (so they can check "yes" rather than "no" boxes). (Almost none of these policies and procedures is required by the federal tax law.)

A nonprofit organization filing this return is required to report the total number of voting members of its governing body and the number of these members who are independent. The organization must indicate whether a trustee, director, officer, or key employee has a family relationship or a business relationship with any other trustee, director, officer, or key employee.

It must report whether it delegated control over management duties customarily performed by or under the direct supervision of trustees, directors, officers, or key employees to a management company or other person. The organization must indicate whether a copy of the annual information return was provided to each member of its governing body before it was filed. The organization is required to indicate whether it contemporaneously documented the meetings held or written actions undertaken during the year by its governing body and/or each committee with authority to act on behalf of the governing body. The organization must describe whether and, if so, how it makes its governing documents, conflict-of-interest policy, and financial statements available to the public.

This annual information return references 12 types of written policies or procedures that nonprofit, tax-exempt organizations may be expected to adopt. The filing organization is asked whether it has a conflict-of-interest policy, a whistleblower policy, and a document retention and destruction policy. If the organization reports that it has chapters, branches, or affiliates, it must indicate whether it has policies and procedures governing the activities of these entities to ensure that their operations are consistent with those of the organization. A filing organization is asked whether it invested in, contributed assets to, or participated in a joint venture or similar arrangement with a taxable entity during the year. If the answer to this question is yes, the organization must report whether it has adopted a written policy or procedure requiring it to evaluate its participation in joint venture arrangements under the federal tax law and has taken steps to safeguard its exempt status with respect to these arrangements.

The organization must state whether the process for determining compensation of its chief executive officer, executive director, top management official, and/or other officers or key employees included a review and approval by independent persons, comparability data, and contemporaneous substantiation of the deliberation and decision. If an organization reports that it holds one or more conservation easements, it is required to indicate whether it has a policy regarding the periodic monitoring, inspection, and enforcement of the easement or easements. If the organization makes grants to recipients outside the United States, it is required to describe its procedures for monitoring use of the grant funds. If the organization is functioning as a hospital, it must report whether it has a charity care policy and a debt collection policy.

An organization must indicate whether it is following a policy regarding payment or reimbursement of expenses incurred by trustees, directors, officers, and key employees regarding first-class or charter travel, travel for companions, tax indemnification and gross-up payments, a discretionary spending account, a housing allowance or residence for personal use, payments for business use of a personal residence, health or social club dues or initiation fees, and/or personal services (such as for a maid, chauffeur, or chef).

SUBSEQUENT IRS GUIDANCE

The IRS has abandoned its draft of good governance practices for charitable organizations, stating that current IRS positions on nonprofit governance "are best reflected in the reporting required by the revised Form 990" and the components in this document as part of the agency's Life Cycle educational tool. The IRS stated: "Good governance is important to increase the likelihood that organizations will comply with the tax law, protect their charitable assets and, thereby, best serve their charitable beneficiaries."

The contents of this document follow, albeit condensed in places, with the stated text essentially verbatim.

Introduction

The IRS believes that a well-governed charity is more likely to obey the tax laws, safeguard charitable assets, and serve charitable interests than one with poor or lax governance. A charity that has clearly articulated purposes that describe its mission, a knowledgeable and committed governing body and management team, and sound management practices is more likely to operate effectively and consistent with tax law requirements. Although the tax law generally does not mandate particular management structures, operational policies, or administrative practices, it is important that each charity be thoughtful about the management practices that are most appropriate for that charity in assuring sound operations and compliance with the tax law.

Mission

The IRS encourages every charity to establish and regularly review its mission. A clearly articulated mission, adopted by the board of directors, serves to explain and popularize the charity's purpose and guide its work. It also addresses why the charity exists, what it hopes to accomplish, and what activities it will undertake, where, and for whom.

Organizational Documents

Regardless of whether a charity is a corporation, trust, unincorporated association, or other type of organization, it must have organizational documents that provide the framework for its governance and management. State law often prescribes the type of organizational document and its content. State law may require corporations to adopt bylaws. Organizational documents must be filed with applications for recognition of exemption.

Governing Body

The IRS encourages an active and engaged board, believing that it is important to the success of a charity and to its compliance with applicable tax law requirements. Governing boards should be composed of persons who are informed and active in overseeing a charity's operations and finances. The IRS is concerned that, if a governing board tolerates a climate of secrecy or neglect, charitable assets are more likely to be diverted to benefit the private interests of insiders at the expense of public and charitable interests. Successful governing boards include individuals who not only are knowledgeable and engaged but selected with the organization's needs in mind (e.g., accounting, finance, compensation, and ethics).

Attention should also be paid to the size of the board, ensuring that it is the appropriate size to effectively make sure that the organization obeys tax laws, safeguards its charitable assets, and furthers its charitable purposes. Small boards run the risk of not representing a sufficiently broad public interest, and of lacking the required skills and other resources required to effectively govern the organization. However, very large boards may have a more difficult time getting down to business and making decisions.

A governing board should include independent members and not be dominated by employees or others who are not independent individuals because of family or business relationships. The IRS reviews the board composition of charities to determine whether the board represents a broad public interest; to identify the potential for insider transactions that could result in misuse of charitable assets; to determine whether an organization has independent members, stockholders, or other persons with the authority to elect members of the board or approve or reject board decisions; and to ascertain whether the organization has delegated control or key management authority to a management company or other persons.

If an organization has local chapters, branches, or affiliates, the IRS encourages it to have procedures and policies in place to ensure that the activities and operations of these subordinates are consistent with those of the parent organization.

Governance and Management Policies

Although the federal tax law does not require charities to have governance and management policies, the IRS will nonetheless review an organization's application for recognition of exemption and annual information returns to determine whether it has implemented policies relating to executive compensation, conflicts of interest, investments, fundraising, documenting governance decisions, document retention and destruction, and whistleblower claims.

Persons who are knowledgeable in compensation matters and who have no financial interest in the determination should determine a charity's executive compensation. The federal tax law does not, however, require charities to follow a particular process in ascertaining the amount of this type of compensation. Organizations that file Form 990 will find that Part VI, Section B, line 15, asks whether the process used to determine the compensation of an organization's top management official and other officers and key employees included a review and approval by independent persons, comparability data, and contemporaneous substantiation of the deliberation and decision. In addition, the Form 990 solicits compensation information for certain trustees, directors, officers, key employees, and highest compensated employees.

The IRS encourages reliance on the *rebuttable presumption*, which is part of the intermediate sanctions rules. Under this test, payments of compensation are presumed to be reasonable if the compensation arrangement is approved in advance by an authorized body composed entirely of individuals who do not have a conflict of interest with respect to the arrangement, the authorized body obtained and relied on appropriate data as to comparability prior to making its determination, and the authorized body adequately documented the basis for its determination concurrently with making the determination.

The duty of loyalty, which requires a director to act in the interest of the charity, requires a director to avoid conflicts of interest that are detrimental to the charity. The IRS encourages a charity's board of directors to adopt and regularly evaluate a written conflict-of-interest policy that requires directors and staff to act solely in the interests of the charity without regard for personal interests; includes written procedures for determining whether a relationship, financial interest, or business affiliation results in a conflict of interest; and prescribes a course of action in the event a conflict of interest is identified.

Increasingly, charities are investing in joint ventures, for-profit entities, and complicated and sophisticated financial products or investments that require financial and investment expertise and, in some instances, the advice of outside investment advisors. The IRS encourages charities that make these types of investments to adopt written policies and procedures requiring the charity to evaluate its participation in these investments, and to take steps to safeguard the organization's assets and tax-exempt status if they could be affected by the investment arrangement. The Form 990 inquires as to whether an organization has adopted this type of policy. Also, the form asks for detailed information about certain investments.

The IRS encourages charities to adopt and monitor policies to ensure that fundraising solicitations meet federal and state law requirements, and that solicitation materials are accurate, truthful, and candid. Charities are encouraged to keep their fundraising costs reasonable, and to provide information about fundraising costs and practices to donors and the public. The Form 990 solicits information about fundraising activities, revenues, and expenses.

The IRS encourages the governing bodies and subcommittees to take steps to ensure that minutes of their meetings, and actions taken by written action or outside of meetings, are contemporaneously documented. The Form 990 asks whether an organization contemporaneously documents meetings or written actions undertaken during the year by its governing body and committees with authority to act on behalf of the governing body.

The IRS encourages charities to adopt a written policy establishing standards for document integrity, retention, and destruction. This type of policy should include guidelines for handling electronic files; it should also cover backup procedures, archiving of documents, and regular check-ups of the reliability of the system. The Form 990 asks whether an organization has a written document retention and destruction policy.

The IRS also encourages a charity's board to consider adopting and regularly evaluating a code of ethics that describes behavior it wants to encourage and behavior it wants to discourage. A code of ethics will serve to communicate and further a strong culture of legal compliance and ethical integrity to all persons associated with the organization.

The IRS further encourages the board to adopt an effective policy—a whistleblower policy—for handling employee complaints and to establish procedures for employees to report in confidence any suspected financial impropriety or misuse of the charity's resources. Form 990 asks whether the organization became aware during the year of a material diversion of its assets and whether an organization has a written whistleblower policy.

Financial Statements and Form 990 Reporting

The IRS is of the view that a charity with substantial assets or revenue should consider obtaining an audit of its finances by an independent auditor. The board may establish an independent audit committee to select and oversee an auditor. Form 990 asks whether the organization's financial statements were compiled or reviewed by an independent accountant, audited by an independent accountant, and subject to oversight by a committee within the organization. Also, Form 990 asks whether, as the result of a federal award, the organization was required to undergo an audit.

Practices differ widely as to who sees Form 990, when they see it (before or after its filing), and the extent of the reviewers' input, review, or approval. Some organizations provide copies of the return to the members of the board and other governance or management officials. Form 990 asks whether the organization provides a copy of the return to its governing body and requires the organization to explain any process of review by its directors or management.

Transparency and Accountability

By making full and accurate information about its mission, activities, finances, and governance publicly available, a charity encourages transparency and accountability to its constituents. The IRS encourages every charity to adopt and monitor procedures to ensure that its Form 1023, Form 990, Form 990-T, annual reports, and financial statements are complete and accurate, are posted on its public web site, and are made available to the public on request.

Form 990 asks whether and how an organization makes its returns, governing instruments, conflict-of-interest policy, and financial statements available to the public.

BOARD MEMBER RESPONSIBILITIES

One of the principles that has been in the law for centuries is that trustees of charitable trusts are deemed to have the same obligation (duty of care) toward the assets of the trusts as they do toward their personal resources. Their responsibility is to act *prudently* in their handling of the nonprofit organization's income and assets. The trustees are *fiduciaries*; the law (for now, largely state law) imposes on them standards of conduct and management that, together, comprise principles of *fiduciary responsibility*. Most state law, be it statute or court opinions, impose the standards of fiduciary responsibility on directors of nonprofit organizations, whether or not the organizations are trusts and whether or not they are charitable.

Contemporary Standards

The contemporaneous general standard is that a member of the board of a nonprofit organization is required to perform his or her duties in good faith, with the care an ordinarily prudent person in a like position would exercise under similar circumstances, and in a manner the director reasonably believes to be in the best interests of the mission, goals, and purposes of the organization.

Thus, one of the main responsibilities of nonprofit board members is to maintain financial accountability and effective oversight of the organization they serve. Fiduciary duty requires board members to remain objective, unselfish, responsible, honest, trustworthy, and efficient in relation to the organization. Board members are stewards of the entity, and are expected to act for the good of the organization rather than for their personal aggrandizement. They need to exercise reasonable care in all decision making, without placing the nonprofit organization at unnecessary risk.

The duties of board members of nonprofit organizations can be encapsulated in the *three Ds*: duty of care, duty of loyalty, and duty of obedience. These are the legal standards against which all actions taken by directors are tested. They are collective duties adhering to the entire board and require the active participation of all board members. Accountability can be demonstrated by a showing of the effective discharge of these duties.

Duty of Care

The duty of care requires that directors of a nonprofit organization be reasonably informed about the organization's activities, participate in the making of decisions, and do so in good faith and with the care of an ordinarily prudent person in similar circumstances. This duty, therefore, requires the individual board members to pay attention to the entity's activities and operations.

This duty is carried out by the following acts:

- Attendance at meetings of the board and committees to which assigned
- Preparation for board meetings, such as by reviewing the agenda and reports
- Obtaining information, before voting, to make appropriate decisions
- Use of independent judgment
- Periodic examination of the credentials and performance of those who serve the organization
- Frequent review of the organization's finances and financial policies
- Oversight of compliance with important filing requirements, such as annual information returns (see Chapter 10)

Duty of Loyalty

The duty of loyalty requires board members to exercise their power in the interest of the organization and not in their own interest or the interest of another entity, particularly one in which they have a formal relationship. When acting on behalf of the organization, board members must place the interests of the entity before their personal and professional interests.

This duty is carried out by the following acts:

- Disclosure of any conflicts of interest
- Adherence to the organization's conflict-of-interest policy
- Avoidance of the use of corporate opportunities for the individual's personal gain or benefit
- Nondisclosure of confidential information about the organization

Although conflicts of interest are not inherently illegal—in fact, can be common because board members are often affiliated with different entities in their communities—how the boards reviews and evaluates them is important. Conflict-of-interest policies can help protect the organization and board members by establishing a process for disclosure and voting when situations arise in which board members may actually or potentially derive personal benefit as a consequence of the organization's activities.

Duty of Obedience

The duty of obedience requires that directors of a nonprofit organization comply with applicable federal, state, and local laws; adhere to the entity's articles of organization and bylaws; and remain guardians of the mission.
The duty of obedience is carried out by the following acts:

- Compliance with all regulatory and reporting requirements, such as overseeing filing of annual information returns and payment of employment taxes

- Examination and understanding of all documents governing the organization and its operation, such as the bylaws

- Making decisions that fall within the scope of the organization's mission and governing documents

Personal Liability

Generally, if a director carries out his or her duties faithfully, and in adherence to the three Ds, the director will not be found personally liable for a commission or omission. Personal liability (see p. 287) can result when a trustee or director—and an officer or key employee—of a nonprofit organization breaches standards of fiduciary responsibility.

LAWSUITS AGAINST NONPROFIT ORGANIZATIONS

Nonprofit organization can be sued under federal, state, and/or local law. Although criminal prosecutions are rare, in the civil laws lurk many occasions for missteps leading to lawsuits. For the most part, nonprofit organization can be sued for the same reasons as for-profit organizations.
Here are the usual bases on which a nonprofit organization can be sued:

- *Nonpayment of income or property taxes.* Governments seeking unpaid taxes bring these suits. The nonprofit organization may be generally tax-exempt but the IRS may be after one or more of the private foundation excise taxes (see Chapters 4 through 8) or unrelated business income tax (see Chapter 8) or a state may be looking for real estate tax as to a parcel of real property that allegedly is not being used for exempt (usually charitable) purposes.

- *Violation of a state's charitable solicitation act.* A charitable (or similar) organization may be raising funds in a state without complying with the registration, reporting, or other requirements. A state will not proceed directly to litigation for a violation of this nature. If, however, after a few requests, the organization refuses to obey this law, an injunction or some other form of civil (or, infrequently, criminal) litigation may be initiated.

- *Defamation.* If an organization produces a libelous publication or one of its spokespersons uses terms or makes statements that another person finds offensive, it is not uncommon for a defamation suit to erupt in response.

- *Antitrust law violation.* Membership organizations are particularly susceptible to a charge of antitrust transgressions. For example, an association may wrongfully exclude or expel a person from its membership. (This can be a form of restraint of trade.) Or an association may enforce a code of ethics and conclude that a member acted unethically; this finding could lead to a defamation charge or, if the person is expelled from membership, to an antitrust law violation complaint.

- *Employment discrimination, wrongful termination, breach of a lease or other contract, and personal injury.* These are increasingly common bases for lawsuits. As an example of a personal injury suit, recently a nonprofit swim club was sued by an individual and his spouse because of personal injuries he suffered when he fell, after swimming, in a stairway leading to the club's locker room; his spouse sued for loss of consortium.

Private foundations, of course, are not likely to be engaged in fundraising or an activity constituting an antitrust law violation. The other above-referenced bases for litigation apply to foundations, however. A foundation once was sued because of failure to make a requested grant.

In most of these lawsuits, the only party sued is the organization itself. There are exceptions, however, such as the liability that can be incurred by an organization as the result of something done (commission) or not done (omission) by another organization. For example, two or more nonprofit organizations may be involved in a partnership or other form of a joint venture. As a consequence of this arrangement, the conduct of one organization may bring liability to it and/or to another organization. Technically, the liability (if any) may be that of the venture but this form of liability can quickly attach to the underlying parties.

Another illustration concerns national organizations and their chapters. It is possible for a chapter to incur liability and cause the national entity to be sued as well. (This is termed *ascending liability*.) The national organization may have done something or failed to do something in conjunction with the chapter. More commonly, however, the national entity is sued simply because it has the most resources. The outcome of this type of litigation often depends on whether the chapters are considered separate legal entities or whether they are integral parts of the national organization.

INDIVIDUALS AS DEFENDANTS

For the most part, as noted, the defendants in lawsuits involving nonprofit organizations are the organizations themselves. Seldom will the charges include other parties, such as individuals. It can happen, though, and when it does, the individuals (including those acting as volunteers) who can be dragged into the fray are trustees, directors, officers, and/or key employees.

Conduct by employees in their role as such is generally considered conduct by the organization involved. If an employee's actions are outside the scope of his or her employment, however, they can be held responsible as individuals.

When an individual is personally sued because of something done or not done in the name of a nonprofit organization, the potential liability is termed *personal liability*. Its occurrence is rare but when it happens it is usually for one or more of the following reasons:

- An individual had a responsibility to do something in connection with the operation of a nonprofit organization and failed to meet that responsibility.

- An individual had a responsibility to refrain from doing something in connection with a nonprofit organization and did it anyway.

- An individual failed to dissociate himself or herself from the wrongful conduct of others.

- An individual actively participated in a wrongful conduct.

For example, a nonprofit organization may have wrongfully terminated the employment of an individual on a discriminatory basis. If the termination was the result of discrimination by a manager who was an employee of the organization, the entity may be found to be the only wrongdoer. If, however, a member of the organization's board of directors actively conspired with the manager to cause the discriminatory firing, the director may be found personally liable. If another member of the board knew of the discriminatory action (and the conspiracy underlying it) and did nothing to thwart it, that board member may be found personally liable as well.

This example involves *commission*: One or more individuals committed a wrongful act and were found liable (along with the organization). But liability can also result from a failure to act. The members of a finance committee of a nonprofit organization may fail in their obligation to oversee the investment practices of the entity. Money may be lost or valuable resources may be squandered as a result. These individuals could be found personally liable for their *omissions*.

Thus, personal liability in the nonprofit (often charitable) context can flow out of a violation of fundamental principles of fiduciary responsibility (discussed earlier in this chapter).

PROTECTION AGAINST PERSONAL LIABILITY

Self-protection, stemming from prudent behavior and fulfillment of fiduciary responsibility, can go a long way to ensuring that personal liability is avoided. There are, nonetheless, some *structural* and *formal* steps that can be taken to provide a greater shield against personal liability.

One is *incorporation* of the organization. The incorporated organization is clearly a separate legal entity (aside from shams); the corporate form generally protects against personal liability. That is, liability is generally confined to the organization and thus does not normally extend to those who set policy for or manage the organization. (This is one of the principal reasons a nonprofit organization should be incorporated.)

Another step is *indemnification*; if state law permits, an organization can indemnify its directors and officers (and perhaps others). This occurs when the organization agrees (usually by provision in the bylaws) to pay the judgments and related expenses (including legal fees) incurred by those who are covered by the indemnity, when those expenses are the result of a misdeed (commission or omission) by those persons while acting in the service of the organization. This assumes that the indemnity is provided in cases of liability where the individuals acted in the interests of the organization and otherwise in good faith. The indemnification cannot extend to criminal acts; it may not cover certain willful acts that violate civil law. Because an indemnification involves the resources of the organization, the efficacy of it is dependent on the economic viability of the entity.

A nonprofit organization can purchase *insurance* to protect its directors and officers in similar circumstances. Instead of shifting the risk of liability from the individuals involved to the nonprofit organization (indemnification), however, the risk of payment for a liability is shifted to an independent third party—an insurance company. The responsibility for certain risks, such as criminal law liability, cannot be shifted by means of insurance (because it would be contrary to public policy). The insurance contract will likely exclude from coverage certain forms of civil law liability, such as defamation, employee discrimination, and/or antitrust matters. An organization can purchase insurance to fund one or more indemnities it has made of its directors and officers.

The fourth step is to determine what state law is on the subject of *immunity*. Immunity is available when the law provides that a class of individuals, under certain circumstances, is not liable for a particular act or set of acts or for failure to undertake a particular act or set of acts. Several states' law provides for immunity from lawsuits, under certain circumstances, for nonprofit (usually charitable) organizations, and for their directors and officers, particularly where these individuals are serving as volunteers. (In the case of the swim club and the personal injury lawsuit [discussed earlier], a court held that the nonprofit organization was immune from liability pursuant to the state's charitable immunity act.)

If a director or officer maximizes use of the *four I's*—incorporation, indemnification, insurance, and immunity—he or she can almost be guaranteed that personal liability for service for a nonprofit organization will be avoided, and in some instances the organization itself will be protected. There are additional guidelines that directors of nonprofit organizations can follow to lessen the likelihood of personal involvement in litigation:

- *Board book.* Each board member should have, and keep up to date, a board book. In this book should be (at a minimum) the board address list (discussed later in this chapter), copies of important documents (such as articles of organization, bylaws, mission statement, and conflict-of-interest policy), copies of recent board meeting minutes, a copy of the ruling from the IRS recognizing the organization as a tax-exempt entity, a copy of the most recently filed state annual report, a copy of the most recent financial statements, and a copy of the most recently filed annual information return. Other documents that may be included are recent committee reports, a copy of the organization's application for recognition of tax exemption (see Chapter 3), and a copy of the entity's most recent unrelated business income tax return (if any) (see Chapter 10).

- *Board address list.* Each member of the board should have, and keep in the board book, a current list of the organization's board members. This list should contain each individual's mailing address, telephone numbers (office, home, cell, car, pager), fax number, and email address.

- *Email communications system.* There should be a system by which the board members can communicate by email. Each member should have a group listing of all of the board members on his or her computer. (Board members should exercise some caution about what is said in email messages; everything should be written from the perspective that it may someday become public.)

- *Minutes.* Careful consideration should be given to board meeting minutes. There should be minutes of every board meeting. These documents are summaries of important actions, perhaps accompanied by one or more resolutions; they are not transcripts of the proceedings. Some organizations have their legal counsel review drafts of board minutes before they are circulated to the directors for their consideration and review.

- *Meetings.* It is essential that directors attend board meetings (or, if by telephone, participate in them). If a board member cannot be involved in a meeting, the minutes should reflect that fact. A board member cannot exercise the requisite degree of fiduciary responsibility without attending meetings and interacting with the other directors. Directors should participate in the decision-making process; silence is deemed to be concurrence. If a director is opposed to an action to be undertaken by the organization at the behest of the board, the director should speak up and have his or her dissent noted in the minutes.

- *Understand the organization.* The directors should comprehend the legal form of the organization and its structure. For example, if the organization is a corporation, the directors should be intimately familiar with its articles of incorporation and bylaws. They should constantly compare the organization's actual operating methods with the structure and procedures that are reflected in these documents, and be certain that operations are not inconsistent with provisions in these documents.

- *Understand the organization's activities.* Board members should understand how the entity operates—the purposes of its programs, their rank order of priority (presumably as mirrored in the budgets), their number, possible overlap, and membership (if any) interest and support.

- *Understand the organization's other operations.* Committees, subsidiaries, directors' "pet projects," members' personal interests or contacts, or community needs may have introduced activities (and expenditures) that were not properly authorized. Some may deserve more recognition and support, while others may be innocently jeopardizing the organization's tax-exempt status.

- *Ask questions.* Directors should never be afraid to ask about any arrangement or information that is unclear to them. An individual with fiduciary responsibility has the obligation to ask these questions. This pertains to subjects such as the organization's form and structure, its finances, use of subsidiaries, involvement in joint ventures, and affiliations with other organizations.

- *Web site.* Directors should periodically visit the web site (if any) of the organization they serve. They should understand everything that is posted there. It is to be remembered that these sites may be visited by officials of the IRS, attorneys general's offices, and other governmental agencies, as well as the media, other organizations, and prospective donors.

- *Conflict-of-interest policy.* While for the most part it is not required as a matter of law, a nonprofit organization—particularly a charitable one—should give serious consideration to adoption of a conflict-of-interest policy. This policy enables an organization to identify its disqualified persons (see Chapter 2) and to know about any potential conflict at the time it is entering into a transaction with such a person.

- *Self-dealing rules compliance.* Board members of private foundations need to be aware of the self-dealing rules (see Chapter 6). This is the case if only because the penalties for violation of these rules can be imposed on the disqualified persons with respect to the organization. These persons include the entity's directors and officers.

- *Use of the organization's lawyer.* Access to the lawyer or law firm representing the nonprofit organization by the board is a matter of great sensitivity. Some boards never interact with the organization's lawyer; this is left to the officers and executive employees. Other boards will not meet without a lawyer present for the entirety of the meeting. (In some instances, boards want to have some time with their lawyer without staff present.) Concern about legal fees is often a factor in this, of course, but nonprofit boards should be certain they are making the best use of their lawyers.

- *Materials and seminars.* Books, articles, and newsletters about the law of nonprofit organizations and the proper role of their directors and officers abound. These individuals are well advised to continually update their knowledge of permissible and innovative practices and current developments in the law concerning nonprofit organizations. Seminars and conferences on these subjects are plentiful. Directors should take advantage of these resources (and document what they did).

MANAGEMENT COMPANIES

It is becoming more common for a nonprofit organization to utilize the services of a management company. (This is not a common practice by private foundations, yet the law being developed by reason of this practice generally may impact foundations.) There are many variations on this theme. Some organizations rely on a management company to assume responsibility for all of their administrative needs, while others delegate only selected functions (such as meeting planning or fundraising). A management company may provide services in connection with the operations of programs. A popular term these days is *outsourcing*, the idea being that certain administrative (sometimes termed *back office*) functions should be handled by an outside company so as to make the operations of the nonprofit organization more economical and efficient. Still other nonprofit organizations that are tax exempt elect to spin out functions that are unrelated businesses to such a company, to eliminate exposure to the unrelated business income tax (see Chapter 8).

There is nothing inappropriate about the use of a management company by a nonprofit organization. Indeed, use of a company of this nature may be one of the ways in which fiduciary responsibilities are met and legal liability avoided. The basic difficulty with this approach is that government officials—in particular, those with the IRS and offices of states' attorneys general—are suspicious of the practice. Management companies are almost always for-profit corporations; these individuals are constantly on the lookout for instances where the resources of a nonprofit (particularly a charitable) organization are being improperly transferred to or used by persons in a private capacity.

The management company structure that inevitably attracts the highest scrutiny is the arrangement where there is director and/or officer overlap between the two organizations. The worst of these situations, from the standpoint of the regulators, is the management company that was established by the same individuals who started the nonprofit organization, and they simultaneously serve on both boards in a majority capacity. Government authorities almost always view this circumstance as a siphoning off of charitable resources for private gain.

This type of management company relationship can result in application of the private inurement, private benefit, self-dealing, and/or excess business holdings rules (see Chapters 3, 6, and 8). At a minimum, it is essential to be able to show that the management services are necessary and in furtherance of exempt purposes, and that the management fees are reasonable. Even where those elements can be demonstrated, however, the IRS may conclude that the arrangement is inappropriate and violative of the private benefit rules. Even where the management company is not of suspicious origins, and where there is no overlap of directors and officers, it is nonetheless prudent to be able to demonstrate that the management company is necessary and that its fees are reasonable.

An illustration of the application of these principles is found in advice offered in 2004 by the IRS's lawyers as to the ability of certain credit counseling organizations, under investigation by the agency and the Federal Trade Commission, to qualify for tax exemption as charitable and educational entities. Relying on the private inurement doctrine, these lawyers recommended application of this body of law because of their findings of "extensive dealings of [these] exempt organizations with back-office service providers, . . . often owned by the principals." They also invoked application of the private benefit doctrine, writing that the credit agencies "appear to be operating to benefit these service providers rather than to serve any public purpose."

If the relationship between a nonprofit organization and a management company is too close, the IRS may contend that the arrangement is a joint venture. This argument is reflective of the fact that a joint venture relationship can be imposed as a matter of law on the operations of two affiliated entities.

WATCHDOG AGENCIES

From a compliance perspective, nonprofit organizations are principally concerned with operating in conformity with the law or rules of the accounting profession. There is, however, another consideration with which some organizations must also cope: the role and influence of the *watchdog agencies* that monitor and publicize the endeavors of nonprofit entities, principally those that solicit contributions from the public. These agencies have and enforce rules that sometimes are inconsistent with or attempt to supersede law requirements. The agencies rarely take action with respect to private foundations but their standards may pertain to foundations' governance practices. For example, these standards may include requirements about board composition and frequency of board meetings.

A charity watchdog agency basically has three functions:

1. It writes standards to which charitable organizations are expected to adhere.

2. It enforces the standards, in part by rating organizations in relation to the standards and by making the ratings public.

3. It prepares and publicly circulates reports about charitable organizations.

The principal set of these standards is the *Standards for Charitable Accountability* issued by the Better Business Bureau Wise Giving Alliance. Included is a rule that the board of the organization should have a policy of assessing, at least every two years, the organization's "performance and effectiveness and of determining future actions required to achieve its mission." Solicitation and other information materials should be "accurate, truthful, and not misleading." There should be an annual report, including a summary of the past year's program service accomplishments, basic financial information, and a roster of directors and officers.

The organization's board of directors should provide "adequate oversight" of its operations and staff. This entails regularly scheduled appraisals of the chief executive officer and sufficient accounting procedures. There should be a board-approved budget. The charity's expenses should be "accurately" reported in its financial statements.

Audited financial statements should be obtained for organizations with annual gross income in excess of $250,000. For charities with less gross income, a review by a certified public accountant is sufficient, although where annual income is less than $100,000, an internally produced financial statement is adequate. Financial statements should include a breakdown of expenses (such as salaries, travel, and postage) that also shows the portion of the expenses allocated to program, fundraising, and administration.

A charitable organization is to "avoid accumulating funds that could be used for current program activities." Net assets available for program use should not be more than the greater of three times the size of the prior year's expenses or three times the size of the current year's budget. "Material conflicting interests" involving the board and staff are prohibited. At least 65% of total expenses must be for program; no more than 35% of contributions may be expended for fundraising. An organization that cannot comply with these percentages is permitted to demonstrate that its use of funds is nonetheless reasonable.

The organization's board of directors must be comprised of at least five voting members. There must be at least three board meeting each year, "evenly spaced," with a majority in attendance. Only one of these meetings can be by conference call.

No more than one individual on the board or 10% of the board, whichever is greater, can be compensated by the organization. The chair and treasurer of the entity cannot be compensated. One of the transgressions embedded in these standards is failure to respond promptly to matters brought to the attention of the Alliance or local better business bureaus.

The media, funders of charitable organizations, and governmental agencies tend to embrace and rely on standards such as these. As federal and state governments evolve best practices guidelines, it may be anticipated that some of these rules will take on the force of law. As an illustration of this probability, the staff of the Senate Finance Committee in mid-2004 prepared a discussion draft of proposals for reforms in the law of tax-exempt organizations, including best practices. These proposals included rules (or guidelines) that boards of these organizations be comprised of between three and 15 individuals, no more than one board member could be compensated by the organization, the board's chair or treasurer could not be compensated, and (in the case of public charities) at least one board member or one-fifth of the board would have to be independent. In addition, an individual that is not permitted to serve on the board of a publicly traded company due to a law violation could not be a member of the board of a tax-exempt organization. An individual convicted of a federal or state charge of criminal fraud or comparable offense could not serve on the board or be an officer of an exempt organization for five years following the conviction. An exempt organization and its officers that knowingly permitted such an individual to be a board member would be subject to a penalty.

SUMMARY

This chapter focused on existing and emerging concepts of what has become known as corporate governance. These principles primarily concern the matter of the boards of directors of charitable organizations: their functions, duties, and responsibilities. Abuses in the for-profit sector and resultant statutory law have created governing principles that are quickly being imported into the realm of nonprofit organizations. The chapter also addressed the subject of legal liability for nonprofit organizations and board members personally; as to the latter, the chapter sketched steps board members can take to minimize (or maybe eliminate) personal liability. The chapter also revisited the law as to nonprofit organizations' use of management companies. The chapter concluded with a look at the import in this context of watchdog agencies' guidelines. Of the chapters in this book, this one describes a body of law that is poised to be most informed and expanded by law as yet unwritten but imminent, about to be manifested in emerging statutes, regulations, rules, and forms, all of which could significantly transform the law of nonprofit organizations.

Index